GOUZENKO
The Untold Story

GOUZENKO
The Untold Story

JOHN SAWATSKY

Macmillan of Canada
A Division of Gage Publishing Limited
Toronto, Canada

Canadian Cataloguing in Publication Data

Sawatsky, John, date.
  Gouzenko: the untold story

ISBN 0-7715-9812-2

1. Gouzenko, Igor, 1915– 2. Canada — Politics
and government — 1935-1957. 3. Spies — Biography.
I. Title.

FC601.G68S28 1984   327.1′2′0924   C84-098973-3
F1034.3.G68S28 1984

Edited by Maggie MacDonald
Designed by Don Fernley
Back cover art by Duncan Macpherson

Macmillan of Canada
A Division of Gage Publishing Limited
Printed in Canada

For
Patrick Nagle,
who gave me an opportunity

With special thanks to
Professor Joe Scanlon
and the School of Journalism,
Carleton University

Contents

Acknowledgements

Many people played a role in the preparation for this book. Of course, most important are the many people who were interviewed. Their names are listed in Appendix F. In addition, there are those whose names do not appear in Appendix F because they were not formally interviewed; nevertheless they gave valuable assistance in providing names of people who should be interviewed and where to find them. Learning the names of the people to interview was an undertaking of its own and here I am particularly indebted to individuals such as Len Starmer, Peter St. John, Peter Newman, Armand Baril, Bill Dewan, Phil Eustace, Elinor Kellock, Naomi Lightbourne, and many others, including some names I cannot mention. Thanks also go to Janet Inksetter, Ron Haggart, David Camp, Bill Curran, and Lilias Massey. The art work on Gouzenko was generously made available by Duncan Macpherson, who did the drawings, and Kevin Doyle and Nick Burnett of *Maclean's* magazine, which owned first rights. I am also indebted to the *Toronto Star*, especially John Miller, for making available their exclusive pictures of Igor Gouzenko.

Only one of the interviews in this book — that of Cecil Bayfield done for a television documentary — was not done by my research assistant or myself. I would like to thank the CBC and the National Film Board, and particularly Gary Marcuse and Jim Littleton, for making this interview available.

I am extremely indebted to Ron and Herta Thiessen, Jay and Marta Armin, and Adele Armin-Riley and Doug Riley, as well as to Michelle Swenarchuk.

I would like to thank the Parliamentary Press Gallery, especially André Pratte, Aileen McCabe, and John Ferguson, for some crucial assistance that helped put me into the position of being able to start this book. Bruce Carr-Harris took time out of his busy schedule to review the manuscript.

The unsung hero of this project is definitely Ralph Curtis, my computer advisor, without whose counsel the preparation of this book would have been much slower and more difficult.

Doug Gibson and Maggie MacDonald of Macmillan of Canada provided wonderful support.

Erin McKelvie, my research assistant, threw herself into the project with her usual dedication and penchant for work. She did more than her fair share of the unglamorous chores that a book like this requires.

Without any doubt the individual I am most indebted to is Professor Joe Scanlon of the School of Journalism at Carleton University, who, along with student Gillian Rutherford, voluntarily and enthusiastically invested a lot of work in this project. Their main — but not only — task was to find the residents of Gouzenko's apartment building in Ottawa at the time of his defection and their success was amazing. How they tracked down Gouzenko's neighbours of nearly forty years ago is in itself a story worth telling. Needless to say, without their work this book would have been significantly poorer.

Introduction

There are two things about this book that I feel obligated to explain at the outset: first, why I compiled it, and, second, why I chose the oral history form.

My reason for doing this book goes back to 1980 and the publication of my first book, *Men in the Shadows: The RCMP Security Service.* It contained a chapter on Igor Gouzenko that highlighted his defection in 1945 and briefly sketched some of his subsequent problems in Canada. It was a reporter's account dug out mainly by consulting public material and by interviewing people who had dealt with him. When the book appeared, Gouzenko promptly issued a writ claiming I had libelled him. My first reaction was to check some of my sources — most of whom were RCMP — to see if I had done something wrong and if, in their opinion, I had libelled Gouzenko. They responded unanimously that I had not and that, if anything, I had been too easy on him. Gouzenko had sued, or had threatened to sue, a dozen or so people before me and virtually every one of them had retracted, including those who felt they had been right. I decided not to settle and undertook to maintain the accuracy of my account in court. Since Gouzenko was only one element in a book about the Canadian security establishment, my research into him still had blank areas. The suit forced me to focus more directly on his story, and in doing so I discovered, with some amazement I remember, that despite all the publicity that always seemed to follow him, Igor Gouzenko, the person, was largely unknown. I had always assumed that most of the Gouzenko story had been told, but as I delved further, I realized how little had been revealed. Moreover, it became apparent that even the people who thought they knew him actually knew little. Many people knew particular aspects of Gouzenko but not many saw the whole picture. For instance, I had always thought that Gouzenko sued people because he wanted money and publicity. Clearly he liked both. It took me a while to realize I had misjudged him. The real Gouzenko, it appears, saw himself as a historical figure. When something unflattering was published, Gouzenko felt obligated to take legal measures to have it erased from the record for the sake of his standing in history.

As the libel suit dragged on and I probed deeper, I came, I think, to understand at least partly why he was so sensitive to having his motive for defecting challenged. My research revealed that virtually everybody who had known Gouzenko in the early years believed he did not defect for ideological reasons, as he claimed. They believed his motives were much less noble. Some felt he had gotten into trouble in the embassy — which explains his early recall to Moscow — and had fled for his personal safety. Others said he simply wanted to enjoy the wealth and materialism of the West. Any writer implying anything of this nature was served with a writ, and for more than three decades Gouzenko largely suppressed such comments. Gouzenko died before the trial began but from having talked with colleagues in the press it was clear to me he had intimidated the media, and this alone, I felt, was a story worth pursuing. Gouzenko sued me to maintain his image. It is ironical that it caused me to probe deeper and unearth information that has done precisely the opposite.

The Gouzenko story can be told only now. No author or publisher would willingly go through the legal harassment this book would have created prior to his death in June 1982. If the unmasking of Gouzenko wasn't feasible before June 1982, delaying any longer would mean many of the ingredients of the Gouzenko story would have withered away as people died or forgot. Even now, scores of valuable interview subjects — Mackenzie King, St. Laurent, Diefenbaker, Pearson, and half a dozen RCMP commissioners, to name just a few prominent individuals — are gone. However, plenty of people with good memories still live to provide a good insight, so it was still not too late.

Why an oral history? People have strong feelings about Gouzenko, both for and against, although his critics outnumber his admirers. It is difficult for a reporter to reconcile these differences in a traditional narrative, so I decided to let the interviews carry the story. Also, with the participants themselves telling the story, the reader gets a better feeling of the quality of Gouzenko's social interaction.

I should make it clear at this point that I personally believe that Gouzenko, in September 1945, performed a valuable service by exposing the details of Soviet espionage in Canada. His subsequent activities do not detract from that accomplishment. As far as this book is concerned, both for his defection and for his subsequent life in Canada, I am acting as a chronicler and not as a judge. This is one of the reasons I leave the Gouzenko story in the hands of other people.

Many people were interviewed. Since the names of those whose contributions appear in this book are listed in Appendix F, it is not my intention to mention individuals here except for Svetlana Gouzenko, who was interviewed in some depth. Nothing in this book about Igor Gouzenko is intended to reflect on Svetlana Gouzenko. She differs from her late husband in many ways. Several years ago, while preparing my legal defence, I came to learn Gouzenko's hidden name and the location of his home. Last February I used this information to phone Svetlana Gouzenko at her home and ask for an interview. She agreed. Svetlana Gouzenko had already by this time let me know through intermediaries that she was concerned about my research. She already realized that I knew her identity because neighbours had informed her that Erin McKelvie, my research assistant, and I had been around asking questions. When I asked her where she wanted to be interviewed, she said simply: "Why don't you come over here? You know where it is."

Erin and I arrived at the Gouzenko house on the morning of March 12, 1984; we sat down around the dining-room table and discussed for an hour the terms of the interview. Svetlana Gouzenko immediately impressed me as a warm, gregarious, giving woman with an enjoyable sense of humour. Each of us wanted a concession from the other. Svetlana Gouzenko wanted me to withhold her legal name and the whereabouts of her residence. I wanted pictures. I offered to yield to her request if she yielded to mine, but she adamantly — although good-naturedly — refused. "Impossible," she said. She wanted to save her exclusive pictures for her own memoirs or to sell them. The interview proceeded with no deal being struck; I was encumbered by no conditions whatever. She asked me not to reveal her identity to prevent Soviet agents and sympathizers who have infiltrated western society from persecuting her children and grandchildren. I did not find her fears credible and I believe very few people would. However, I have decided not to publish her name for other reasons. I am of the opinion she really believes her family will be persecuted if her name becomes public. Besides, Svetlana Gouzenko has other concerns today, and in the past she has often faced difficulties that were not of her making. As well, no great issue of public importance is served by the release of her identity. It is not the intention of this book to reflect in any way, bad or good, on Svetlana Gouzenko and her family or to cause them difficulty.

What struck me at virtually all stages of my research was how little digging Canadian journalists and historians had done into the Gouzenko defection. Gouzenko's flight from the Soviet Embassy in September 1945 has become virtually a legend of Canadian history and yet I discovered basic errors in some of the most elementary parts of the story, which were routinely repeated many times without checking. For example, popular legend has Gouzenko walking into the newsroom of the *Ottawa Journal* on the night of September 5, 1945, with documents he spread out before a disinterested night city editor who told him to go away because the story was too big. I believe I have interviewed every living adult who was in the *Journal* newsroom that night and the account of what really happened is different. Gouzenko produced no documents and, paralysed with fright and speaking incomplete English with a heavy accent, could not articulate his concerns. He was simply incomprehensible. It was the following day when Gouzenko returned with his wife before he made himself understood — but not believed — and it was then that the *Journal* turned him away. In other words, Gouzenko flubbed his first effort to defect and later, when he wrote his autobiography, may have been too embarrassed to admit it, so rearranged the events somewhat. This single example reveals how dependent the public has been on Gouzenko's self-serving autobiography published in 1948 and how little his story has been checked. It is particularly amazing in that all the people who knew what really happened inside the *Journal* newsroom that night were journalists trained to go out and get stories. Yet none of them — even in later years — wrote the story that unfolded in their own newsroom. In this present book I seek to accumulate as best I can the real story about Gouzenko. If it punctures some myths, that's fine. If it uncovers some warts, that's okay. The same goes whether it makes the RCMP look bad or good, or bolsters the political biases of either the left or the right. The purpose of this book is to retrace the life of Igor Gouzenko from September 5, 1945, to June 25, 1982, and maybe give some glimpses of how he affected our country. Much can be learned from his experience, but that's for the reader to grasp.

John Sawatsky
Parliamentary Press Gallery
Ottawa
April 1984

1 Gouzenko

Don Fast, *retired RCMP officer who handled Gouzenko*

Shortly after Gouzenko came to live in my home we were in Toronto one time and we passed a supermarket. He insisted on stopping. He always wanted to go into the supermarket. We walked in there and he spent about an hour browsing through it with his eyes wide open. He was more interested in the meat and bread sections. He stood there for five minutes just looking at the bread. He said: "This is what it's all about. Forget politics and all the other things. This is what is most important. Look, no line-ups, no coupons, no rationing. Having been hungry for months and months and cold and without privacy, this is an unbelievable paradise. We were told about hardships and persecutions in the western world and had no idea of what was really here." He said that if people in the Soviet Union could really see this and believe it they would all be breaking down the doors. I believe honestly it was food and not politics that motivated him to defect. He wanted to eat regularly. You can't blame him for that. But his motive wasn't to try and help Canada.

A. Clare Anderson, *Gouzenko's neighbour prior to the defection*

Gouzenko always kept a picture of Stalin in his living-room window. If you looked up from Somerset Street, that was the first thing you saw. I don't know if that meant anything or not. He didn't seem to be a guy who would defect. He never talked about personal things or anything like that. If you mentioned the weather to him, that was the end of that. He was a very quiet and well-behaved gentleman. He didn't seem to do anything much except to go to work and come back. I never saw he and his wife out together. He would come in and pretty well stay in for the evening. He seemed to keep to himself.

Svetlana Gouzenko, *widow of Igor Gouzenko*
We were saying usually very few words in the apartment because we were always considering that we could have some microphone there. So usually we go out in the park and he would leave the [baby] carriage a few feet away because the carriage could have a bug. And we would walk away a little bit and then we would discuss and we would never come near the same tree to discuss any matters. We were cautious.

A. Clare Anderson
A Packard limousine would come every once in a while and park in front of the apartment building and two or three men would get out and go up to his apartment. We couldn't take our car to Ottawa on account of the gas situation, so we had to take the train. But they would come with this big limousine and always leave the motor running and they would be up there for an hour. It used to bother my wife that we couldn't drive our car and they wouldn't even shut off their motor. We never knew who they were. We think they were a couple of Russians from the embassy.

Dr. Robert D. Howland, *neighbour*
He had a little boy there. Instead of going into the bathroom, the baby used to stand on the balcony upstairs and take a leak over the side. He would just stand at the edge and let it go.

A. Clare Anderson
They kept the stroller for their little child downstairs in the hall. We heard a commotion down there — the building was really quiet — and Gouzenko looked out the window and saw a fellow stealing it. He ran downstairs and took after him down the street and caught him about four blocks away and wrestled him to the ground. The guy got away but Gouzenko got the stroller back all right.

David M. Conlan, *neighbour*

I lived downstairs and he lived above me. I remember very little about him. He was a very quiet chap, a mousy type of fellow. Inoffensive. I generally met him at the door coming in or going out. It was wintertime when I saw him more often. You couldn't carry on a conversation with him. For one thing he was Russian and we had little or no common ground to talk about. What do you do when you see a fellow about five minutes a week and never meet anybody else of his crowd or family? So it didn't amount to anything.

Svetlana Gouzenko

He is the one who decided. I was really very much an obedient wife. At that point I didn't know what actually is involved in his work. I didn't know he was a cipher [clerk]. He never told me and I didn't know what they're ciphering and what ciphering and espionage is all about. I didn't know a thing.

Margaret MacDonald, *neighbour*

He was a little man. And he was friendly. And he was a gentleman. He'd say good morning and take his hat off. He seemed to want to be friendly with us.

John MacDonald, *Margaret MacDonald's son*

It was a constant amazement to him. My mother was a civil servant. There was just two of us living on a very modest income and yet he considered our lifestyle — radios, furnished apartment (I guess it was a huge apartment by his standards) and what he found in department stores and the way people were dressed — as amazing affluence. And that's about all he could ever talk about. In hindsight it was easy to see the seeds of motivation being planted in his mind. We were not surprised by it. Maybe even then we wondered if he would go back and what kind of a devoted communist was he if he felt so much of the affluence in the western world. I think it was a real eye-opener to him. . . . He always struck me as one motivated a great deal by worldly possessions.

Robert D. Howland

I heard he was being transferred back to Russia. I had an apartment downstairs and he had a slightly bigger one upstairs. These were war days when you couldn't get apartments. I went up and talked to him. He had a little boy there. Well, he said, he'd think about it and so on. These were the days when you talked about furniture; sometimes you had to buy the furniture. I talked to them and when I went back downstairs I told my wife: "I don't think he wants to go back to Russia."

John MacDonald

He was interested in what we paid for the apartment, how much Mother made, what salaries were like, what you'd have to make to own a car, and a record-player. How much furniture you would have. He would ask a lot of things about the average Canadian family. So he was interested in material possessions — the lifestyle of western society — a great deal. I never saw the apartment but Mother remembers it as being quite plain, sparsely furnished. He was in the living room at our place. He would know what the average, middle-class, civil servant apartment looks like. And ours was hardly luxurious. But he always considered it quite exceptionally luxurious for a working woman. His conversations came back to that one way or another.

Margaret MacDonald

I think they were happy here and they were going to make a life here. But then I think he got afraid. He was afraid. He didn't want to go back. I came in and he was packing up furniture and stuff and he wanted to know where he'd get the boxes to put his furniture back because he was going back to Russia. . . . He didn't get the boxes.

Peter Worthington, *journalist*

The minute he was recalled I think the seed was planted and I think he knew that if he was recalled it was nothing but trouble and that it would be the end of a nice life. But I think they're adequate motives.

Robert D. Howland

I never got the impression that he took those documents from the embassy out of respect for Canada and disrespect for his own country. I had the impression he just didn't want to go back. . . . That's how crude I was about it. I didn't ever get the impression he had a sincere moral conviction in exposing the stuff he did. It wasn't an informed opinion. It was just a busy young man's impression.

Robert Reguly, *journalist who met him frequently*

Gouzenko said that while he was in Ottawa the Russians were very tight on expenses and that one of the Intelligence Officers in the embassy had kited his expenses by fifty dollars. In other words, saying he had paid out fifty dollars Canadian to a source when he actually hadn't. Gouzenko said they brought him back to Russia, shot him, and then sent word back to the staff that this is what happens to people who hype their expense accounts. They snuffed him for fifty bucks.

Robert Keyserlingk, *paperback publisher of Gouzenko's autobiography*

He had never lived in a society where you could obtain things so easily. He was used to rations and certain stores and coupons. He told me: "You take your wife to the movie at night. I don't do that. She and I go to the IGA and just look at the things in the store, just to see all these things and to know we could take this can and this bag and buy the things." He was so impressed with it that I have a strong feeling that somewhere he was a little careless when he went back to the embassy from a walk like that and told them the story in the same way he was telling it to me.

David M. Conlan

I was on holidays at the time he defected. When I came back I could almost feel something in the atmosphere. The tailor across the street gave us the whole story.

Willson Woodside, *writer for* Saturday Night *magazine*

Gouzenko heard a Greek fruit merchant in Ottawa say he was

going to sue the city. He was impressed with the fact you could sue the city and talked about it in the embassy. They became suspicious of him. At that time Stalin was calling back all kinds of people.

Peter Worthington
The initial recall would scare the bejesus out of any sane person. When the Soviet system recalls you, if you've got any other place to go I'd go there quickly, especially in Stalin's time from what we know now. Everybody is in trouble in the Soviet Embassy in the days of Stalin. Nobody knew who was safe and that is why the system wasn't working. If it hadn't been for the war, you can make a very powerful argument that the system would have collapsed. The war gave them a chance to start over.

John Picton, *reporter and friend*
It suddenly occurred to him he had never seen any cipher clerks come back from these foreign postings and he suspected that that's what was going to happen to him too. Because they get to know too much. Whatever reason he defected, the fact that he did it is all we should be concerned with in the West.

John MacDonald
He was getting himself in trouble and we didn't pay any attention to him. So what help did he have from us? None. He must have been bitter. Mackenzie King didn't listen to him. Who listened to Gouzenko at first? Nobody.

Robert Keyserlingk
I don't think we can construe the idea that he found Marxism to be wrong. At university I had to read *Das Kapital* and things like that and I tried to engage him in conversation and he didn't know a damn thing about it. He was not a Marxist or an ideological communist. He was a practical man. He was a very efficient operator on those things they put him to.

Don Fast
Gouzenko sold himself on the idea he liked living in a democ-

racy. He learned about democracy and communism after he came here. If you could get a copy of the transcripts of the spy trials, you will notice he embellished his testimony. At the first trial he said he did a certain thing for a certain reason. In later trials he came up with additional reasons for having done the same thing. At first he gave one point and in the end he was citing a whole number of reasons. But he was fairly strong and it was enough to impress the judge. He sure learned a lot about communism since he came here, which is why he was so good at denouncing it.

George Mackay, *retired RCMP officer, one of his first bodyguards*
The Soviet Embassy has a caste system where everybody had his place. That I would imagine would be difficult for him. The amount of information that passed through his hands would make him feel tremendously important. Maybe they do it the wrong way. Maybe the cipher clerk should be at the top of the heap.

Don Fast
Before Gouzenko came to Canada he didn't have enough to eat. When he landed at Edmonton, where he switched to rail travel en route to Ottawa, he saw a pile of oranges. Gouzenko had only once before tasted an orange. He and one of his companions each spent their entire allowance on oranges. They didn't have enough bags to hold the oranges and got them into boxes and managed to get on the train just in time with their cargo. They were eating oranges all the way to Ottawa. Oranges were rolling up and down the aisle. I think one of the reasons Gouzenko wanted to stay in Canada is that here he always would have enough to eat. I firmly believe he defected because he wanted to eat regularly.

William McMurtry, *lawyer*
He was obsessed with this idea that not enough Russians were defecting because he believed there were hundreds of people like himself in a position of great knowledge who because of the fact the Russians had somehow brainwashed them into thinking

"you can never successfully defect, we will get you and destroy you one way or another" and therefore if they couldn't destroy him they were content to destroy his image. The last thing the Russians wanted was to let the world know this man defected over reasons of idealism. If he defected over money, they could laugh and say: "You see, he's as evil as the West." The party line. And he felt that our people were awfully stupid. He just felt we were so naive that we could not see how the Russians manipulated news and images. He would sometimes just scratch his head and say: "I don't understand how we can be so stupid; that people don't understand it."

Lydia Black, *widow of Mervyn Black, RCMP civilian member who translated Gouzenko's autobiography*
He came over here because he wanted to improve his life and get money. He said differently but people could see it was not true. It's the way a man acts. It doesn't matter what he says. If he was a man who defected only for an ideal, he wouldn't have sought the luxuries that he did. He would live a simple, peaceful life and be thankful for what he's got. You can splurge a little, but you have to be careful too. He said Russia was so bad and he wanted to live the way Canadians lived. But he wanted to live way higher than that. My husband also agreed that Gouzenko was after the money.

Roma Joy, *who housed Gouzenko shortly after his defection*
The motive for his defection was materialistic. Very definitely. The whole thing started when he realized that if he turned this material over to the Canadian government he would benefit by it and be able to keep his family here in Canada and give them some luxuries — luxuries as far as food was concerned which he had never had in Russia. He wanted this. Once he started and realized he could get anything and everything out of the Canadian government, he went boring right ahead. The RCMP guards were very unhappy with his attitude.

Willson Woodside
Gouzenko couldn't handle money. He simply couldn't handle

money. He let money slip through his fingers. His wife used to give him twenty-dollar bills and he would put them in his inside pocket and he would pull papers out of his inside pocket and they would fall on the floor — twenty-dollar bills and fifty-dollar bills. He was no good at all with money. He went through several fortunes.

George Mackay

Superintendent Rivett-Carnac and I went to see him. He was by that time living in his own house. I went there because I knew where the place was, so I drove him out. When we came back we were sitting in the car and he asked me if I would go out and see him every once in a while. I said: "If you're making that an order I'll do it, but otherwise I don't want to see the guy again." He said: "If that's the way you feel, then forget it." And that's the last time I saw Gouzenko.

. . . I don't know where the feeling arose but it was in me. I felt that he was going to be a problem. You just sense it, and I didn't want to be part of the problem either in fomenting it or solving it. That was my whole reason. I felt he would never be happy, that there would always be something more that he would want. He got what he wanted in the way of citizenship. I don't take away anything from the service he performed. It's just unfortunate — well, his ego got the better of him. I had this feeling within me back in 1946 that he wouldn't be prepared to stop, that he wouldn't be prepared to go away and say, "I've done my job and am living in a country where I can say what I like and move around freely and spend my money as I want and leave the rest behind." He just couldn't do that. Don't ask me how I felt that; it was just in there.

Doug How, *former Canadian Press reporter*

I remember at one time there was a Mountie who was one of the ones who spent time with Gouzenko. I forget his name. He was just a corporal or constable and one day I asked him: "What's this fellow like?" He said: "He's a very difficult fellow. For instance, he seems to be torn by two desires. One is to be known as the Great Gouzenko, the fellow who sprung the trap on the spies. At the same time he knows bloody well it's not in his own interest to have it known who he is. So he seems to be torn." I said: "How does this come out?" This was all off the record at the time because they didn't want any indications of it, so I just salted it away in my mind. He said: "I've seen him get on a bus and he'll bump people. You get the feeling he's on the verge of shouting: 'I'm Igor Gouzenko, goddammit. You should be looking at me. I'm important.'" He never did, but he said he always had that feeling there were these strong forces churning around inside him.

Eddie Goodman, *lawyer*

He had seen himself in the headlines and a lot of people never recover from that. He thought that he should continue to be a matter of public attention for ever after, and, of course, these things come and go.

William Kelly, *retired Deputy Commissioner of the* RCMP

I can tell you that there was a time when Gouzenko thought that only two men in the world mattered: Winston Churchill and himself. And probably he took priority.

Don Fast

I have thought this thing over and come to the conclusion he did not defect for any high motive. He defected simply for selfish reasons that either he was afraid or that he wanted to eat regularly. That was the one thing that was on his mind: food. So I came to the conclusion he defected for personal gain. And then all his actions after that supported this thesis. Everything he did was for himself. He was bright enough to build up reasons after the fact, and very quickly too.

Peter Worthington

If he had been part of the [Soviet] system, he would have been a tyrant. Can you imagine him as ambassador in some Soviet embassy? I guess there's a point when he goes one way or another way, and he certainly went the democratic way and then used all the instruments of democracy to do what he could and fight for himself. If he had gone the totalitarian way and used all the instruments and weapons to advance himself, he would have been in Brezhnev's position, that kind of thing.

Peggy Blackstock, *Gouzenko's editor*

Mr. [Cecil] Eustace and I took him to lunch. When we were walking back, I was walking with Gouzenko and Cecil was walking with the Mountie, and Cecil asked the Mountie if anybody would still take a pot shot at Gouzenko. The Mountie said if anybody is going to, he hoped he'd get the first chance. Cecil told me about this later.

Irene Eustace, *wife of Cecil Eustace*

He came to lunch on Sundays and on other occasions. I had absolute instructions that the luncheon I had to serve would be plain so he could see what he was eating. Gouzenko was very dubious about tasting the food until we put our children with him in the dining room. I always remember he sort of looked at everything and then waited to see that everybody had something to eat before he did. He was a suspicious little man. Highly suspicious.

John Picton

He told me he never took public transportation in Canada. And indeed from the day he defected he never went out of Canada. He wanted to stay totally within Canada, within Mountie jurisdiction. As he put it to me, public vehicles can be hijacked. Airplanes can be hijacked. Buses can be hijacked. Trains, places where he can be taken hostage, can be hijacked. He always stayed within Canada and would only go places where he could drive so that he could have the security of his own vehicle.

Robert Reguly

We would go down the street and right to the door of a restaurant. He said: "Have you made a reservation?" I said no. "Did you pick this restaurant?" I said yes. He said: "Okay, we don't go there. We go to another restaurant." He would never go to restaurants that you picked out. Subsequently I asked him why he was so ultra-cautious in the choosing of restaurants. He claimed that during the latter part of the war it was a favourite KGB way of assassination, that they would mix a teaspoonful of radioactive thallium — an odourless, tasteless white powder — and put it into things like spaghetti. Nothing would happen for six months or so and they would then get cancer or leukemia and there would be no connection as to cause and effect. He claimed this was done regularly.

Herb Spanton, *retired RCMP officer*

He had a right to be suspicious. He was brought up in circumstances where there was suspicion from the day he was able to walk. He was thrust into this cipher's job and extreme prohibitions were put on him. He told me of some of the degrading things that had happened to him. I could never blame the man for being suspicious of me or anybody else. I had the greatest admiration and respect for him and for what he had done.

William McMurtry

I think it's very important when dealing with Gouzenko to look at the totality of the man. It's very important. I think if you look in a segmented way, at one comment or one transaction or one issue in his life, it will be a great disservice to him. And I think this is where most people went wrong in assessing Gouzenko.

Peter Worthington

I could understand all the journalistic prejudices toward Gouzenko because he was a real pain in the ass at times and an awkward guy to get along with. But I found him terribly rewarding. He had a tremendous analytical capacity and insight. He was a very, very bright man. If he had ever been harnessed or used, there was no end to what he could have done. He could have helped our Security Service just endlessly if they had ever used him. And they never did.

Robert Fulford, *writer and editor*

There is one thing I have noticed during my life in journalism, which is more than thirty years, and that is, journalists, who are lower-case liberals or NDP, have always been eager — not willing but eager — to generate and circulate gossip against Gouzenko. Any nasty little thing they have heard, no matter how distant the source, no matter how shaky, they have always been very glad to put him down. If you said he's a bit of a nut case or is leeching off the government, it always got a very welcome reception from the journalists I have known. That is the most human response. He brought us a message we did not want to hear. And even twenty years later, people did not want to hear it. Metaphorically we were shooting the messenger.

William McMurtry

Here's a man who was so bright and brilliant in high school he was sent away on a state scholarship to a school which is basically military engineering. And he so excelled there — he stood first — and made such an impression that they did a very rare thing and allowed him to take whatever discipline he wanted. He chose his first love, which is architecture. There he so distinguished himself and so attracted attention by his brilliance that the army came in again and took him out and put him into military intelligence. He came over to Ottawa as a very young cipher clerk.

Robert Glasgow, *former* Time *correspondent in Canada*

He was a stereotype of the passionate, larger-than-life person who overreacts to all events. When they're depressed they're at the bottom, and when they're elated they're jumping and doing the sword dance. Gouzenko had a lot of that. I thought he had fairly wide mood swings. I think also there was something of a charlatan about him. He was such a self-promoter.

Franc Joubin, *once an acquaintance*

I viewed him as being totally unreliable. He was a curious character, not directly a thief but living in a dream world, thanks probably to the Canadian press, which made a hero out of him. He believed he was a hero and should be generously dealt with that way.

Don Fast
> He had a double character. One was bold and up front. The other extreme saw him scared. In one day Gouzenko could run the whole gamut of emotions from fear to defiance and promptly go out and do something dumb.

George Burnett, *Gouzenko's trust officer at National Trust*
> You knew that he was a mover. I always had the impression that some day that man was going to make a killing. I always had the impression that sooner or later this man would hit it big. Actually I was rooting for him.

Marilyn Maxey, *neighbour*
> All the properties were for sale. He advised the other neighbours to go for a certain price; I even forget which. And they all thought he was nuts. But he wasn't. He said it was going to get X number of dollars for his and that's what he got. He got his price. In fact, I think he even helped the other neighbours to bring up their property because it was valuable property at that time.

Don Fast
> He would have been easier to understand and you would have been able to get along with him, but you wouldn't be able to surmount that ego. He had a certain quality there that would make you wonder and then you would get the other extreme.
>
> He was two people. He would flip-flop. He was this cunning, sly person who was always on the top and then he was the ordinary guy. You would see flashes of that when he had been drinking. He would really go low and then all of a sudden he would come up with some brilliant idea and away he'd go on that level. So you were never comfortable with him. He kept wavering between these two people.

John Dean, *retired RCMP officer*
> I spent a little over two and a half years with that guy, that was 1945 to the latter part of 1947. And from 1947 until now my problem was to try and forget it. They're the worst two and a

half years I've ever had, and the idea is to forget it. And if anybody wanted to talk about him I didn't want to listen. I just didn't want to hear any more about him.

John Picton

His recall was excellent. Apparently he had masses of files in his home. And names. The most obscure name from thirty years ago would come up and Gouzenko would be right in on it. The amount of reading and filing and clipping the man must have done. Of course, he lived this. This was his life.

William McMurtry

He was not physically remarkable in any way. In fact, he had a way of speaking which was not very forceful. He had an accent. He might even fumble for words, but he always got the right word. But it was one of those things; the longer you spent with the man, the more impressed you became with his intellect. I must say I found myself quite often just sitting and talking about things. I got a kick out of hearing his view of history and current affairs and his assessment of various presidents and things that had been said and done. He was very, very interested in international affairs and the relationship with the Soviet Union, to the point of being almost obsessed.

Robert Reguly

He had continuing suspicions on things, and when we tried to pin him down on what he based it on, you found it was all supposition. He was taking a bit here, a bit there, and another bit there, and coming up with a grand scheme. But when you pressed him on the suppositions, you found his arguments, to my mind at least, were built largely on sand. You couldn't go with him. I finally determined that anything after 1948 I would have to let go.

Arthur Cole, *retired broadcaster and newspaperman*

It's a shame what this country did to him in my opinion. They did provide him with a very small pension, not enough to live on. And for a while they provided him with protection, but it wore off after not so many years. For quite a few years he was really virtually on his own.

Hon. E. Davie Fulton, *former Minister of Justice*

I feel Gouzenko did a great service to Canada at real risk to his life and safety and that he should be assisted and protected by the Canadian government. It was just too darn bad that he made it so difficult. There is no doubt he made the task as difficult as could be.

William McMurtry

I'm sure he was a nuisance. I think he became a nuisance. I think they created it. I don't think they handled him with sensitivity or intelligence. I think they looked upon him as "All right, we've got some of the information out of him, now how do we get rid of him? We just don't want to be bothered by him."

Peter Worthington

I must say I liked Gouzenko and I admired the man in many ways. I could see why people would be frustrated with him. I think he got a raw deal in Canada. We could have been a little more generous with him considering what he did. Don't look at the motives necessarily, look at the achievements. Certainly he considered himself a Canadian. He lived here longer than he did in Russia. It wouldn't have hurt us to have given him a little bit of recognition.

William McMurtry

I had an affection for him. I think I had an understanding for where he had come from and appreciated his thought process. The more you did that, the more affection you did have for him because you realized he was very misunderstood by some people. He wasn't a lovable character. Calculating is the wrong word, but he was a very analytical man. Very analytical. Some people would say he was paranoid.

James Eayrs, *historian*

I must say I'm very ambivalent about him. I think he was a very interesting figure, a very complicated person, very talented, very intelligent, but very limited. All these things. A very difficult person to get a perspective on. The overwhelming impression he left me with was utter lack of self-knowledge. Here was an extraordinary person, a man who had to live on his story. That was basically his predicament. He had a story. That was the only property he had. And he had to live off this story. His whole being was bound up with his story. And yet I was struck by the fact that he absolutely lacked perspective from which to step out from that story and to see himself in any detached way. I was very struck by that.

Robert Glasgow

His defection was the central event in his life and there was no damn way he would ever be able to top that again. Yet his appetite for recognition and awards was insatiable.

Robert Fulford

If he was more interested in himself and his own future than in ideology, then he was like the majority of human beings. That's why most people defect from really rotten environments — not because they want to save the world but because they want a better life. When you meet an immigrant in Canada from the Ukraine or Argentina or Chile or wherever, he may have a political point of view but he's here because he wants a better life. It's usually for his children as much as anything.

Dave Ghent, *retired reporter*

My opinion of Gouzenko is that he was just a little fink. I'm sorry that he's been adulated by the media and various other people as being a national hero. I know he had bugged and threatened to sue people and done all kinds of things over a long period of time. As far as I am concerned the guy was a fink. The guy was in a trusted position in his government, which he didn't have to be in if he didn't want to, and he took advantage of it and took off.

Irene Eustace

A traitor is a traitor in any language. It was for our benefit after all he did sell out his own country. You can't deny that fact. It was for his own good that he did it — for money. It wasn't for the love of Canada, I'm sure. You can't admire a traitor regardless of who it helps. I don't.

Peter Worthington

I think it's a very impetuous statement to say that Gouzenko is a traitor, because I'm not sure we can apply it. Gouzenko could make a good case that he wasn't a traitor. Would you brand as a traitor somebody who escaped from the Nazis? It may be technically, but it doesn't qualify emotionally as treason.

Svetlana Gouzenko

What's he a traitor [to]? He was born there. He didn't choose that country. He didn't choose the system. He never even voted for that system.

Eddie Goodman

I definitely got the impression every time I saw him that the world owed him a lot and never realized how much it owed him, and no one was prepared to do what the world should have done for him. The government. The public. Everybody.

Peter Worthington

I think more than anything that if Canada made a mistake it was in not appreciating him. Why wouldn't they ask to interview him at the Royal Commission on Security? The second one. I'm sure it didn't occur to them. They would probably say: "What has he got to offer? Why would we bother?" But just for historical reasons to place his past achievements, hear what he has to say. It's far easier having Gouzenko testifying before you and appearing in a booklet form than having him run off to newspapers saying, "They're afraid to have me testify. They're afraid of what I might say." And then people like me wondering why they won't give him the courtesy of hearing him. I think that attitude has marked the Canadian government's treatment of him from early on. Mackenzie King saw him as a God-given chance to save western democracy at one time — almost religious fervour — but it quickly palled.

Sir William Stephenson, *wartime head of British Security Co-ordination*

In light of subsequent events, Gouzenko has proved to be by far the most important defector of all the escapees from Soviet tyranny.

Ben Dworkin, *reporter who covered the spy trials*

My impression was that it was a great big deal about not too much. I was never an admirer of Gouzenko as a patriot or somebody who was doing a patriotic job for Canada. I think Gouzenko was looking after Gouzenko first, last, and always.

2 *The Ottawa Journal*

Svetlana Gouzenko

He decided then [to defect] when Kravchenko escaped and got a reasonably good reception. Kravchenko was an engineer who asked for political asylum in the United States and he eventually wrote a book, *I Chose Freedom.* . . . I didn't speak one word of English at the time, so I didn't read the book. But the news was in every newspaper. And it was discussed in the embassy, but all were blaming him and "Oh, he is such a mean man who leaves his wife.". . . His example was one of the decisive points for us — that it's possible to do.

J. L. Granatstein, *historian*

On the evening of September 5, 1945, Gouzenko walked out of the Soviet Embassy carrying a substantial sheaf of over one hundred documents and went to the *Ottawa Journal* in an attempt to present this material to the Canadian public in a way that would make the most impact.

Svetlana Gouzenko

A hundred and nine documents. Well, he could have taken more of interest but you know he put 109 sheets of paper under his [shirt]. He had to hold his stomach in not to be too bulgy. You know otherwise he would have [looked] like a pregnant elephant.

Cecil Bayfield, *retired RCMP officer*

He was afraid to come to the police in the first place because he didn't trust them. He thought they were all Gestapo. He told us that. He trusted the newspapers but he didn't trust the police because he thought they would have some infiltration or association with the NKVD [predecessor of the KGB].

Andy O'Brien, *ghost-writer of Gouzenko's autobiography*
Gouzenko had been reading the *Ottawa Journal* and got to admire the paper and think of it as a good place to unload his secrets.

J. L. Granatstein
He had an exaggerated view of the power of the press in this country. He had been in Canada for two years and had seen the press operate in an election and I assume he knew the *Ottawa Journal* was a Conservative or an Opposition paper. I guess he was impressed with the way the newspapers had attacked the government in the election a few months before.

Ken Parks, *former* Ottawa Journal *reporter*
I was in the newsroom when Gouzenko showed up. I remember seeing him but I didn't talk to him or have anything to do with him. I hadn't been at the *Journal* very long and was the lowest form of humanity, a night reporter. I was doing obits that night and I remember he came in and was standing in the door and everybody wondered what he wanted. He just stood there looking around. He was a small, unimpressive guy. Somebody said: "See what that gentleman wants." I guess one of the office boys went over to speak to him first.

George Paterson, *night editor of the* Ottawa Journal *in 1945*
The office boy brought this Gouzenko to me. I said I was night editor but I don't think he understood what I was saying. I passed him to Chester Frowde, the night city editor, because I couldn't understand what the hell he was talking about. There was no indication that he could be somebody important. He spoke very broken English. If he had been a normal person I would have talked to him. I talked to anybody who came in. But since I wasn't communicating with him, I directed him to Chester Frowde and then went to lunch.

Chester Frowde, *night city editor*

I remember it was a hot, humid night — September 5, 1945 — when the night office boy led a man to my desk. This man was short, with a tubby build, and was as white as a sheet. He beckoned me to leave the desk. I gathered he wanted to talk to me in private somewhere, so I led him into what is called in the newspaper the morgue on the other side of the main office. He backed against the wall. The first words he spoke were: "It's war. It's war. It's Russia." He said those words as if he had them prepared to frighten people. Well, that didn't ring a bell with me because we were not at war with Russia — World War Two was over —and I didn't get the connection. I talked to him at least ten minutes in that room. The door was open and the sports editor, Bill Westwick, was making a pot of tea at the time and saw me talking to someone in there but he didn't see Gouzenko. So finally I asked him if it was a police matter, because if it was, I would be glad to show him to the headquarters office of the RCMP on Wellington Street which was not far from the *Ottawa Journal*.

Bill Westwick, *sports editor*

We used to eat in a little room at the back of city desk. I came over from the sports department and passed the morgue when Chester was in there with this little guy. I stuck my head in the door and said: "We're having tea. We'll see you there later."

Chester Frowde

I didn't follow it up, perhaps, as much as I should because I put it down as a wild statement because we weren't at war with Russia and there was nothing in the paper lately about a war with Russia. I think I may have told him we're not at war with Russia and don't expect a war with Russia. Our relationship with them was apparently quite normal. Perhaps I should have followed it up more about the war with Russia, I might have drawn him out a little more.

I plied him with questions. I said: "Where are you from? What is your complaint? What do you want to tell me?" and questions like that. "Is it a matter for the police? Is there anything we can do?'' And he just stood there apparently paralysed with fright and refused to answer. I was wearing a green eye-shade at the time and later in his book he referred to the fact that an older man didn't quite grasp what he was saying. He didn't want to tell me any stories at all. If he would, I would have been right on the job.

If the man had been anybody other than Gouzenko and not been so frightened, I would have gotten more information out of him. No one could say I brushed him off that night. I think I showed plenty of patience. Now, looking back at the incident, I wish I had spent more time working on him. I've had thirty-eight years to think about it.

Marcel Schnobb, *deskman, sports department*
The Belle Claire Hotel was next door and we had drunks come in night after night. We even had the police come. Guys would come in and argue with Westwick on whether somebody scored one goal or two goals and they would become inflammatory after a few beers. Guys would get into an argument in the Belle Claire and then say: ''Let's settle it.'' So they would come over to the *Journal*.

I was a deskman in the sports department, which was in a closed office in the corner. So I would go from my cubicle and walk across the editorial room into the teletype room, where Westwick, Paterson, and Jones that night were having their lunch. In those days the sports was interspersed with the news on the wire and I would tear the sports out of the news and drop the news on their desks and bring my stuff to the sports desk and edit the copy. As I walked by there I saw Chester with this man. I went back to my room, which was totally closed in. I couldn't see Chester from where I was sitting. When I walked back I said: ''Chester, what the hell was that all about? Was that another drunk from the Belle Claire?'' I forget what he answered.

Chester Frowde
I led him to the elevator. He didn't seem to object at all to the way I dealt with him. He showed no disappointment. He wouldn't even give me his name, which is what troubles me

most today. If I had even had his name we could have checked in some way or other. It's one of those things that could have happened to any newspaperman. Some people, mainly the Ottawa *Citizen*, our rival, thought we had missed a big scoop. Even the president of the *Journal* at that time, E. Norman Smith, said: "We often had kooks call at the *Journal* at night." My conscience doesn't really bother me, except the pride that any newspaperman would have in having a story like that slip through his fingers. I still think of it.

Ken Parks

I was sitting at my desk and heard Chester saying afterwards, "I don't know what the guy wanted. He seems to think somebody wants to kill him. He keeps saying 'kill me, kill me' or something, he thinks he's going to be murdered. We're not running a police protection service here." He sent him on his way. He left the office after some time. It was quite late at night, I remember.

Bill Westwick

Chester joined us later [in the lunchroom]. I was in there with George Paterson, the night editor, and, I think, Reg Jones, the telegraph editor. I remember him saying: "Jeez, you meet some pretty odd people up here." Some of the guys would come up from one of the hotels all hot about something and wanting to write an editorial. But Chester said: "He mentioned something about atomic bombs and things. I couldn't understand him." Somebody jumped in and said: "What the hell is this all about?" Chester said: "I don't know. I couldn't make it out. He couldn't speak English very well. I told him he didn't need a newspaper but the police. I told him which direction to go in."

Ken Parks

We had all kinds of nuts come into the office. We had one guy who used to come in at night and claim they were watching from the empty building across the street and putting electric waves on him. We frequently had cases like that.

J. L. Granatstein

He then went to the Department of Justice and got to a commissionaire who effectively said: "The offices are closed after five o'clock. Come back tomorrow." He then had to go back home obviously in a high state of nervousness because he couldn't know when the fact that documents are missing would be discovered at the embassy.

Svetlana Gouzenko

. . . it was some young constable, whoever he was, and of course he cannot decide. Suppose [somebody] would rush in to the RCMP and say: "The Prime Minister's cottage is on fire." They will wake up the Prime Minister. They will wake up the whole cabinet: "The Prime Minister's cottage is on fire." Now here comes a man and says: "Here I have documents to prove Soviet espionage. The country is being taken from inside. Your country is on fire." And he says: "No, we can't reach him. He is away on a weekend, holiday. This is Labour Day weekend. I can't reach him. You have to come tomorrow morning." That was beyond our comprehension. Would something [like that] happen in Russia, whoever did not pay attention would be shot. He, his relatives, and friends and neighbours half a mile around would be shot for this kind of miss.

3 The Ottawa Journal Again

Cecil Bayfield

Then in the morning they decided they would both go to see the Minister of Justice. They went to see the Minister of Justice in the Justice Building.

Svetlana Gouzenko

They were all panicking. They were all just in a panic. Didn't know what to do. Didn't know what to do. To see them it is a live atomic bomb sitting in the middle of this building and they're running around. Don't know what to do. Finally St. Laurent made the decision that he doesn't want to see [us] . . . and [they] say: "Go back to the embassy and return the documents." I remember that point and I even told Igor: "You tell them that those are Canadian secret documents. Why return them to the embassy?" I don't know whether he told them or not because I couldn't speak English. Well, that was the decision of St. Laurent, the Minister of Justice. . . . When St. Laurent sent us away we were sure the decision was made by some bunch of Soviet agents because no minister of a country could decide not to be interested in that.

Don Page, *historian, Department of External Affairs*

He sat in there hoping he would see St. Laurent himself. Finally word came out he wouldn't be able to see him. He was very distraught but he had given enough information to an officer at that point that people were concerned about what was happening.

J. L. Granatstein

By this time the fact that he made these two tries with the Justice Department had come to the attention of someone who had informed the Department of External Affairs, because Norman Robertson, the Under-Secretary, knew of Gouzenko's appearance and informed Mackenzie King. So in some fashion the word that a Russian of some sort with documents was trying to see someone in authority in Canada had penetrated up the chain of command.

Greg Guthrie, *former reporter,* Ottawa Journal

I was at Lansdowne Park waiting to be discharged from the army and decided to go and see Mr. Lowry, who was the managing editor of the *Journal,* about returning to work at the *Journal.* I had worked there before the war. I can remember coming up the elevator and into the newsroom. It was a short step from the elevator to the newsroom doors and off to the right there was a place they called the library, which was really a little rotunda where the publisher's secretary sat. It was normal for visitors to wait in the library until they were ushered into the newsroom. There was this mousy little rather dishevelled-looking man standing there. I hardly noticed him and didn't have anything to do with him. It wasn't until later that I learned this odd-looking character was Gouzenko. It was a panelled room with heavy bookcases. He looked out of place in the surroundings. It was the only reason I noticed him at all.

Phyllis Wilson, *former reporter,* Ottawa Journal

The war was over, so we must have stopped running casualty lists by then. Very often couples would come in bringing in pictures of sons who had been killed overseas. I edited the casualty list, so it was very often my job to get the details about the boy and his life. You got so you could spot them because they looked so sad and unhappy. And when these two came in, all I remember is that they were two very unhappy or disturbed people. I didn't think any more about it.

C. C. "Chuck" Milne, *acting city editor*
I was acting city editor on the day he and his wife came into the *Journal*. It was noon, and when you're putting out three editions a day and one is due up you don't have much time to pay attention to detail. I mention that because I was on a deadline. Miss Pass, who was the receptionist at the editorial desk, came in and said there was a man and a lady there who wanted to speak to somebody in the newsroom. I told her to bring them in. I turned them over to one of our reporters. Her name was Elizabeth Fraser. Miss Pass took them over towards Elizabeth at one of the desks and as they came into the room I watched them.

Elizabeth Fraser, *former reporter,* Ottawa Journal
I was a reporter on duty in the newsroom at the *Ottawa Journal* at the time. There was a receptionist-librarian out in the lobby next to the elevators on the sixth floor. She was an elderly woman and she brought this young couple and a small child to me. It was one of the duties of the duty reporters not only to answer the phone and take obituaries from the funeral directors but also to talk to whoever wandered into the office with news or requests. We did the screening before we relayed them to senior editors. He did not give me his name but made it clear he came from the Russian Embassy and had documents, and that the Soviets were chasing him and that he was in great danger. He certainly knew English but it was fractured. It was not only heavily accented but rudimentary. It was a bit beyond pidgin English but he did not speak clearly, although he spoke understandably. His syntax was a step or two up from pidgin English but not fluent and not correct. She was very heavy with the next child and, speaking no English, was obviously perturbed and exchanging words with him in Russian. She was terribly anxious but not as agitated as he was. He was utterly agitated, almost incoherent. He blurted out on the first encounter: "It's dess if you can't help us" and then proceeded to try to convince

me that his situation was indeed as dangerous as he felt it to be. He said he had evidence with him of terrible Soviet spying activities against the western countries and that he wanted to save Canada from their perfidy, all of which, given the political climate of the time, sounded to me utterly fantastic.

He looked fairly young at the time, young enough to cast some doubt on his story. He didn't look like a high school kid. I didn't doubt that he was from the Soviet Union. But he was claiming he had been very important in the embassy and had all sorts of inside-track information and did not seem to fit either the man or his appearance. I had been on the diplomatic beat and had phoned the Russian Embassy about three times a week and talked to Nikolai Koudriatzev, the press attaché, who was a man of some bearing and sophistication. He had a great deal more polish than Gouzenko had, and, of course, a better facility in English. The comparison was obvious to me since I knew some of the diplomatic people and I didn't know any who seemed quite as ragged and raw as he did. I thought he was probably in trouble with the Soviets for some completely different reasons and was probably trying to seek asylum with this story. I became convinced he was paranoid and had not only delusions of persecution but of grandeur that he held information that would change the course of western history. His wife was so concerned for his well-being that I felt she was humouring a sick man along.

His story was unbelievable at the time. This was 1945. We had been hearing great propaganda stories all through the war about our marvellous allies, the Soviets, and we were being invited constantly to Canadian-Soviet Friendship League meetings. I covered a couple of them for the *Journal*. The hype was all in that direction. At the time, he was so agitated I was quite sure he was suffering from delusions. All I could do was to try to find out the correct procedure for them to follow if his story were true. It was obviously not something the newspaper could risk doing anything about. I went to a senior editor for advice and came back with the advice that he must go not to a newspaper but to the police.

Chuck Milne

Elizabeth said they had taken something from the Russian Embassy and they were afraid for their lives and they didn't know what to do. She wanted to know what they should do about it. You have to think of this in one context and that is that this was the capital of Canada and the Russians were still our allies and the embassy grounds were Russian territory. They said they couldn't go back to the embassy and they didn't know what to do. So I told Elizabeth to tell them that in that situation they should go straight to the Mounted Police and see what they could do for them. Because they had stolen something from an embassy — that's what they had admitted doing at that time.

Elizabeth Fraser

So I told him that this was not a story that the newspaper could print under present circumstances. It would have to be authenticated through the government. We had just finished the war but we were still very much in the ambience of controlled news. We had absolutely no concept at that point of investigative journalism of the sort that now is fairly common. It was just too hot to handle, not so much a matter of fear of consequences so much as genuine public-spirited fear of doing damage at a time when the world was desperately trying to regroup in a United Nations and at peace conferences, of damaging international relations. There was just no feeling that they could risk taking unauthenticated stories from someone who might very well be mad. It had to go through government channels. The ethos of journalist attitudes to government has changed enormously. It was just an entirely different way of thinking about things. We trusted our governments in those days.

I took them to the sixth-floor newsroom window and pointed out the Supreme Court building within easy view and said: "Over there. Go there and ask them there". He pleaded. He didn't protest. He pleaded. I can't remember the actual words he used. Besides, the words were not that coherent. The more upset he got, the more incoherent he became. I have a strong picture of a man who believed he was in very great danger for reasons he could document if he could get to somebody who could read his documents. We had no one who could read Russian. We simply saw the potential for damage being far too great. He had to go to the police for protection. We thought, they'll protect him one way or another, whether it's in a mental hospital or whatever. There was more pleading back and forth and finally, as kindly as I possibly could and with real concern for their pain but with very little belief in the story, I ushered them out of the office. I didn't believe his story, but he was so perturbed I later on a number of occasions thought: "I wonder how that poor man fared. I hope he got some help." It just didn't occur to us that his claims could be a possibility. We were very naive, I suppose. And it wasn't until the whole story broke with the arrests of the suspects many months later that I had any reason to believe that they in fact had been telling the truth.

Chuck Milne

I gathered from Elizabeth they never said exactly what they had stolen. It wasn't a case of coming to Elizabeth and saying: "We have some secret information about spies in Canada." It was not as abrupt as that. If there had been, I don't know, we might have taken a different step. Of course, this was the first inkling anybody had of spying operations.

Phyllis Wilson

I believe it was that day that Elizabeth Fraser and I went to lunch together in Murray's Restaurant on Queen Street and she told me about this interview she'd had. We talked about it: Could this possibly be true? I think she told me she had shown them the Justice Building on Wellington Street through the back window of the newsroom and had told them that that's where they should go. This is a long time ago to remember a conversation but it seems to me we decided that if this was true we would get a report that the police had found a body in a ditch somewhere.

I. Norman Smith, *later editor of the* Journal

I was away on assignment during and after the Gouzenko affair, but it always seemed to me the *Journal* was right to urge Gouzenko to go to the police. After all, it was the middle of the night when the stranger came in out of the dark. He was a very disturbed and frightened man. Had the *Journal* not resisted the lure of having a sensational scoop, whose facts could not be checked, the Russians would probably have sent Gouzenko back to Moscow under close guard with or without his wife and two-year-old boy to prison or worse. Chester Frowde's quiet handling of Gouzenko on the midnight visit and the subsequent decisions of restraint by others the next day enabled Gouzenko to give the Canadian government and RCMP his comprehensive testimony on Russian spying and much else under skilled, friendly, patient questioning in his own language.

Andy O'Brien

I don't blame the *Ottawa Journal* a bit. At the Montreal *Standard* we used to get nuts walking off the street by the dozen. The trouble was that after the Gouzenko thing I was always afraid to let them go. . . . Gouzenko felt he had gotten short shrift from the *Ottawa Journal*. He told me: "They did not give me a chance." You're not going to get much of a chance from an editor in a busy newspaper office.

Svetlana Gouzenko

You see, we a little bit overestimated the free press and what it could do. We thought the free press would right away grab the story and print it, then we would be safe. The Soviets would not attempt anything immediately if it would be in the press already.

Ben Dworkin

I don't think any newspaperman would have touched that story. It was just in the postwar period and we had more cranks coming into the newsroom than you could shake a stick at. There is no reason anybody would have taken this guy more seriously than anybody else. I never blamed the *Journal*. I probably would have done the same thing. Of course we at the *Citizen* had a smug attitude about it.

John Dalrymple, *former reporter*, Ottawa Journal

After that incident every kook who walked through that news-room door got a thorough, thorough interview. I went home with a half a dozen people with secret documents from the NATO alliance. Oh man. No story was too nutty.

Marjorie Nichols, *columnist*

The consequences of the Gouzenko saga on the *Ottawa Journal* were monumental. I'm ashamed to say that when I arrived at the *Ottawa Journal* in 1966 as cub reporter — it was my first job — I had never heard of Igor Gouzenko, but I think it took me only the matter of a month where I had a verbatim account about this man. Igor Gouzenko was permanently imprinted in my brain because it was regarded as this collective blemish on the *Ottawa Journal*. It was like the House of Atreus — this curse — had been cast upon us and we would all have to put shoulder to the wheel and try to somehow work harder. So every kook who walked off the street was interviewed as a matter of interest because people said "remember Igor Gouzenko". I remember when I was a reporter so junior I was still waiting word from management whether I would become a permanent employee and this very odd-looking elderly couple arrived in the news-room. The managing editor flagged me over and said: "Go and interview these people." They told me that they owned the crown jewels of England. It took hours to get this story out and I kept thinking, "What in the world am I doing here?" I thought: "Well, orders are orders." They had traced the family tree and they wanted us to be the last to know before they left by ship for England and they were simply going to march up to the palace and announce that they owned the jewels. I went back to the managing editor and said in a very humble manner — as I was in that position — that I ran through this "and that quite frankly I think they're nutty as nits." And the managing editor, Bill Metcalfe, just laughed and said: "That's great. As long as we've checked it out." So that was the great Igor Gouzenko legacy. This was twenty years later and we still felt it. It was something you lived with every day — like a wooden leg.

4 "The Russians Are Here"

Cecil Bayfield

[The *Journal*] told him to go to the police. He said no, he didn't want to do that. So they then sent him to the Crown Attorney's office in connection with naturalization because a young lady at the press said: "If you want it so the Russians can't pick you up, get naturalized." That is why he went to the Crown Attorney's office, to see if he could fill out some forms to get naturalized. His wife was with him at the time, the afternoon of the sixth.

Fernande Coulson *(née Joubarne), secretary to Crown Attorney*

It was probably 2 P.M. or shortly before or after. The assizes of the Supreme Court were opening and I was working for Raoul Mercier, the Crown Attorney, and he had to be in court at two o'clock to present his indictments to the grand jury and he had already left.

This man and his very pregnant wife came in. He was short and stocky and looked like a Russian peasant. He was very ordinary-looking and so was she. In very limited English he told me he wanted to apply for Canadian citizenship. I first had to find out whether I could accept his application, because an applicant had to be a landed immigrant, and after one year as a landed immigrant he could apply and file a declaration of intention to become a Canadian. Then he had to wait an additional four years. After being a landed immigrant for a total of five years he could apply for citizenship. So I put the questions to him. I said: "Do you live in Ottawa?" "Yes." I said: "Have you got your landed-immigrant card?" He didn't seem to understand, so I said: "How long have you been in Canada?" He explained to me then that he was Russian and he was working at the embassy. I said: "Oh, you cannot be a landed immigrant because you are actually on Russian soil." He said: "No more. I left last night and I'm not going back and I want protection." I said: "What do you mean you left last night?" So he went on to explain to me that he was a cipher clerk at the embassy and that he knew that Canadians were spying for Russia and he wanted protection and for Canada to know. I said: "Well, I cannot accept your application for citizenship because you have to be a landed immigrant and you have to be in Canada one year before I can apply your intention to become a Canadian." He was desperate and said: "Nobody will listen to me." I said: "What do you mean?" He said: "I have papers inside this jacket to show." He had a pocket inside and it was bulging with papers. He said it was proof of what he was saying and that he had stolen the papers from the embassy the night before. His wife had an old-fashioned black strap purse. It was old-fashioned even in those days and it was bulging. He told me it was full of papers. And he also had papers on his person in his jacket. So I said to myself that that man can't be lying. I told him: "Sit down. Just wait one minute."

Svetlana Gouzenko
. . . this woman was the smartest out of all these politicians. She realized right away that this was something of tremendous importance for Canada . . . that it is not a crackpot mumbling something something in half-broken English. So this is to her credit. I'll say put more women into the security service, because they are smart.

Fernande Coulson
I ran upstairs to the courtroom because I had seen Eddie O'Meara arrive a few minutes earlier to cover the assizes for the *Journal*. I was all alone in my office. I ran upstairs and told

Eddie I had this man downstairs who had left the Russian Embassy the night before with documents to prove that Canadians were spying for Russia. I said to Eddie: "Come down with me and I'll put you in Mr. Mercier's office. Look at those papers and tell me if what he's saying is true." So I ushered them through my office into Mr. Mercier's office and shut the door. He was there about fifteen minutes or so and when he came out I said to Eddie: "What I told you, is it true?" He said: "Yes, but I can't touch it." I think I had told Eddie that Gouzenko had told me that he had gone to the *Journal* that morning and whoever he talked to thought he was a nut. And that he had gone to the RCMP and had been turned away. Gouzenko told me all that in his faltering English. Eddie said he had to go back to court to cover the assizes for the *Journal*. I thought: "Gee, he's not helping me."

Svetlana Gouzenko

I think he was smart enough to realize it's a very big thing. But he also realized that it was a decision to be made by the RCMP and the government.

Fernande Coulson

Then I think I called the *Journal* and probably spoke to the editor. I knew them all. Then I called the RCMP criminal branch because they're the ones I dealt with every day. The Crown Attorney's office deals with the police every day. I spoke to somebody I knew there and said: "I want one of your men in my office." I told them who I had and everything. They said okay and sent a Mountie and, again, I put him into Mr. Mercier's office with Gouzenko and his wife. When he came out I said: "What I told you, is it true?" He said: "Yes, but there's nothing I can do." And away he went. Well, I was getting mad.

I was getting desperate. Mackenzie King's private secretary was Sam Gobeil and father of Charlotte Gobeil and Madeleine Gobeil. He was a good friend of Mr. Mercier's. I called Mackenzie King's private office and spoke to Sam Gobeil and told him who I was and where I worked and who was in my office. I said: "They need help. Somebody has got to protect these people or else they will be killed by the Russians." He said: "Give me your name again and your phone number. I'll call you right back." I hung up and Gouzenko continued talking to me. She would interrupt in Russian and he would speak back in Russian. Finally I said: "What is she asking you and what are you telling her?" He said: "She ask what you say to me and what I say to you." A few minutes later Gobeil phoned me back and said: "Do you want to listen to good advice?" I said: "What good advice?" "Have nothing more to say or do with that man. Get rid of him as soon as you can." I said "thank you" and hung up. By this time I was boiling. I was really mad. I thought: "What do I do now?" I phoned *Le Droit* and they said: "Oh, we couldn't touch it." The RCMP would have nothing to do with it and the Prime Minister through his private secretary sends me a message to get rid of him. I was getting a bit shaky. But I was mad at the same time.

I phoned Inspector Leopold of the RCMP. We dealt with him an awful lot, so I called him up and he started by telling me there was nothing we can do, that we can't help him. I said to Leopold: "You've got to do something. You have to see him. And I mean it." I was really frantic. He didn't want to see him but I guess Leopold felt that because of my insistence there might be something to it. I said: "What I'm telling you is true." So finally he said: "All right, I'll see him tomorrow morning. Tell him to come to my office at 9:30." I've forgotten the number of his room but it was in the Confederation Building at Bank and Wellington. I said: "All right." I told Gouzenko: "I've got you an appointment with Inspector Leopold" and wrote his name, room number, and address on a piece of paper and gave it to him and told him:"You have to go there tomorrow morning."

Svetlana Gouzenko
And she was phoning, phoning, trying to find someone and explaining to everyone in English and in French — phoned finally her priest, and couldn't get anywhere.

Fernande Coulson
In the meantime I had phoned the man who later became my

husband. He was the associate historian for the RCAF. I also had a very good friend who was a chaplain, an air commodore, in the RCAF and I spoke to him too. I said to myself: "Somebody might come up with a good suggestion and we might get help." The last thing I did was set up this appointment with Inspector Leopold. It was after five o'clock by that time. Gouzenko then begged me to keep all these documents, and after what I had been told by Sam Gobeil I was saying to myself: "Suppose I am wrong." It could cost me my job maybe. So I decided not to keep those papers. And he begged me. His wife by this time was crying. She was very pregnant. I said: "No. You need them. You have to have them tomorrow for Inspector Leopold anyway." So that was a good excuse for me. He was afraid to leave my office with those documents on his person. He said: "They will kill me."

Svetlana Gouzenko

I think she did advise to go to the RCMP and the government and just keep going and going because she felt it was important, but she cannot personally herself do anything. "If I can do anything I'll do [it]."

Fernande Coulson

He left, and in those days there were streetcars and I looked out the window of my office facing the corner of Nicholas and Daly and I stood in the corner and watched his wife and him leave my office, go down the steps to the corner, and get on the streetcar. As I watched him I said to myself: "That man may not be alive tomorrow." It was about 5:20 by this time. . . .

Svetlana Gouzenko

And that's when we went home. [We] were too tired already.

Fernande Coulson

In February, after this all came out, Mr. Mercier said to me: "You were so right. And that Sam Gobeil, what he said to you — " He was quite upset by the whole thing. So, knowing the man as well as he did, he phoned him up in Mackenzie King's office and said: "Sam, do you remember a certain phone call my secretary made to you last September?" You know what Gobeil answered? "No, Raoul, I don't remember." Mr. Mercier said: "You don't?" and hung up and said to me: "The son-of-a-bitch doesn't want to remember." About five minutes later the phone rang. It was Gobeil, wanting to speak to Mr. Mercier. He said: "Raoul, about that phone call, I would like to ask you a favour. Forget it was ever made." So Mr. Mercier hung up and repeated it to me and I said: "Like hell I'll forget."

Cecil Bayfield

In 1945 I was a staff sergeant in Ottawa in charge of Special Branch in A Division. On September 5, 1945, in the late evening, we received information about a man from the Russian Embassy in Ottawa who was possibly going to defect. However, this information came to us in a roundabout way and on the afternoon of the sixth I took up surveillance of a man who later turned out to be Igor Gouzenko, a cipher clerk in the embassy of the USSR in Ottawa. His wife was with him. . . . They went from the Crown Attorney's office and then up to the Justice Building. I think they wanted to see the Minister of Justice. However, I then went over and saw them go home to apartment four at 511 Somerset Street West. There is a park right across from his home and I then took up a position there on a park bench and waited.

J. L. Granatstein

It was now a whole day since he'd been gone. By this point he knew the Russians must have realized that he had hopped the fence and carried documents with him. Understandably he was very frightened. He knew what the NKVD could do to someone in his position and was scared.

Svetlana Gouzenko

We didn't answer [the knock on the door], but I think next door one of the next-door neighbours opened the door and looked and said: "They are not home," because he was banging too much and was too loud on the door. And at that moment Andrei ran across the living room. We were in the bedroom trying to hold [him]. And for one second you just leave the child and he just ran through the room into the kitchen. And whoever was knocking on the door heard the child running and then started calling "Gouzenko, Gouzenko." Well, [we] grabbed Andrei, towed him back, and didn't open the door. Maybe that was the time the neighbours heard and said: "They are not home." And he went away. . . . So we know that they know and they would be after us.

J. L. Granatstein

He saw the police sitting outside and didn't know they were police and thought he was being watched.

Cecil Bayfield

He looked out the window and saw two men watching the apartment. One of those men was myself but he didn't know that.

Svetlana Gouzenko

Suddenly two men, husky men, appear there. Sitting there staring at our window. Well, it doesn't take too much to put two and two together, you know. We felt it was Soviets. . . .

Harold Main, *then an RCAF corporal and Gouzenko's immediate neighbour*

We knew something was going on next door but we didn't know what. Their bedroom and our bedroom were right next to each other with a thin wall between. We could hear everything. Unfortunately they spoke mostly in Russian.

Mildred Main, *neighbour*

We thought they weren't getting along. When there's talking back and forth and it's getting hotter and hotter all the time and it's in a different language, you just surmise what's going on.

Svetlana Gouzenko

This is when Igor went to the neighbours. . . . This man also understood right away.

Harold Main

We each had a balcony at the back and he asked if he could come over to see us and talk to us. So he came over.

Mildred Main

He said his life was in danger. He thought he would be dead before the night was over. And he wondered whether we would look after the little boy.

Harold Main

It wasn't too surprising to us at all because with all the noise and shouting we knew that something was going on. It finally came out what was going on.

Svetlana Gouzenko

[He said:] "I realize it is really big but first things first. We have to make sure that you are secure, so I will go to the police and get police protection if they will attempt to kill." He was a military man and to tell him that one man can kill another was not new to him.

Harold Main

I didn't call the police. I went to them. I hopped onto my trusty bicycle and rode down to the police station. I didn't call them because we didn't know who was listening on the phone.

Mildred Main

I said I didn't feel that we could take the child. In fact I didn't want to be mixed up with it. We had a little girl of our own about the same age. We told Mrs. Elliott [another neighbour] about it and then Mrs. Elliott went over and offered her place. . . . In the meantime Harold went downtown to call the police. We felt we needed some protection. We didn't know whether they would know the right apartment or what they would do. I think if we would have taken the child the Gouzenkos would have just disappeared. They would have made a dash for it. I'm sure they would have disappeared for the night.

John Mockett, *former reporter,* Ottawa Journal

I was in the police car that night. We managed to get into the patrol cars to a certain extent and often got rides to run out to the assignments. They had a call to go to this apartment. The car drove up and parked on Somerset directly in front of the building. I didn't leave the car. You would seldom interfere with their call as such. You were in a privileged position. In fact, at that time we didn't know exactly what was going on. It was indicated as a domestic-squabble situation. That's the way they explained the call. Although I think they knew a lot more than that, that's the way they classified it as far as we were concerned.

Cecil Bayfield

At about eight or nine o'clock that night the Ottawa City Police arrived, two of them, Constable Walsh and a Constable McCulloch, and while they went inside I sat outside and maintained my surveillance from the park bench.

John B. McCulloch, *retired constable, Ottawa City Police*

Tom Walsh and I got a call on the radio to go there to see the corporal in the Air Force. It was at 511 Somerset Street between Lyon and Bay. They lived upstairs. I went up alone to see what the call was about. Gouzenko, the wife, and the little boy were there with the corporal. I stood at the doorway of the corporal's apartment. The corporal did most of the talking at the time and he was explaining why the Gouzenkos were there and why they thought something should be done about it. He said they had been to everybody and nobody paid any attention. They didn't know what to do next. So they called the police. She showed me her bag with everything they had taken from the Russians. "Don't ever touch that bag." She wouldn't give that bag to anybody. She held on to it all the time. Not him. Her.

Mildred Main

The police came around to the place but they said they couldn't do anything because Gouzenko's apartment was Russian property. They could give us protection but as far as what was going on in the apartment they couldn't do a thing.

Svetlana Gouzenko

They [Mrs. Elliott] had a couch to pull open and make into a double bed. So she made it for us and she fixed the bed. We were exhausted really and we lay down. Of course, I fell asleep right away and had a good healthy sleep. Igor didn't sleep. . . . I think Mrs. Elliott was not sleeping. She was nervous. She was that type, too, that was nervous.

Constable McCulloch

So we went back to the police station and were going to have our lunch and the call comes: "The Russians are here." So we turned around and beat it back again. When Tom and I got upstairs, they had smashed the door into the Gouzenkos' apartment at the end and four of them were in there.

Cecil Bayfield

At about ten o'clock or so, four people went up and one went into the apartment upstairs, I presume, and then came out. Then at about eleven o'clock these four individuals all went into the apartment block. They later turned out to be from the USSR Embassy and were looking for Mr. Gouzenko.

John MacDonald

My bedroom window was on the ground floor next to the court-yard. The Russians were looking into it and I was looking out at them. It was kind of strange. There were three or four of them with a Russian-movie sleaze look to them. People might glance into a window but these guys were peering in. Now, whether or not they thought Gouzenko was with us, I don't know. But they were taking as much of a look as they could. When they saw me they sort of pulled back a little and went back onto the street. But they were persistent enough. If I left the window they would come back. This went back and forth two or three times.

Margaret MacDonald

John noticed them, a lot of men, outside around the house. And he came in and said: "Mother, what are the men doing around the house?" And I ran to the window and I saw these men.

John MacDonald

We had the apartment right below him. My bedroom window was right on Somerset Street. There were figures flashing back and forth. There was so much commotion that my mother put her head out the window and a policeman very abruptly told her to, for God's sake, get back in. "Don't show your head out here." We knew then it was exciting.

Harold Main

They broke the door in. You didn't have to work very hard to break those doors in. As far as I know they just put a shoulder to it. I couldn't see what was going on because our door was in a little alcove in the hallway. I could only hear what was going on.

John MacDonald

The Russian Secret Service was pounding on the door, and fortunately he had left. There was an awful lot of noise. The Russians tried to get at him. They thought, I guess, he was still in the apartment and they were pounding on the door. The Ottawa police came along and there was a great deal of loud chat.

Constable McCulloch

We got upstairs and here was the door smashed right open. I walked in with the gun in my hand and had the whole four of them in the parlour as you go in. There were four of them and each one of these Russians was dressed in a different suit. The head one was the blue suit. The second one was in uniform. The next one, I think, was a brown suit. They were searching the apartment. They were looking under the bed and couldn't find Gouzenko. They didn't know where he was. . . . They came out from under the bed, the toilet, and the various rooms and just stood and looked at me. I was in uniform. Tom was in plainclothes. I wanted an explanation of why they were there and why they broke in the door. And they told me who they were; they were from the Russian Embassy and they were after Mr. Gouzenko, the cipher clerk; he had disappeared and he had certain papers with him and they wanted him. But they didn't know where he was.

Svetlana Gouzenko, *looking through the keyhole from Mrs. Elliott's apartment*

Igor was watching, and when the police walked in, Farafontov [one of the Russians in the Gouzenkos' apartment] just fell into the couch. Not sit down. He just collapsed on the couch. He knows he is a cipher clerk. He knows he has no diplomatic immunity.

Constable McCulloch

Tom went back to call the station and I had to stay with the Russians. I had them there and kept them. I got all their names and ranks. Wrote it all down. And the Inspector comes back with Tom; they didn't talk to the Russians at all. The next thing I know is that they went away again. They were trying to get Gouzenko placed somewhere, as far as I know. The head guy from the Department of External Affairs at that time was there. They wanted to move the Gouzenkos away to Quebec — to the big lodge on the other side of Gatineau.

Cecil Bayfield, *still sitting outside on the park bench*

. . . Constable Walsh of the Ottawa City Police came out and looked around and came over to me in the park and wanted to know what I was doing. I said I was just out getting the air. He said I had better move on and I said I didn't see why I had to. It was a warm night and I was just sitting out there. "Well," he said, "I'm telling you to go. Move." I didn't disclose my identity. I said "All right" and got up and circled around and surreptitiously entered the park again and took up my same spot.

Constable McCulloch

They [the Russians] wanted to leave and I wouldn't let them leave until I got permission to let them leave. In the meantime I waited for Tom and the Inspector to come back and they didn't come back until after the Russians were gone. I waited and waited and they demanded to leave. They said there was no way

I could hold them there because they were immune from anything. I had to let them go. When they were leaving, they said they would be responsible for any damage that they caused.

Svetlana Gouzenko

... [Igor] was ready to run out and shake the policeman and say: "Those two don't have diplomatic immunity. Arrest them."

Cecil Bayfield

After the embassy staff had left — it was after midnight — I went into the apartment building and went upstairs and to apartment four, which I knew to be Gouzenko's apartment. The door was locked ... and I opened it with a skeleton key, went in, looked, and saw the place in a shamble. Drawers in the dresser had been turned out and balls of wool and children's clothes were scattered all over the place. Anna Gouzenko, Gouzenko's wife, had been expecting another child and she had been doing some knitting. All this was thrown all over the place. They had made a real thorough search. The closet doors were open, so I just looked around, didn't touch anything, and went back out and back to the office.

Don Page

Bill Stephenson, later Sir William Stephenson, the Man Called Intrepid, had been invited to have dinner with Norman Robertson at the Royal Ottawa Golf and Country Club. He had come up from British Security Co-ordination headquarters in New York and stopped in Montebello, Quebec, and phoned Robertson from there to inquire about the time he was supposed to be at the country club for dinner. Robertson alerted him that there had been major moves here and he must come down immediately. On the chesterfield at the country club Robertson informed Stephenson about what was going on. It was Stephenson then that gave Robertson a tremendous support for not carrying out the Prime Minister's orders for turning Gouzenko back to the Russians.

George Glazebrook, *retired External Affairs officer*

Stephenson was coming to Ottawa for another reason. I don't remember what it was and the case broke on that day. A dinner was already arranged for Stephenson at the country club. That went through its normal course, but I have a photographic memory of Robertson and Stephenson sitting on a sofa and Stephenson having this story told to him for the first time. Later on he went and hid behind the bushes, watching the building in which Gouzenko was hiding.

Constable McCulloch

External Affairs wanted to take them away that night. I'm not sure but Tom and I wouldn't let them move them at the time. We were going to stay all night with them and they weren't going to take them any place until the government took things in hand. And they took over the next day. . . . They were trying their damnedest to take Gouzenko over into Quebec to a big lodge there. But they didn't get them because we wouldn't let them take Gouzenko out of the apartment. We wouldn't let them touch him. We didn't know what they were going to do with him. The guy said he was from the Department of External Affairs, but who was he? He didn't show any credentials.

Don Page

The mysterious people who went to call on Gouzenko's apartment that night in addition to the police and people from the Soviet Embassy were Stephenson and Tommy Stone, the key person in security matters in External Affairs. They had gone on their own up to the apartment to see if they could contact Gouzenko and find out where he was, and they hid in the bushes for some time and so found out something about what was going on. I think the credit for the fact that Robertson was encouraged not to carry out the Prime Minister's orders really belongs to William Stephenson.

Sir William Stephenson

Then we returned to Norman Robertson's house and I induced Norman to telephone RCMP rescinding the previous order and to place the Gouzenkos under surveillance and later protective

custody until further orders. It should be noted that Robertson
and I had complete confidence in each other, and indeed there
was a close friendship.

Constable McCulloch

The next thing we knew we ran into the chauffeur and another
guy coming up the stairs. The Russian car was outside the door.
I had the number and everything. He demanded to go up to the
apartment and we told him he couldn't go. We pushed him
back down the stairs again. They had to leave. That was as far as
they got.

John MacDonald

We must have thought that he [Gouzenko] was escaping because
he didn't want to go back [to the Soviet Union]. We didn't know
that he had secret papers or anything. We didn't know he had
all these files. We just thought he was skipping the country. Or
asking for asylum.

Margaret MacDonald

And that night we went to sleep and the next day I saw all these
men around, walking around our place. They were just watching. They were the police. And this one policeman said: "Don't
worry. They can't touch you. It's the Russians. But you're all
right."

John MacDonald

The police told us to keep this very quiet. It didn't break publicly
for a number of months, so we weren't supposed to tell anybody
that this had gone on. The spy scares were not in the wind those
days. This was the first one. What we did think was that they
came to drag him back to Russia. We had no idea about the spy
angle and we knew pretty well that he certainly didn't want to
go back.

Mildred Main

We didn't talk very much about it. A couple of days after it
happened, two men arrived at our door and wanted to use the

phone and I told them we didn't have a phone. I'm sure they were from the embassy. The police told us if we were asked any questions by anybody coming to the door that we were supposed to deny it. They said: "If they ask about a phone, deny that." So I did. They wondered where they could use a phone and I told them where there's a corner grocery store.

John MacDonald

The police watched the apartment for quite some months. If you lived in the neighbourhood you could always spot a plainclothesman. They would sit on the park bench across the road. We came home from a party one time. My mother had brothers and sisters and one of her sisters is a bit of a cut-up. And when we came home and got out of the car she started speaking a little bit of Gaelic. And the plainclothesman guy — this would be maybe November — in the park came right over to my uncle's car and asked an awful lot of questions, thinking that this awful-sounding language was Russian.

5 Hiding

Svetlana Gouzenko

Igor was proposing what to do immediately. Like grab the other one [cipher clerk] while he knew which man is the cipher for the secret police line. The NKVD. . . . Igor said: "Just see that he walks out of the embassy. Just arrest him under the pretext of crossing the wrong lane of the street or anything. As long as you get him in your hands you've got the whole information." He would not be able to return to Russia because the Russian secret police would not trust a man who was in the hands of western intelligence.

John Batza, *retired RCMP officer*

It was the fourth of September when I came back off holidays. I remember somebody saying there was some kind of a Russian bomb walking the streets of Ottawa. I was a sergeant in Special Branch and second in charge at the time in A Division. Bayfield was the staff sergeant of the whole works. Inspector Williams was the officer, and he explained the whole thing to me in the afternoon. Gouzenko was inside the Justice Building at this time being interviewed to determine whether he was a genuine defector. He was — so they took him over. That was the word go.

Svetlana Gouzenko

We stayed in a motel. And it was a one room and both sides were motel rooms with Mounties, maybe four Mounties, six Mounties, there. Oh, they were guarding us really well because the Soviets would just strike my husband then these papers would be of no value.

. . . All we can hear is their walking, their bang, bang, bang. The motel walls are very thin. You can hear them and they're walking and walking and walking there. And Igor say "Go to sleep" and he couldn't. Well, then they took us to one cottage.

John Batza

The next thing I knew it was five o'clock and we had a car ready in the backyard and Williams told me: "You're taking Gouzenko and his family. Take another man with you and some arms. Take him out of town. Go wherever you like but make sure you bring him back alive." Those were my instructions. Ottawa was a dangerous place for Gouzenko, and the RCMP wanted to get him out of town. The feeling was the Russians would shoot Gouzenko on sight if they ever spotted him. Williams said: "Nobody will know where you are. Phone me from there and I'll transmit it to the Commissioner. It will be only the Commissioner, me, and you."

I chose Happy Harris to come with me. He had just returned from overseas service. He was a captain there and would stand up under fire. I was looking for somebody who wouldn't cringe and run under fire. We went out to the car and Harris and I sat in the front while the Gouzenkos sat in the back seat.

John "Hap" Harris, *retired RCMP officer*

Jack Batza and I didn't know what was going on. We were suddenly told to go home and pack a bag and get ready to go out. When we got back to the Justice Building, we were told we were to take the Gouzenko family out of town and find some place to stay and phone back and give our location. At that time there weren't many motels around in the countryside and I had been away from Canada for five and a half years during the war so I had forgotten the location of things, so we had some difficulty.

John Batza

The Inspector told me: "We'll send several cars to follow you out to make sure nobody else is following you." As we drove out, Gouzenko said: "Where are we going now? Where are we going now?" "I don't know. It's up to us to find out when we get there." We drove and drove, and every time he looked back and saw a car he said: "Mountie, there's a car following us. A car is behind us." He said this all the time. He was worried and really a nervous character in that respect. He was scared of every Tom, Dick, and Harry that he saw. He was a spy. I said: "It's an RCMP car." He said: "But they've got spies in the RCMP too." Those are verbatim the words he shouted from the back seat. There were two or three Mountie cars and then eventually they pulled back and we were alone. We were free.

John Harris

Oh hell, he was always saying: "Okay, they're going to get me and they won't stop for you." This sort of thing. I had been away for five and a half years and had forgotten about the area. I thought Batza would know more about it than I did, but he didn't seem to know where the hell we were going either.

John Batza

We drove out towards Smiths Falls. We didn't know what to do and it was getting close to supper and we needed something to eat. I saw the hotel on the main street and stopped the car and went inside, and, as luck would have it, a friend of mine was running it. Walters, who used to run the beer parlour in the Château Laurier. I was in the anti-sabotage section and he had been a contact man of mine. When I told him I had a Russian defector to look after, he understood immediately and didn't ask too many questions. He said: "There's nobody here. The girls have all gone home. Normally I would say no, but I'll unlock the dining room and serve you myself." He locked us into the dining room so nobody else could get in. We couldn't have it any other way. If anybody else had been there, Gouzenko would have never walked in. You couldn't have forced him in. He [Walters] opened the door once to come in and asked something and Gouzenko dove under the table. He was completely underneath. I said: "Come out of there, Gouzenko. He's a friend." So he came out.

An hour later we packed up and left. Then I asked myself:

"Where do I go from here? I can't go much further or else I'll be too far away to come back in the morning." So I swung east along the Rideau Canal and went all the way through to Kemptville. "Where do I go from here? I'd rather drive north." So I turned north a few miles and crossed the bridge and on the bridge I looked to the left and saw three cottages.

John Harris

There were three cottages there and a house. In fact I think the woman who was in charge of the house wanted to turn us away because she said there was no room. I said: "Well, we've got a sick baby and it's crying." So she said: "Just a minute." She wanted us to go into the rooms in the house and I said nothing doing, the baby is sick. After all, they were speaking Russian. Then she said: "Well, there's two cottages available. We'll clean them up and put you in there." So that was it. Eventually she told me she recognized me. I used to work up in that area before the war.

John Batza

He went to bed and apologized. "We sleep in the nude," he said. That didn't bother me, I had seen nude people before. Harris would stay awake for an hour and then I'd stand guard for an hour. We'd have a gun in our lap. An intruder would have to swim from across the river.

We got up at eight o'clock in the morning to get some milk for Little Joe. We called him Little Joe for Joe Stalin. We gave Joe his milk and then thought about how to get them back to Ottawa alive. During the war, the hotels wouldn't give you a room — nothing. I went to the hotel in North Gower and told the manager: "I'm on a secret mission and I don't want anybody to know. Can you give us something to eat? Anything at all." He said: "We're not in business. We're closed, but I'll make you something. What would you like?" I said: "Ham and eggs or something like that." We were eating at the table and all of a sudden Bayfield, who had come down from Ottawa to see me, opens the door and comes in. Gouzenko dropped underneath the table again. Bayfield said: "What's he doing?" I said: "We're trying to hide him from all this stuff." So he came out again.

Bayfield informed me there had been a change in plan: "Leopold wants to interview Gouzenko in the morning." The next morning was Sunday. "Go back to where you were and stay there." Bayfield went back to Ottawa and we finished breakfast and went back to those same cabins.

John Harris

When we got back, we took our two cabins back but we didn't think of taking the third one. We should have done that because later somebody else took the cabin and it caused Gouzenko a lot of concern. This fellow came in and took a briefcase and typewriter out of his car and went into his cabin and pulled down the blinds, turned on the lights, and started typing. We went out to dinner at Kemptville and when we got back his car was gone. In the meantime we had checked out his licence number to see who he was. It was an awful hot night and eventually he came back and started typing again.

It was midnight, I guess, and Batza and I were sitting out there and suddenly out of the other cabin came Gouzenko in the nude. "That's him. That's him. He's one and there will be more." He heard the typing and thought this was a set-up.

John Batza

I jumped up and here was Gouzenko standing outside the front of the cabin completely naked, both arms raised over his head, hollering "Help! Help!" — screaming to beat hell.

John Harris

We told him to go back to bed and we'd take care of the thing. That's when we thought we had better organize. So we went into shifts. At about four o'clock in the morning there was some creaking from the next cabin, and I thought, if anything is going to happen, it's going to happen now. So I went out and told Batza: "I think we better split. You be over here and I'll be over there." We saw this character come out with a briefcase and got into his car and drove away. That relieved us. We found out later he was a schoolteacher from Smiths Falls or somewhere and he was out there writing a thesis.

John Batza

The next morning we waited for Leopold but it wasn't until about noon that he arrived. Leopold interviewed Gouzenko inside the cabin while she and Little Joe were outside. Gouzenko's English wasn't too good and Leopold's Russian wasn't very good, so they had a time getting things straight, but he eventually seemed to get to the end of it. While Leopold and Gouzenko were inside, I stretched out on the grass in the back of the cabin and actually fell asleep. All of a sudden I felt something on my face and woke up and looked up and here was the little boy peeing right into my ear.

Leopold said: "Stay here until tomorrow morning and at eleven o'clock there will be a rendezvous outside of Ottawa. Make sure you're there. A party will be waiting for you." The meet was set for a point beyond the west side of Ottawa.

John Harris

The next morning we went to North Gower, but the hotel was shut so we kept on going. The hand-over was supposed to be somewhere near Carleton Place, so we went to Carleton Place and had breakfast there. We had a blowout on the way.

John Batza

The roads were pretty crooked and narrow and windy and all of a sudden, bang, there was a flat tire. The road went one way and the car was pulling the other way. We were doing about fifty miles per hour and I was trying to slow down the car while the flat tire was trying to pull us into the ditch. The car teetered and nearly turned over. I said: "My God, that's all we need. What would have happened if we had upset the car with these people in it and the police come and we have to reveal everything." I could see the worst coming and my career with it. Gouzenko got out and helped Harris change the tire. We did it in about fifteen minutes flat. We had breakfast and when we came back we drove slowly around that corner.

When we got to the rendezvous point at Ottawa there were all kinds of cars lined up one after another. Williams and some of the other officers were there. I shook hands with Gouzenko and said goodbye and that was it. That was the end of my tour with Gouzenko.

John Harris

That was that. I didn't know where they were taking him. My wife didn't know where I was for three or four days. She wanted to know where I was going and how long I would be and I said I don't know. At that time I didn't. But then when I came back, she asked a few questions and I told her there was nothing I could tell her.

Svetlana Gouzenko

One cottage we were at several days and it was cold already. And already maybe a week passed and we didn't have a bath. I had a bath last time in the motel. Igor went with Andrei to swim — the lake was cold. I can't go to swim [because of my pregnancy]. I am not going to make a spectacle of myself, but it was terrible. All I was using was a washcloth and wiping myself. And being already spoiled for being two years Canadian with my own private bath. I always had a bath every day because I enjoyed it.

Lydia Black

They called my husband in at that time and he started to take translation. He spoke Russian and wrote Russian. But I didn't know where he was. I hadn't seen him for two weeks. I asked McClellan: "Where is my husband?" "Oh, Mrs. Black, you know I'm not a liar. I can't tell you at the moment." So I let it go. My husband was away from home for a whole month.

John Batza

In October I was detailed by Inspector Williams to look for another place, because that place was too cold. I checked and checked and checked, spent two or three Sundays doing nothing but driving around, but couldn't find anything better than the cottage we spent our holidays at. It was a big cottage at Otter Lake with three bedrooms and a big stove and lots of stove oil. I knew the lady in Smiths Falls who owned it and she knew me because I had rented it once before. So Gouzenko moved there for the rest of the time he was in the Ottawa area. After that, McClellan, who was in charge of CIB [Criminal Investigation Branch] in Toronto, came down with some other guys and they picked him up and took him to Toronto. He had everything lined up for him down there. So Gouzenko left the Ottawa area and we were free.

Greg Guthrie

I did learn about some of his doings from the Mounted Police in the special section who were in charge of him. One was Blackie Campbell, who told me that they fixed him up in a cabin on a lake. He told me stories about Gouzenko expecting them to act as chambermaids and cooks and everything else. They got pretty fed up. When he ordered breakfast one morning, they told him to cook it himself. Apparently he knew nothing about cooking and dumped the eggs in the pan without grease. The result was a great cloud of smoke. They were down at the lake and had to rush back. They thought the cabin was on fire, suspecting that somebody was trying to get at Gouzenko. I gathered from them they weren't too enamoured with Gouzenko, that he was not the pleasantest house guest.

John Batza

Bill Campbell stayed with them at Otter Lake. He moved in with them and helped them buy groceries. Campbell was a good guy to look after him. They got to know him. In the end Campbell hated him. He said he was nothing but a big show-off. He said he'd go out and buy the damn store if he didn't stop him. He said he didn't have too much money but he'd buy caviar and stuff like that and then didn't eat it. He said: "Half of the stuff I took back and turned in for other stuff." Gouzenko had no inclination to make friends with people. It was a case of "what I say goes". He was used to that from when the guys came down to interview him — what he said went. They never argued and he got used to that. So he thought Canada was that way.

6 Camp X

Herb Spanton

I think it was day three when George B. McClellan, who was stationed with me in Toronto, phoned me at home around nine o'clock and said we've got a job to do that required us to be in Ottawa at ten o'clock sharp. He said: "I'll pick you up at your place at 4 A.M." Now he didn't say any more and we didn't ask questions over the phone. He picked me up and while we drove to Ottawa he told me what had happened. We arrived at RCMP headquarters in the old Justice Building. I didn't meet Gouzenko at that time. I learned about the situation and studied some background. We were asked to do a study to find a place to put him that was secure but not totally isolated — preferably in the Toronto area. We left Ottawa at around nine o'clock that night. George B. was driving and oddly enough we both thought of the same place at the same time. He said: "Camp X." I said: "The old farmhouse." He said: "Yes." That's how we chose the farmhouse at Camp X as the place to lodge Gouzenko.

George Mackay

I was a corporal in charge of the Enemy Alien Registration Office, which was down from the old post office on Adelaide Street. Every day I'd have to take my mail over to headquarters at Bay and Front to post it. So I was over there one afternoon walking down the hall in October 1945 and the door opened and Herb Spanton said: "I've been looking for you." I went into the office, which belonged to then Inspector McClellan, and was told I would disappear for at least six months and that I was going to have to look after a certain individual and I would be staying in a certain place. I was caught completely by surprise with the whole thing. I learned only later it was Igor Gouzenko. I was told to go to one of the senior NCOs, who I believe was put into the picture, and was supplied with such things as mattresses and stoves and was told I would be allowed to take the truck. So I went with Spanton to Camp X and within the week Gouzenko and his family arrived. He didn't have anything to say about the place that we were in. It was no palace, believe me.

Svetlana Gouzenko

We were told we were going to a different place but we were told that it would take several hours driving away from the Ottawa region where the Soviets could go freely. We were to go to the Toronto area. We didn't know it was the Toronto area either but they told us we were to go to that one area where the Soviets will need to ask permission to go. . . . We came and that is the one where there was a bathtub. And the first thing I did was take a bath. After three, four weeks, you can imagine that.

George Mackay

I was his personal guard. I was armed at all times. I slept in a room down the hall at the head of the stairs. Later on I shared it with other constables. Downstairs there was a kitchen, living room, and big bathroom. It was heated with wood stoves.

Outside, just a short distance away, there was a guardroom with soldiers who had been employed at Camp X and were still there. I presume they were armed. I never paid too much attention to them. We got along with them fine and they were very helpful. It meant that nobody could get to our farmhouse without having to pass them or else going way around across country. It was a fenced area. It was really a farm. Camp X itself was really within a farm. But there were no pretentious fences indicating something important was there, just ordinary barbed wire fences with cows across the road. It was a typical rural scene. I was in plainclothes of the type you would wear working around the farm except for the presence of a shoulder holster.

Herb Spanton

The location was perfect. It was wide open, so the security was good. It was a big piece of land that nobody bothered paying any attention to during the war. There were antennas and everybody looked upon it as a CBC broadcasting place. The odd time somebody would come down the road to the beach, but we had a very good view.

John Dean

The tension was pretty high. We slept with our revolvers. I didn't wear anything. It was about three o'clock in the morning and there was a noise outside the window. I got up with revolver in hand and went out through the front door and tried to sneak to the back where I heard the noise. It was a damned cow. There I was running around the place naked with a revolver in my hand. It's funny now but it wasn't funny at the time. Incidents like that happened all the way through.

Don Fast

It was a typical old farmhouse. I would say about forty-fifty years old. Two storeys. Stove-heated. Not very comfortable. Not very imposing. She was pleased as punch with it because she thought it was real nice. It wasn't. It was very awful. She was thinking in terms of one room and three people in a room. Here she had three bedrooms upstairs.

George Mackay

It was a farmhouse that hadn't been used for quite a long time. It was an expedient to get him out of the way and afford him protection. We fixed it up as well as we could. Basically it was warm and clean. The Gouzenkos had quarters to themselves. Of course, I had a room to myself also. We got along as two people who had been brought together under a common umbrella. He understood my position and I understood what I had to do.

Svetlana Gouzenko

It was a nice little farmhouse, an old farmhouse. And we had an upstairs, a bedroom, and all the Mounties were cramped. Usually it was one Mountie with his wife in one of the bedrooms upstairs — a three-bedroom house. And downstairs one of the poor Mounties was sleeping on the couch. Mounties are huge, big, long-legged, and the couch is small . . . it was always like a grasshopper then in the morning-time.

George Mackay

Shortly after that, he was being interviewed by various people in the Mounted Police and some MI5 people. These people were coming and going. There was information our people had to get from him in relation to establishing the names and whereabouts of the people his documents indicated were passing information to the Soviets.

Don Fast

A lot of the debriefings took place in the car. They were trying to get him away from the noise and the child and whatnot. I think most of the briefing and debriefing had been done before he got there.

George Mackay

In the early part it might be four or five hours a day. Then he'd get tired, trying to think, and confusion would set in. I must say he never became impatient. He realized the necessity of it. The die was cast as far as he was concerned. He was now dealing with a lot of strangers. You will recall he didn't want to go to the Mounted Police in the first place because he was satisfied there were Red agents within the force.

Svetlana Gouzenko

There were so many of them coming. Once six or seven of them would be all downstairs at this big farm table and they would be sitting there. Or each of them would look for some point that he wanted clarified. Very often it would be a mistake. Once Leopold built it all up how the Soviet system worked. A chart. He made a chart and it was all wrong.

Herb Spanton

Johnny Leopold [late RCMP officer who once infiltrated the Communist Party of Canada] did a great deal for this country. I took him to Camp X, where he met Gouzenko. The next day we left for Ottawa and Igor came with us, but he wouldn't ride in the same car as Leopold. He said he was a spy. We stopped in Kingston for lunch and Igor got up and left the table. He told me: "You don't believe me." Of course I didn't believe him, but I just said: "Let's forget about it." Leopold had more secrets than I would ever dream of knowing, and one of the most loyal people I had ever met in my life. Yet he was convinced. "Don't ever have that man around me again." As far as Igor was concerned he was a spy. He had learned that Leopold had been undercover for some time and I suppose he felt that if he worked undercover there he would be working against me, too. I don't really know what his thinking was.

George Mackay

He was thoroughly frightened as to what his fate might be. He and I would go on walks together, but I was never that far away that he couldn't call me. He wanted somebody with him all the time. At that particular time he had a real apprehension. I never experienced any problem in the time I was there with anybody being around. Camp X was winding down and it wasn't long afterward that these chaps outside the guardrooms were gone. Mind you, we had access to a telephone that would give us Camp X itself if any assistance was needed. He had a good reason to feel apprehensive. His life was in danger, because if they caught up with him, if they couldn't kidnap him, they'd kill him. That was the attitude in those days. Things have changed greatly since then. Defectors are just shrugged off as another one lost now. It was a different story in Stalin's days. Then Gouzenko would have been the example. So he had a good reason to feel apprehensive.

John Dean

We'd walk outside but never off the grounds. The property went from the rail line to Lake Ontario. So we could do quite a bit of wandering around. The property was quite big. Nobody knew about Camp X. That was a secret, a real secret. Nobody knew we were there.

Svetlana Gouzenko

I have about a thousand hobbies, so they kept supplying me with all kinds of materials to do with my hobbies. Crocheting, knitting, and I knit babies' clothes and I am sewing. They bought for me a sewing machine, so I was sewing finally a dress that would fit me. And Igor was writing a lot. He would write in Russian and then it was given to Mr. Black, the translator.

Herb Spanton

There was some acrimony, but it was a reasonable thing to expect. Here was a man in a very delicate situation for many months. He was almost a displaced person. Security around him was very tight. He appreciated this, but at the same time it was difficult for him to comprehend that we were the responsible body and if anything happened to him it happened to us at the same time. He didn't see it quite that way. Often little things would come up that he wanted to do that we just couldn't arrange.

George Mackay

Sometimes we had a lot of fun. Unfortunately, or fortunately, they weren't card players that you could sit around the table at night with. Anna — we called her Anna — was always busy with something of an artistic nature. She was a good painter and very good with her hands. So quite frequently, particularly when Black would come out and stay — there was a room for him also; he might stay three or four days — we might spend the night around the table discussing the situation as he knew it, his future, the events of the day and their meaning. He considered himself somewhat of an analyst as far as the news was concerned. He was an avid reader in everything, particularly in the political field. He would go through a newspaper back to front.

Sir William Stephenson
I had a request from the RCMP to send a layette to the camp for Mrs. Gouzenko, as layettes were not available there. I had not the slightest idea what a layette was until enlightened by one of my secretaries. The problem was: was it to be blue or pink? And we finally settled on white. It was purchased from Saks, Fifth Avenue, and it was duly delivered by hand of Captain Herbert Rowland, a Canadian member of BSC [British Security Co-ordination] from Owen Sound, Ontario.

George Mackay
There was the night the baby was born. I said: "Sure as hell it will come at four o'clock in the morning" and I was right. I was asleep. But when I came downstairs, she was sitting there doing her toenails, just as calm and collected as all get up. If she was suffering any labour pains, she certainly didn't show it. We tore into the hospital. Merv Black was there. He was the father. I was the taxi driver who took them to the hospital.

Svetlana Gouzenko
Well, we waited and waited and waited. The thing is, they had been on alert, you see, from about the twenty-sixth of November. On alert. The car was there standing and two Mounties will take me to the town and some four Mounties will be staying with my husband and Andrei. So it was terrible, the waiting and waiting, and it is ten days past.

Wes Harvison, *son of the late RCMP Commissioner, Cliff Harvison*
Mrs. Gouzenko was very pregnant at the time and she spoke nothing but Russian and was going to pop at any time and they didn't want to identify her. Meanwhile, they had her in this farmhouse and the little kid was tearing around. Apparently the little kid they already had was a horror. They nicknamed that one Little Iodine. They said: "We have to do something about the delivery." Black spoke perfect Russian, but he also did the best Russian shtick you ever saw. They figured the hospital questions would be mainly concerned with who pays. There was no hospitalization in those days. So they gave Black a wad

of bills that would choke a horse with, in the best Mounted Police tradition, mostly ones on the inside and the big bills outside. He got into a farmhand mode, acting like a poor immigrant farm labourer who "not speak too good English". Black takes Mrs. Gouzenko to the registration desk and he answered all the questions the best he could in his halting English. When it got to the point where the questions get a little touchy, he reaches into his pocket and pulls out this great wad of bills and says: "I pay now." There were no more questions.

Svetlana Gouzenko

A nurse recognized me. She was in the nursing hospital in Ottawa when my Andrei was born. And she looked at me and said: "Didn't you have a baby some two years ago? I was working in Ottawa. I thought a woman . . . resembled you very much." Well, I knew a few words in English and she kept saying: "In Ottawa — you had a baby in Ottawa." And I told her no and she then came to the conclusion all those newcomers all look alike.

George Mackay

During the first Christmas, somebody somewhere threw into the air the idea of Christmas-tree ornaments and we still have a couple that go on our tree, but that whole place was covered in Santa Clauses — little ones — made out of papier mâché. We bought out Woolworth's entire supply of toilet seat paint, which is an enamel, red and white and gold. The bathtub was filled with rolls of paper being soaked. They made moulds. We were all in on pressing these things into the moulds. We had Santa Clauses, geese, Christmas trees, and other things. For a while, everywhere you looked in the house these things were drying, either having been painted or having been moulded.

Svetlana Gouzenko

I was making some Christmas decorations — ornamental — to relax more or less. Then the Mackay family locked themselves in their bedroom and all we can hear is this paper [rustling]. What on earth are they doing there with this paper? If they would be typing then it would be typing paper. What on earth are they doing with this paper? And Igor was getting nervous, saying: "What are they preparing there? I can hear all the time the rustling of the paper." They were wrapping presents.

George Mackay

We had a turkey and did the whole thing up in a traditional Canadian Christmas. Presents were bought by the police and we had a Christmas tree with lights. Behind it all was to assimilate them into the Canadian way of life. We had a Thanksgiving dinner. These are things they had never heard of. Later on in the following year there was Easter.

Don Fast

On his first Christmas they decided they would give him a real Canadian Christmas with a turkey and all the trimmings. So they prepared a big table with the whole works. The living room had a stove with a chimney that ran up and across the room and into the roof. Little Georgie [Andrei] went upstairs and had a pee on the stovepipe. It ran along the pipe and all over the place and onto the turkey. It was splattered all over. She took a towel and wiped off the turkey and said: "It's all okay. It's lovely." Guess who got the first piece.

Herb Spanton

He had to go to a dentist, so I went to my own dentist and told him about a friend who had just come from Yugoslavia who hadn't had proper care. My dentist understood that. I said: "I'd like to make an appointment on a day that will be quiet." I told him there would be no conversation, that he would look after his teeth and that's all there would be to it. Both Igor and his wife went, and that's when the fence came down a little bit. I waited in the lobby downstairs. My wife went up with them and it would have only increased the suspicion if I had gone up too. Some time later the dentist said to me: "I'd like to ask you a question because I wouldn't want to make a mistake. If my suspicion is correct, then that will be the end of it." He had figured it out. He was suspicious because of the way it had been arranged, and the newspapers were full of Gouzenko at that time. So I said: "I'm not going to name any names, but let your suspicion be your guide." As far as I know, he was the only one who found out.

John Dean

We drove him as a witness from Camp X to the preliminary hearings in Ottawa and Montreal. We stopped at Kingston. We had chicken and we all got salmonella trouble. We all felt pretty grim. Of course, he thought an agent was involved. It was just lousy chicken in the restaurant.

Herb Spanton

I was the only one in the group who didn't have the chicken and I was the only one who didn't get sick. I had a roast beef sandwich or something. Dean particularly was ill. It was quite serious. We ate in Kingston again, but we never went back to that place, not because of the bad chicken but because of his suspicion.

7 Arrests and Headlines

J. L. Granatstein

Gouzenko's biggest revelation was the fact that civil servants on a fairly broad scale were breaking their oaths and clandestinely supplying information to the Soviet Union. That's the major revelation. The next most important thing was that Allan Nunn May, a very senior scientist who was heavily involved in the construction of the Chalk River reactor, was part of the Soviet spy ring. It's fair to say he knew everything about Canadian-British-French atomic research and knew, I'm sure, a good deal about the American atomic research as well. He was a big fish. The next most important revelation was that Fred Rose, a Member of Parliament, was acting as an agent. The idea that somebody elected by the people of Canada had turned himself into a conduit of information to a foreign power was not something that Canadians at that point had contemplated. Next was the fact there was a spy in the British High Commission, Kathleen Willsher. She was as far as I can tell the secretary to the British High Commissioner and had access to nearly everything and had been passing documents for seven or eight years. She had been passing material to Fred Rose. That came as a serious shock. Another big revelation was that there was a Russian agent in the office of the United States Secretary of State. The reference was a little vague but it seemed to be an assistant secretary in the office of the Secretary of State, and of course that was the first finger pointing at Alger Hiss. There was also a reference in the Gouzenko materials to an agent in the U.S. Treasury Department and it appeared to be pointing to Harry Dexter White, the senior civil servant in American treasury and a figure of very substantial importance. Gouzenko revealed much more, but these sit at the top of the list.

Cecil Bayfield

After Gouzenko had been taken into protective custody there was a special detail to attend to that. Constable Campbell and myself maintained twenty-four-hour surveillance on all the suspects — eleven of them — in the Ottawa region. We would see them go to work, see them go home. Some of them lived up in the Gatineau — Benning and Gerson who worked in Munitions and Supply, they had cottages up in the Gatineau around Glen Eagles. We maintained surveillance on those individuals to see who contacted them, if anybody did. That was my job then. Every day I would submit a report to the officer in charge of Special Branch, Superintendent Rivett-Carnac. I worked also with Inspector Leopold of the Special Branch and Inspector Parsons. It was a tight-knit group. Practically nobody else in A Division knew there was such an investigation going on, apart from the officer in charge of CIB, Inspector Williams, and Constable Campbell, and myself. We maintained strict secrecy on that investigation.

Don Page

The problem was, once they found out that people had been involved in this ring both within External Affairs and the British High Commission, they had a major decision to make. If they arrested these people immediately, then they were not sure how many others could possibly be involved. Gouzenko admitted he didn't know everyone and that there could be more people involved than he knew about. Nor did he know whether this was the only so-called spy ring. There may have been others. The problem was, how were you going to communicate this information to Washington and London on a secure communications base knowing that the British High Commission's link was compromised, that External Affairs' communication link was compromised, and the hope was that they could continue to operate the way they had in the past until they could identify who had been passing these messages on and what was involved?

The key here was that through British Security Co-ordination's connection with Ottawa they had a secure link to Washington, New York, and London, and because of that link we could carry on communications with our allies and allow our compromised communication system to carry on until we could positively identify who in that system actually was passing on the secrets.

William Kelly

Although the RCMP had suspected espionage, there was nothing very definite. The feeling was that if espionage can take place in other countries it can take place in ours. But they never, until Gouzenko, had come to grips with this kind of thing. Of course, the Gouzenko case was one of the greatest revelations, not only to Canada — the British, Australians, and Americans were all amazed at what was going on: the fact it was going on to that extent anywhere in the world. Up until that time it was just the odd master spy and so on. This changed the whole picture.

Wes Harvison

I was about eighteen. My father had always been in Montreal and then the Mounted Police shifted him to Winnipeg, which didn't make any of us very happy. We had hardly got to Winnipeg when orders came through that he was supposed to report to Ottawa *ex post haste*. He was pretty sore about it. He said: "If the so-and-sos wanted me in Ottawa, why didn't they transfer me there?" Because we wouldn't have minded Ottawa. "I just hope they've got an excuse for this kind of nonsense." They told him to be prepared to be there for a few weeks. So he left me and my mother by ourselves. There hadn't been a word of what this was about. When he came back I said: "Well, has it been justified or not?" He said: "Ohhh yes, it was fully justified." I said: "Give. Let's have the story." He said: "Sorry. Not a word." He used to tell us things that strictly speaking he shouldn't have, but we were privy to a lot of secrets during my growing up. He knew he could tell us, but on this one not a word. He said: "I'll be getting another call and will be going down again and then it will become obvious what this is all about." I said: "When you get that call, you'll be able to tell us?" He said: "Nope." I said: "Well, when are we going to find out what this is all about?" "You'll read it in the paper." When the call finally came, I said: "Now you can tell me." He said: "No, but you'll see it in the paper." I said: "There are a lot of stories in the paper. How will I know which one?" He said: "Oh, you'll know."

J. L. Granatstein

I think it is quite proper to say the RCMP at this point appeared to have known nothing whatever about espionage out of the Soviet Embassy. The potboiler histories of the Mounted Police make it sound as if they knew everything that was happening and they were just waiting for the chance to crush the Russians. They had, as I understand it, a grand total of two people working on counter-intelligence in Ottawa in this period. It seems quite clear they knew nothing whatsoever about any espionage being launched by the Soviet Embassy or any other embassy. It's for this reason that soon after Gouzenko came over, that Ottawa had to ask the U.K. to send some counter-intelligence people over. So Peter Dwyer and Roger Hollis came over to play a role in the debriefing of Gouzenko and work in the counter-espionage aspects of this case.

George Glazebrook

Stephenson lent us two people from New York. I remember meeting them at the railway station and we went over to the Château Laurier and they turned on the taps so nobody could hear anything. I told them what had happened thus far and then they got into the act. They were experienced people.

Don Page

Now, we were quite aware that the Russians were very intent on spying on our legation in Moscow. We saw this and [Ambassador Dana] Wilgress often reported on it by the fact that employees were given theatre tickets next to an NKVD agent so as to be watched. When there was a bachelor on the staff, for example, there were indications of efforts to have him date certain Russian girls. . . . So there was enough suspicion —opening of parcels,

difficulty with customs — that they were quite aware of the
NKVD's activities. What they didn't know was that this extended
into Canada.

Robert Keyserlingk

I read and translated some of these documents and I must say he
[Gouzenko] was pretty bright in the things he picked out. It was
a pretty thorough collection. I would imagine it was the most
thorough collection we got from anybody at that time.

Hon. Jack Pickersgill, *then head of Prime Minister Mackenzie
King's office*

It [the revelation of Soviet spying] was a terrible shock to Mr.
King, as he indicates clearly in his diary, and it was also a shock
to Mr. St. Laurent that these gallant allies were at the same time
engaged in this kind of activity. Now that perhaps suggests they
were both pretty naive. I don't think it was as great a shock to
Norman Robertson, and even less of a shock to Hume Wrong,
who were the two officials in External Affairs who knew about
it. But it was kept very, very secret. It was one of the best-kept
secrets in Ottawa. I knew something was going on because these
meetings were being held in Norman Robertson's office, which
was just along the corridor from my office in the East Block.
But I made a practice, which I believe is not widespread in the
public service, never to inquire into things I didn't need to
know. I thought it was much better to be able to say honestly
and truthfully "I don't know." So I made not the slightest effort
to find out what this obviously cloak-and-dagger business was
all about. The day these people were arrested, Norman Robertson sent for me and told me the story, told me what had happened, told me they were being arrested that day and they were
to be held incommunicado.

W. L. Higgitt, *retired RCMP Commissioner*

I understood that perhaps he [Mackenzie King] even wanted to
go to Moscow and see Stalin personally about this and say sort
of: "Let's tidy this thing up." But he didn't follow through. He

was advised by his cabinet or by somebody against that thing. How far he had actually crystallized it in his mind I don't know.

J. L. Granatstein

Atomic energy was a closely shared secret of the ABC powers — the Americans, the British, and the Canadians — even though the Canadians and the British did not have all the details on what the Americans had done. Canada was in a privileged position. So King felt obliged to raise the question of Soviet spying with his partners. . . . He travelled to London first and then to Washington. The trip was camouflaged under other purposes.

In Washington there was a tripartite discussion on how to play the Gouzenko case. It seems revealing that the three allies decided not to hype it up. They decided not to create a great war scare out of this and not to create a great anti-communist scare. . . . They decided at that meeting it was all to be kept quiet and to allow for co-ordination of investigations and arrests. The Americans were not at this point entirely satisfied that either Alger Hiss or Harry Dexter White were spies and wanted to further their investigations. The British were still carrying out their investigations around Allan Nunn May, and matters were simply left in abeyance for a time. The fact that matters were left in abeyance suggests that people like Mackenzie King hoped that the Gouzenko case could possibly blow over.

Don Page

One of the big problems was: what do you do with people when you don't have sufficient proof? Do you allow them to function in their present position or not? External Affairs agonized over this. What they did is they took these people and moved them out of sensitive areas to clerical work. . . . One clerk in particular they were very suspicious of because of things that Gouzenko had said. But he was never publicly identified because there was not proof of this. A number of circumstantial pieces of evidence caused people to be concerned, so they simply gave him a very routine type of job. Soon after that he quit and went off because he didn't like doing routine work.

Hon. Jack Pickersgill

Mackenzie King was reticent in taking action because he had a pathological fear of having the Government of Canada provoke a war. He wanted to be bloody sure that the British and French had declared war in 1939 before we did, that we weren't one of the original parties. He always held that one of the main reasons why the Japanese ever came into the war at all was because of Arthur Meighen's action in Washington and London — particularly in London — over getting the Japanese alliance denounced. He said: "Well, that turned the Japanese against Canada and against Britain." I don't believe that for one minute, but he did. There's no doubt about it. Then, of course, when the war with Japan came, we declared war first — before the Americans or the British, and Mr. King wanted to do this. He wanted to show leadership. Not two hours had passed when he regretted it, because he said: "You know, we were the leaders on this. The Japanese in the long run are going to hold this against Canada." And there's no doubt whatsoever that his first reaction would be: "If we exploit this Gouzenko business we are going to be the prime targets of the Soviet Union." Again, I don't believe they pick their prime targets that way, but I know enough about Mackenzie King to know he felt this way.

Don Page

The officials in it had come to realize that time was running out and they couldn't keep this secret forever. It was bound to come out and they were much more prepared than King was to the fact that when it came out they would have to act. He would have liked to have seen it gone on for some time but they realized that you just couldn't do this. Too many people were involved. There were too many inquiries going on and somewhere someone was going to start to talk. When you start sending people around about what you're doing at certain times and the nature of your work, people start getting suspicious and enough comes out of just answering questions that you can be assured that sooner or later the press will be tipped off.

Sir William Stephenson
King refused to take the necessary action for fear of offending Stalin. The Soviet penetration in the U.S.A. was so widespread and their agents were preparing to escape. After consultation with Hoover and President Roosevelt's so-called brain-trust co-ordinator, Ernest Cuneo, we agreed that the story should be released by way of Drew Pearson, Sunday night broadcast, *Nationwide.*

J. L. Granatstein
Matters in fact lapsed for roughly four months before any public action was taken. And when public action was taken it was because Drew Pearson, the American newspaper and radio columnist, talked about a spy case in Canada. It has been claimed that Stephenson leaked it to Pearson and maybe that's so. It seemed to me it was just as likely somebody in the United States who wanted to create an anti-communist incident in Washington. Once it became public and people were talking about it, King felt obliged to act. At that point King told the cabinet for the first time about the affair. Prior to this, only two or three cabinet ministers knew. He now told the whole cabinet and advised that he was setting up a royal commission under two justices of the Supreme Court of Canada, Messrs. Kellock and Taschereau. The Commission began its work on the next day, February 6.

W. Kenneth Campbell, *secretary to the Royal Commission*
Mr. Justice Kellock and Taschereau asked me into their office and showed me some of the papers and I was just aghast to see what was there. I didn't think any Canadian could do that. They asked me if I would take on the job as secretary to the Commission and I said I would do my best.

Dave Ghent, Ottawa Journal *reporter*
We didn't know about the Royal Commission or the spy investigation. Eventually we got indications that something had happened. Little things cropped up. The two *Hansard* reporters, one of whom did court work in Ottawa, went missing. The one

who did court work in Ottawa just wasn't there one day. He was a nice guy. We knew him. Was he sick or something? We didn't know. We checked around and discovered that he told his wife he was going on some special job and packed a suitcase and took off. She had no knowledge of where he was or anything else, just that he was doing something very special on behalf of the government. He wasn't coming home at night. He was just gone. He could have been heading down to Tijuana with some chick but that wasn't his nature.

W. Kenneth Campbell

The hearings were all in the Justice Building, I think on the seventh floor. The Commissioners sat with their backs to the Gatineau Hills. The witnesses would come in and sit at a table and I sat directly opposite the witness. When the witnesses were sworn in, the Commissioners were identified. At the other end of the room was another table where the Commission counsel, E. K. Williams, Gerald Fauteux, and David Mundell, were sitting. The piles of necessary paper were put on tables around the side at the back of the room.

. . . Kellock had been one of the leading counsel in Ontario and Canada. Taschereau was a leader in the Quebec bar. E. K. Williams had been president of the Canadian Bar Association and Gerald Fauteux was probably acknowledged at that time as the best criminal lawyer in Canada. He was a leading Crown Attorney in Montreal. He and Williams appeared before the Supreme Court regularly. The four that they got were the best they could get in the whole country. No question about that.

Hon. George McIlraith, *then Parliamentary Assistant to C. D. Howe*

All these lawyers were the very cream of the crop in the country. Kellock and Taschereau were on the Supreme Court of Canada. And E. K. Williams, the counsel, later became the Chief Justice in Manitoba. You were dealing with the very top level of professional men in the country. Either then or looking backwards from now you couldn't put together a better legal team than that.

W. Kenneth Campbell

They [the Commissioners] were amazed when everything unfolded and developed. Each day something new was coming up. The counsel would ask questions and they [the Commissioners] would ask questions and the witness would tell another story and add something else. It all unfolded and the pieces fell into the right place.

J. L. Granatstein

The Commission's hearings began on February 6 and Gouzenko started to give his evidence on February 13. It became clear there were a number of civil servants identified in his documents. The Commissioners presented a report to Mackenzie King saying in effect "that we have sufficient evidence to cause the arrest of twelve people." The arrests were made on the morning of February 15. There had originally been an attempt to grab those people in the middle of the night, but Robertson had stopped it by saying we shouldn't act the way the Russians would act. So they were then taken in daylight hours.

Cecil Bayfield

The time set for the arrests was six o'clock on the morning of February 14 and I was told I had carte blanche and could draw any men I wanted from headquarters staff to man the cars. So I picked forty-four men. We had eleven cars — there were four to a car — since we had eleven to pick up in the Ottawa area. And at four in the morning they were all summonsed to the Justice Building, where I briefed them as to what it was all about. Up until that time none of them knew what they were there for. They did not know. A lot of them thought they were going on a narcotic raid, but it was kept so quiet they didn't know.

I briefed them and they studied the orders they were given. The sergeant, the NCO in charge of each car, was given a certain man to pick up and the place to search. At quarter to six, half past five, depending on what distance they had to go, they all left and the arrests were all made at six that morning.

The places were searched and documents or anything incriminating was brought in. The suspects were taken into headquarters and then taken into Rockcliffe — Rockcliffe is the RCMP's training division — which was set up as the detention area.

Lola Benning, *widow of J. S. "Scott" Benning, one of those arrested*
They came at five or six in the morning. It was very early in the morning. My husband wore glasses. He couldn't see a darn thing without them. They held out a piece of paper. . . . Gave him the glasses and they said: "No!" The landlady had come up with them because we had just rented a few rooms upstairs and she said: "He doesn't see without glasses." So they permitted him to put on the glasses to read whatever they had.

Ben Dworkin
There was a girl, Kay Willsher, who worked at the British High Commission. She lived in an apartment at 225 Kent Street in the centre of Ottawa. It's a brick building and still stands there. By sheer coincidence my apartment was right next door to hers. My apartment was eight and hers was seven. At some ungodly hour one morning there was some terrible pounding at my door — it scared the hell out of me and my wife — and there were the Mounties looking for Kay Willsher. I won't say they smashed into the door. They didn't. They stood at the door and found it was the wrong place and went next door. I had no idea what they wanted her for. This happened before the Gouzenko story broke. I put a little story in the paper, maybe two or three paragraphs. I didn't make a big thing of it — my wife didn't want to get involved any more. Later it took me a while to let it sink in that she was in fact charged as a spy because I just couldn't believe it. Here was this mousy woman who had lived next door to me for three years.

Cecil Bayfield
All [were arrested] but Fred Rose, the Member of Parliament. We couldn't arrest him because he skipped. But I picked him up on the fourteenth of March, a month later. I surprised him up in his apartment at two in the morning.

W. Kenneth Campbell

The Mounted Police picked them up in the early morning hours. They were all down at the barracks in Rockcliffe by eight o'clock in the morning and behind bars and couldn't see anybody.

Peter Benning, *son of Scott Benning*

My father was detained for pretty close to two months, I think. After talking to the others later, it seemed each was detained in pretty much the same condition. Each was given his own barracks. My father was in a barracks all by himself. The lights were on constantly and there was always an armed guard watching over him. My father was a fairly playful sort of person. What he did was to take the mattresses from the two dozen or so cots that they had left in the barracks and piled them all in the corner and make this huge nest of mattresses. And apparently somebody took a picture of that and they threatened to publish it in a newspaper as an indication they were not so badly off.

J. L. Granatstein

They were taken to RCMP barracks at Rockcliffe and subjected to intensive interrogation. They were kept in rather sparse quarters and watched constantly. I understand that lights were kept burning in their rooms twenty-four hours a day. They were denied the right of habeas corpus and for some substantial time could see neither their wives nor families nor their legal counsel.

Peter Benning

The War Measures Act was still in effect. None of them had been told why they were arrested. My mother did not know where my father was for the first ten days. My father was not in communication with anyone during the first ten days. My father was interrogated often and at length before he was allowed to see a lawyer, my mother, or anybody else.

Arnold Smith, *Royal Commission staff member*

It was essential to synchronize the arrests and that was done. It was also essential — so the people planning this thought and I agree with them — to question as many of them as possible before they were given orders from their party superiors that they should under no circumstances say anything. Otherwise we wouldn't learn anything. And the object was learning. So they were held for the first few weeks or days before they were allowed to be visited by their wives or friends or lawyers, because that would have brought them party orders not to say anything.

J. L. Granatstein

After the arrests were made, Mackenzie King made the first public statement on the Gouzenko case. He didn't name Gouzenko and he didn't identify the Soviet Union. He said a foreign power had been found to be committing espionage and a Royal Commission had been set up and some arrests had been made.

Doug How

I'll never forget the day that this story broke in Ottawa. At that time I was in the Parliamentary Press Gallery with Canadian Press and the House of Commons wasn't sitting, so we were down at the office in the old Ottawa Citizen building. We had a reporter at that time called Jack Brayley who was one hell of a reporter. Drew Pearson in Washington was the first one actually to suggest there was something coming up. But Jack was the first one. I don't think we had even seen Pearson's account. Jack came charging into the office one day, it was a dull day and late in the afternoon, and his eyes were bulging out and he said he had one hell of a story. Foster Barclay was the news editor, and the minute Jack told him what it was, he said: "My God, this can't be." He got Jack to sit down and Jack pounded out the first story: that a group of people had been detained by the Mounted Police for conspiring to communicate secret information to an unnamed foreign power. They didn't name the Russians. Back came a message from the general manager saying: "Is this candy?" which is CP inside language for "Are you sure?" Barclay wrote back yes. I think within an hour or so the official announcement came out. I remember asking Jack later: "Where in the hell did you get that story?" He said there was a Mountie

Ottawa Journal staff a few years before Gouzenko walked into the newsroom with his bombshell. Chester Frowde is standing on the extreme right and Bill Westwick is seated next to him.

Chester Frowde

This man was short, with a tubby build, and was white as a sheet. He beckoned me to leave the desk. I gathered he wanted to talk to me in private somewhere, so I led him into what is called in the newspaper the morgue on the other side of the main office. He backed against the wall. The first words he spoke were: "It's war. It's war. It's Russia." He said those words as if he had them prepared to frighten people. . . . I plied him with questions. I said: "Where are you from? What is your complaint? What do you want to tell me?" and questions like that. "Is it a matter for the police? Is there anything we can do?" And he just stood there apparently paralysed with fright and refused to answer.

Bill Westwick

I saw Chester in the morgue talking to this little man. They tell me Gouzenko couldn't speak very much English and it would be very difficult. Another guy might have brushed him off and not too kindly, but Chester was a very patient fellow and very kind. He wasn't at all one of these brusque characters which the movies depict reporters as being.

John MacDonald
We had the apartment right below him. My bedroom window was right on Somerset Street. There were figures flashing back and forth. There was so much commotion that my mother put her head out the window and a policeman very abruptly told her to, for God's sake, get back in.

Fernande Coulson, left, here being interviewed by Betty Kennedy, spent an afternoon frantically trying to arouse official Ottawa about Gouzenko's defection. Nobody intervened, and Gouzenko went back to the streets.

Fernande Coulson
I called Mackenzie King's private office and spoke to Sam Gobeil and told him who I was and where I worked and who was in my office. I said: "They need help. Somebody has got to protect these people or else they will be killed by the Russians." He said: "Give me your name again and your phone number. I'll call you right back." ... A few minutes later Gobeil phoned me back and said: "Do you want to listen to good advice?" I said: "What good advice?" "Have nothing more to say or do with that man. Get rid of him as soon as you can." I said "thank you" and hung up. By this time I was boiling. I was really mad. I thought: "What do I do now?"

When everything else failed, Gouzenko asked his neighbours, Harold and Mildred Main, to take care of his nearly two-year-old son.

Mildred Main
We thought they weren't getting along. When there's talking back and forth and it's getting hotter and hotter all the time and it's in a different language, you just surmise what's going on.

Harold Main
We each had a balcony at the back and he asked if he could come over to see us and talk to us. So he came over.

Mildred Main
He said his life was in danger. He thought he would be dead before the night was over. And he wondered whether we would look after the little boy.

When Gouzenko was finally accepted, John Batza (above) and John "Hap" Harris were the two Mounties assigned to spiriting him out of town and out of reach of Soviet revenge.

John Harris
Jack Batza and I didn't know what was going on. We were suddenly told to go home and pack a bag and get ready to go out. When we got back to the Justice Building we were told we were to take the Gouzenko family out of town and find some place to stay and phone back and give our location.

John Batza
We drove and drove, and every time he looked back and saw a car he said: "Mountie, there's a car following us. A car is behind us." . . . I said: "It's an RCMP car." He said: "But they've got spies in the RCMP too."

Herb Spanton
We were asked to do a study to find a place to put him that was secure and not totally isolated — preferably in the Toronto area. We left Ottawa at around nine o'clock that night. George B. [McClellan] was driving and oddly enough we both thought of the same place at the same time. He said: "Camp X." I said: "The old farmhouse." He said: "Yes." That's how we chose the farmhouse at Camp X as the place to lodge Gouzenko. . . . The location was perfect. It was wide open, so the security was good. It was a big piece of land that nobody bothered paying any attention to during the war. There were antennas and everybody looked upon it as a CBC broadcasting place. The odd time somebody would come down the road to the beach, but we had a very good view.

The house where Gouzenko lived briefly after Camp X.

Don Fast
They selected me because I spoke Russian and had a big home and was living out in the country. It was a nice big stone house which was sitting on a hill, so there would be good security.

Roma Joy
We had a ten-acre place out in Rouge Hills Valley about seventeen miles east of Toronto. My husband [Don Fast] was one of the guards. . . . Our friends couldn't understand why we refused invitations or wouldn't have them in our home. I looked upon it as my particular war effort. I was very happy to do it for the Canadian government. I received a commendation from Mackenzie King for a job well done.

Don Fast sitting in Gouzenko's house in the 1950s.

Don Fast
He wanted a house in the suburb of Toronto something like my house.
Which is what he got. He wanted to be a country gentleman with a home
outside the city.

Roma Joy
Right along the government was trying to find a home for him that
would be out of the way and more or less safe. I wasn't told where he had
moved. When I moved back west and opened my own fashion store, I had
to make trips back east to Toronto and Montreal and also Ottawa. As it
happened, I had some very close friends out in Mississauga and they gave
a dinner for me and at this dinner they were talking about this house that
was not too far from them that was a disgrace. They didn't know who
had it, but it certainly didn't do the neighbourhood any good. And the
more they talked, the more I began to wonder as to who it was. I didn't
say anything because there were about twelve people at dinner that night.
The next day I asked my host if he would like to take me for a drive. I said
I would like to see this house. I did not tell him why. I was still under
oath. When we got outside the house, I said: "You're a very good friend of
mine. Will you trust me? I want you to park the car up the block. I want
to go in here by myself." I went to the door and it was Igor.

Roma Joy
Every time I travelled to Toronto I got in touch with him. One evening
Anna and Igor came in to the hotel to have dinner with me and in the
dining room we were talking about some of his paintings and he went
out into the lobby and got a sheet of hotel stationery and told me: "You
just sit quietly and I'll draw a picture of you to remember this date by."
We talked as he did it. He started pencilling at the table and had it
finished in about twenty minutes. It was no effort whatsoever. He was
very clever in that respect. It's not exactly like me but I guess it's a fair
likeness.

Robert Keyserlingk
I think the Mounties had a little difficulty to understand him and he to understand them. I remember the Mounties once asked me to straighten him out on something. I can't remember specifically what it was but I thought he was not being very intelligent about it. I talked to him in Russian barrack-room language and that appealed to him immensely. His reaction to it was: "Bob, you are my only friend." I had really dressed him down. . . . [I told the Mounties]: "Shouldn't there be some kind of control that would ration out the money to him to make it a little easier?" They said: "No, we can't do that. After all he's a free man." So there was already a certain conflict. How does a man from his background adjust to a free society so suddenly? It was just too fast.

Peggy Blackstock
Mr. [Cecil] Eustace and I took him to lunch. When we were walking back, I was walking with Gouzenko and Cecil was walking with the Mountie, and Cecil asked the Mountie if anybody would still take a potshot at Gouzenko. The Mountie said if anybody is going to, he hoped he'd get the first chance.

in Ottawa whom he had known some years earlier in Saint John, or somewhere in the Maritimes, and in those days it was extremely difficult to get an apartment right after the war and Jack had helped him find one. And this was the guy's way of repaying him. He phoned him up and tipped him off.

It was a shocker at the time — that this kind of thing was possible. The war was just over.

Ben Dworkin

I don't think it has ever happened before or again that a prime minister made an announcement of that kind. It wasn't a big deal. We weren't swamped by terrorists or anything of that kind. But it was a field day for reporters. Everybody was stepping on everybody else. I don't know the stories that others made up but I know the ones we made up. In retrospect I think it was largely politically motivated. I don't say that spying didn't happen, but I don't think it would ever happen that way again. I can't see Trudeau getting up and announcing a spy ring.

J. L. Granatstein

As soon as the announcement was made, the press was saying it was the Soviet Union and nobody was denying this. And five days later, on February 20, the Russians in Moscow owned up to the fact that, yes, there had been some irregularities in the actions committed by their officials in Ottawa and, yes, some misguided people had given documents to the Soviet Union, but because the Soviet Union was so technically advanced by comparison to Canada, nothing of importance had been handed over. In effect they admitted that they had been committing espionage. The fact that they admitted they were committing espionage is surely somewhat unique. It can only be attributed to the fact they realized from what Gouzenko had taken that they were nailed. They couldn't evade that.

Richard Jackson, *long-time parliamentary correspondent for the* Ottawa Journal

The story emerged little by little. The first real development was when they announced — and they gave a list of the names of —

the civil servants who were held incommunicado at RCMP barracks at Rockcliffe. There was Emma Woikin. She came from External Affairs. And there was Gordon Lunan. He was with the Wartime Information Board. It's quite a list. Of course, we all did stories on who they were and what possible access they might have to information that was valuable to the Russians. But we really didn't get anywhere. The lid was on.

Dave Ghent

Gouzenko was the guy who was on the blotter at the city police department. But up until that time his name had not appeared anywhere. It had never been officially identified and no news media had it at that time. I had it and I laid it on Jackson. Now that's basically what happened.

Richard Jackson

I was down there one night pounding out some of this awful stuff for the morning *Journal* when the police reporter for the *Journal* came up to me and said: "Do you want the story?" I said: "Sure." He said: "Go down to the Ottawa police station and ask for the file of September 6. And the whole thing is laid out there." "You've seen it?" "Yes, I've seen it. And I've read it and know what's in it." I said: "I don't want to go down there, tell me what's in it." So he told me. He said the tip-off man in the spy investigation was a Russian cipher clerk from the embassy by the name of Igor Gouzenko who had fled with incriminating papers involving these civil servants and his immediate bosses at the embassy who were involved in espionage. I said: "Why haven't you used it?" He said: "If I had written it no one would have believed it and I would have been in tremendous trouble at the police station. But you can do it because city desk perhaps will use it where they wouldn't for me." So I sat down and wrote it just as he told it to me except he spelled Gouzenko's name wrong — G-o-z-e-n-k-o. And I turned it in to George Paterson, the night editor, and he said: "Is it true?" "I don't know. I think it is." I've got to hand it to him because he had guts and used it, right across the top of the front page. I didn't know this until the next morning. I deliberately didn't go into the *Journal* that morning. I went straight to the Press Gallery and got out of the elevator and heard the phones ringing and the general commotion in the newsroom. And Jim Oastler of the *Montreal Star* came rushing out and yelled: "Dick, you're right. You're right." Wow.

Dave Ghent

The information was publicly available if you knew where to look for it. But it was made as unpublic as they legally could. It was under wraps because that's the way the government wanted it. It had to remain as an official record because that's the way the system was. It had to be put down somewhere but it could be hidden away somewhere else, but it still existed.

Jack Brayley, *retired Canadian Press reporter*

On Sunday my wife and I always rented a couple of horses for two bucks each and went for a ride in Rockcliffe Park from a stable at Eastview. In those days that area wasn't built up at all — it was all maple bush and no houses — and on this one Sunday we took our usual route and went right into the front gate of the RCMP barracks there. We started to ride through and there were Mounties almost in full battle dress with side arms and searchlights and everything. So I knew that's where they were. It was the first time in many years that I hadn't been allowed to ride through and come out at the other end. So I phoned in the story and charged the horse to my expense account.

Hon. Jack Pickersgill

Criticism began to mount about our holding these people incommunicado — having a concentration camp. After all, you have to remember when this was. It was in a period just after we'd had — within a year or so — all these dreadful revelations about Buchenwald and so on. Particularly when somebody got these stories about the lights being kept on all night in the rooms where these people were boarded, and this sort of thing.

Mackenzie King was very upset about these things. What bothered me before it was over — I didn't think of this right away — was the fact that they weren't allowed to have counsel the very first day. That was the biggest mistake made over the Gouzenko business. The curious thing is that I do not think the Gouzenko affair increased the repressive attitude of the government or the public because there were enough people in Parliament and there were enough issues raised about civil liberties and freedom in the debates right away that public opinion was divided over this. I would guess that it was no easier after Gouzenko than it was before to take arbitrary action — maybe a little less easy.

J. L. Granatstein

It became a civil liberties issue. No one was saying spies shouldn't be punished, but many people argued vigorously, not the least John Diefenbaker and John Bracken, the leader of the Conservative Party, and the CCF leader, that these people — most of them — were Canadian citizens and were entitled to the rights of Canadian citizens and that one of those rights was habeas corpus, that they were entitled to legal counsel, and that the government by acting the way it had was acting more like the Russians than the Canadians. For six months at least this was a good hot civil liberties issue in the press. The interesting thing is that Mackenzie King generally tended to agree with the critics.

Hon. E. Davie Fulton

Mr. St. Laurent was Minister of Justice at the time and I remember he and I having an exchange in the House of Commons about that, specifically about Fred Rose. I took the position that the government was breaking the law and that it was entirely wrong to proceed against him as if he was already convicted and that they shouldn't deny him the right to counsel. There was some discussion of the writ of habeas corpus and Mr. St. Laurent said in effect that this writ was available and could be used if there was any suggestion of improper detention, to which I replied how on earth could he get a writ of habeas corpus when nobody knew where he was being held and he had no right to communicate with anybody to instruct a lawyer? St. Laurent then again replied, "My honourable friend is a lawyer, he knows how to proceed," and I said, "Yes, I'm a lawyer but not a magician." Mr. St. Laurent didn't have anything further to say after that.

Arnold Smith

But there was tremendous pressure on Mackenzie King to change this. Tremendous pressure. And Mackenzie King finally did change it and quite quickly. Now everybody we questioned after that would say nothing. It's only people we questioned before that who talked. We wanted a few more days before lawyers and wives were allowed to visit and he said no. And I can understand his political pressures.

At one stage Mackenzie King said: "You know, this is the worst political fix I've been in in my career. You must get out a report" — before we felt we were ready to get out a report. What we did as I recall is do an interim report. It was a very slender one but we were under great pressure to get something out.

We worked until midnight most nights and I was busy writing on Sundays. It was a very intense period and it probably would have been less intense if it hadn't been for the enormous pressure from Mackenzie King to move quickly. But I think that was legitimate. I think he was right politically. People were arrested and held under the War Measures Act. They weren't given bail; the war was over. It was that sort of thing. He didn't interfere at all with the findings, analysis, or anything like that.

Hon. George McIlraith, *then Parliamentary Assistant to C. D. Howe*

It looked like an overthrow of all the governments at first. Today we have all the evidence. But that decision had to be taken when they just got the bare start of disclosures when they had the names of all the departments of government they had penetrated. In the light of that I'm not troubled by it at all. If you are to ask me in the light of hindsight, well that's open to discussion, and ordinarily that wouldn't be tolerable at all.

Hon. E. Davie Fulton

It was a great pity that we had breached civil liberties and were guilty of conduct that allowed people to point their fingers at us. Had it been handled properly the fingers would all be pointed at the Russians.

8 The Spy Trials

Don Fast, *the Mountie whose house Gouzenko moved into after Camp X*

They selected me because I spoke Russian and had a big home and was living out in the country. It was a nice big stone house which was sitting on a hill, so there would be good security. But when I was asked what it would take to handle him, I thought, "Well, I have a good way of getting out of this by naming a pretty stiff price." So I thought it over for a while and thought I had better make it stiffer. So I named a very stiff price for that time and they said yes. And then I was stuck — and knew it. Within two weeks after that he was within my home. I was a little unhappy about it because it meant sitting at home all the time. I didn't go into Toronto to go to work any more. The only thing they arranged was that I would be relieved for one day a week when my wife and I could go into town. The only other relief we had was when we were travelling to the trials in Montreal and Ottawa.

Roma Joy

We had a ten-acre place out in Rouge Hills Valley about seventeen miles east of Toronto. My husband [Don Fast] was one of the guards. The other guards came in the morning and left at night. The RCMP didn't want us to be in touch with our family or close friends because they would ask questions. We had no visitors. Other than the guards, we were absolutely alone. My father couldn't understand what was wrong and it was only when it was all over that I was able to tell him. Our friends couldn't understand why we refused invitations or wouldn't

87

have them in our home. I looked upon it as my particular war effort. I was very happy to do it for the Canadian government. I received a commendation from Mackenzie King for a job well done.

Don Fast

There were difficulties right from the very start. You could see that unless he made certain adjustments he was going to have problems. It was everything from personal habits to dining-room habits.

Roma Joy

His personal habits were bad. We changed an awful lot of that, of course, at least we tried to. I always kept my home spotless and I did a lot of the painting and had just finished doing the bathroom. When he went to the bathroom on the first day he left the lavatory a complete mess and my paint was all scratched off. His refuse was on the toilet as well. So I went out into the living room where the guards were and said: "What goes on?" Then one of the guards, Johnny Dean, said: "Roma, I'm sorry. We should have warned you." Apparently he always stood up in the bathroom and this was just impossible. So we had to train him. And we tried to change his table manners because of the children. If he could eat with his hands he would. By the time he left he was eating with a knife and fork.

Don Fast

I knew that meals would have to be very hefty because I had heard he was a heavy eater. So we put on fairly big meals. He was always the first one at the table and was on his second helping even before we started to eat. It became unpleasant even to sit down and have a dinner. So we had a scheme worked out where we'd sit their family down and feed them first and we would be their servants more or less, and then we would eat afterwards. He treated his knife like a sabre and attacked his food with either knife or fork. And always did. Matter of fact, in travelling we were always nervous because he attracted attention by his table manners and by the fact he would order two or three servings off the menu, enough to feed a few people. "I want this and this and this." You had people watching you.

. . . He'd talk in a loud voice and would be very demanding of the waitress. We'd try to tone it down by saying, "Give us the order, exactly what you want, and we'll tell the waitress." That way we were able not to attract so much attention. We'd all give our orders at once and the girl would be there scratching her head saying: "Well, there's orders here for six meals and there's three people. Have you got some more people coming?" We'd say: "We're very hungry. We haven't eaten for two days." But when the food arrived, sometimes there would be no room on the table to put it. The Force didn't question the expense accounts. But I think we had to from time to time explain there were six meals on this account, four of them were Gouzenko's and the rest were ours.

Roma Joy

He wanted all the Charles Atlas body-building equipment, which he got. That was set up in the home. Being out in the country we went for walks. He would make different things from my daughter's Tinker-Toys. He made a machine gun that actually worked. Anything like that he did.

Don Fast

The second Christmas was at my home and we had a small tree. This time Anna made Santa Claus heads with papier mâché. She said: "You can't see what I'm doing." Before she got through she had five-six dozen of them made for the Christmas tree. By the time we put ours on we could put only five or six of them on. When she left our place she left them all for us. "This is yours." I used to give five or six of them away at a time as a Christmas present. They were beautiful things.

Roma Joy

We were all worried about whether the Russians would retaliate. One winter's day the sun was shining and it was beautiful and we all, plus the guards, went out for a walk. There was a slight hill from our home down to the main road and we had just got there when a car came along and backfired and Gouzenko ran back up the hill. He was sure he was being shot at. That was the end of the walk. He would laugh about it later when he realized it was a car backfiring. But he was always — always — terrified that they would find him.

Fernande Coulson

We had a number of spy trials as a result of Gouzenko and I prepared the indictments. I prepared all the cases of those who were tried in Ottawa, seeing to it that all the witnesses were here and getting the deputy sheriff to serve the subpoenas.

J. L. Granatstein

The government moved to take to court those people named by the Royal Commission. . . . I think the first trial began before the Royal Commission's final report came out in June 1946. The trials stretched into 1949 because Sam Carr was not caught until 1949. There's no doubt that there was a bit of a witch-hunt atmosphere. There's no doubt that there was a great deal of public interest in these cases. "Spies should be punished and these dirty communists should be whipped and beaten." I think that's the public attitude.

Roma Joy

He held the fact that he would not testify against these men over their heads unless he received the finest camera in the world or whatever. But on the other hand there was a softer side. We enjoyed making things together. His wife was very clever. When she wanted to learn more English, I would have her pronounce things and spell them properly.

Don Fast

Before a trial he would become quite nervous and you would almost think he was having a nervous breakdown. But he was recharging his batteries. He was an amazing fellow. He talked himself into it. He hyped himself up. Whatever he did he was a nervous man and was under tense conditions when going into a courtroom. You would think he would not be fit for a trial, but when he came to the courtroom he was in control. He was on stage.

Wes Harvison

At the time of the trial my dad was most impressed with Gouzenko. He said he was an absolutely ideal witness, clean-cut and acting out of conviction. There are people who are good witnesses and there are people who aren't. Gouzenko was just a natural witness. The guy was absolutely solid and had an instinct for what to say and how to confine his remarks to what he could support.

George Mackay

In my opinion he was one of the best. When he said something it was definite and there was no way you could shake him. I don't recall him ever retracting anything. He would stand there with his hands on either side of the witness stand. It was the look on the face and the way he said it. Some lawyers would try to break him down or get him to change it. He didn't bend.

Herb Spanton

He was very well spoken. He spoke directly and in a clear voice and didn't take too much reflection when answering a question.

Don Fast

He became more solid and had more to offer with each successive trial, and the smart lawyers would know that after a while they should withdraw and not press the man because he always had some ammunition in the back. He prepared his stuff in advance. He not only anticipated the questions, if the question wasn't asked he wanted to know why and saw that it was asked. I would say he was brilliant in that area because his mind was working all the time. It's all he ever was thinking about. And if you lived with him for any length of time you could just see it. He would carry on conversations in that area for so long that you had to shut it out. He was testing certain theories and ideas on you.

George Mackay

Herbie Spanton used to say: "Come on now, put on your tie. Leave it alone." By the time we got to the door it looked like he had been pulled through a knothole. He had nice clothes but clothes didn't mean anything to him; you put them on and that's it. So before we took him into a courtroom we made sure we had him pulled tight and straight. And he always looked good in the box. Sometimes I used to think that eating didn't matter to him. He'd be lost in his thoughts on some aspect of something he saw in the paper and he'd be going over and analysing it.

John J. Robinette, *lawyer*

You couldn't trip him up. He was completely confident of himself. He was very definite when talking about the cases. He was an opinionated fellow, too. But he didn't convey that feeling in the witness box. He was opinionated when you just talked to him, but in the witness box he was very good.

Don Fast

Another person presenting that same evidence wouldn't carry the same weight. He had a fascinating personality in that way. When he was onto something he knew and liked, he presented it in such a manner that you at first glance were completely absorbed by it until such time as it would begin to wear on you.

Stuart Keate, *then Montreal bureau chief for* Time *magazine*

The first impression I had of him when he came into the witness stand was his size. He seemed to me a very short person. I would think around five foot four or something like that. Because of what all had been written about him we had conjured up pictures of a great Russian soldier. He had sandy hair and kind of a square, flat face. The other thing I noticed about him was the way he took over the witness box in a somewhat cocky manner, although I also presume he would have been military since he was trained in that field. But he was in complete command of the situation. He threw his shoulders back and barked out his answers. He also managed to convey a slight contempt for everybody who was quizzing him on this.

W. L. Higgitt

People high in judicial circles say that he was one of the finest witnesses that they have ever seen and ever had to deal with. It is my view, too, and I attended almost every trial that Gouzenko was present at as a witness. He had given evidence on different occasions — at trials, preliminary hearings, and the Royal Commission — and some of the most able criminal lawyers were defending their clients before him and I never heard any instance where he was ever found to be at variance with anything he had previously said. And the lawyers would come into court with literally stacks of previous testimony. I remember one very particular case — I don't remember the question — but they would say: "Mr. Gouzenko, last year when you were at a certain preliminary hearing at a certain time you were asked this question and this was your answer." And he read from it. And it appeared to be at variance with what he had just said. And Gouzenko said: "Yes, Mr. So-and-so; if you read the next question you will see that I said so-and-so." And boom, he was right on. He had the most tremendous ability to remember and record incidents. There is no question about it, he was a tremendous witness.

Don Fast

When the lawyers tried to shut him out, he'd say: "Just a minute, I'd like to explain this fully." He would look at the judge for his reaction. If he saw the judge was not going to shut him out, he'd continue. And away he'd go. You couldn't stop him. The lawyers tried many times but they couldn't stop him. He would use words he had picked up somewhere. One of his expressions I remember was: "From what I have heard, from what I have seen, and from what I know, this is my answer" —when a lawyer tried to question him. Then he would go through a whole series of points which he had memorized, which I had heard him repeating beforehand.

Doug How

One day there was a lawyer named A. W. Beament from Ottawa who had been a brigadier in the army. He was a tough guy and he set out to try and demean and to in effect slander Gouzenko. He said: "Really you are a renegade. You're a traitor to your country." Gouzenko said he did not consider himself so. Beament said: "The strange thing I find about you is that when you left the embassy you didn't go straight to the RCMP. I find this very interesting. Why wouldn't you have gone to the RCMP?" I always found this interesting, particularly in light of what came out a couple of years ago about that possible mole in MI5. Gouzenko said: "I didn't go to them because I was convinced the NKVD would have penetrated the Mounted Police." That really stopped Beament. He really shut up. At that time it brought a little bit of a chuckle because nobody could see our glorious Mounted Police being penetrated by anybody.

Wes Harvison

In one incident the defence was trying to set up an appearance of inconsistency. They asked him why he went to a newspaper and he said: "Well, I went to the police and they didn't take me seriously." They said: "Why didn't you go to the Mounted Police?" He said: "Because they were the federal police and I was afraid of them. I thought they might have been sold out to the communists." So the defence lawyer scoffed at this and said: "Do you really believe the Mounted Police could be sold out to the Russians?" And Gouzenko said: "Why not? A Member of Parliament was." It just shattered the defence. A titter went through the courtroom and the steam hissed out of the lawyer.

Don Fast

When he was going into court he'd learn phrases he could use. He'd talk to a few of the guards who were around — mostly to me — and say: "How is this? Is this correct English?" He thought ahead of time, and whenever he was in the witness box some of the best lawyers went after him. If he got into a near miss he'd think about it and later ask: "Do you remember that question? How could I get around that?" After testifying, he would turn to me and say in Russian: "Did I make the right impression?" He was more than image-conscious. He created his image.

Gary Marcuse, *broadcaster*

Joseph Sedgwick, who defended Eric Adams, thought that Gouzenko was an extremely canny witness. He said that Gouzenko frequently testified in Russian and then had it translated into English, although Sedgwick knew perfectly well that Gouzenko knew enough English to make himself clear at this trial. He thought this was Gouzenko's way of gaining a little time to sharpen his wits while the statement was being translated. Statements from other people bear this out. John Cartwright, the prosecutor of the Gouzenko trials, said that Gouzenko was an astute witness who knew his documents inside out and that if he overlooked any possibility that Gouzenko would remind him of the possible use of a piece of evidence.

Merrily Weisbord, *author of* The Strangest Dream

When you look at the trial transcripts you get an idea of the role of Gouzenko. For example, at the Fred Rose trial Gouzenko testified five days straight. Five days. And he did the same thing at the Boyer trial. His job was to get up and scare the shit out of everybody: "fifth column", "third world war was going to be staged by the Russians against the west", "stab our Canadian brothers in the back even though they have given great help", "secret cells impregnated by communist agents" — in other words terrifying rhetoric. And he would always give the whole set-up at the Soviet Embassy with all these scary-sounding foreign names and code names. That was the ritual at both these trials.

Richard Jackson

They had fantastic security. I was writing running copy, giving it to a cop, who would get it to a CPR boy outside the courtroom. You were searched on three or four occasions from the front door, which was well guarded, through to your seat every time you went in.

Ben Dworkin

We were not supposed to take pictures of Gouzenko. Gouzenko came in through the side door from the jail. Joe Finn [fellow reporter at the Ottawa *Citizen*] and I just wanted to show that we could take a picture of him. To get into the court from the prisoners' side entrance, Gouzenko had to go outside and into a laneway leading to the courthouse. There was a little closet with a window overlooking the laneway. Now Joe and I were so well known in the courthouse that nobody was going to pay any attention to us at all. We knew our way around. Joe pasted newspapers over the window so they couldn't possibly see us and left one little hole. I put the camera against the window and shot a picture of Gouzenko as he came in. The picture was never used. We couldn't have used it; otherwise we would have been charged with contempt of court. But we showed the picture around the newsroom. We just wanted to show we could do it, that's all. I tore it up and threw it away.

Doug How

I must have covered six trials, if not more. Each one became fascinating in itself. I've often wondered since where these people got the money, and one can suspect where they got it. They had the absolute cream of the Canadian criminal law fraternity. They had Royden Hughes from Ottawa, who at that time — in the 1940s — was said to be making fifty thousand dollars a year. A. W. Beament was a big-leaguer. I think Maloney was there. They had Joe Cohen. They didn't fool around. They had the absolute cream of lawyers.

Roma Joy

I was very interested in the occult and numerology at that time. When he was going through the period of the trials I would often sit down with him and we would work out numerically — you may think this is crazy — whether he was going to win. I was doing it for something else at the time and he asked what I was doing. I said: "I'm just trying to work out something here numerically." He became interested and said: "I wonder if we could find out whether or not we could win at these trials." I said: "We can try." So we took the names, Rose and the rest of them, one by one and I worked them out every time they went on trial. When the boys picked him up to drive him to Ottawa for a trial, he would always say to me, "Well, we'll see if we win this one." But it never failed. Not once. And he was quite intrigued with that, and once in Ottawa, in front of the officials, he mentioned the fact that I had done this. So I got an order from Ottawa to get rid of my books and see that I did not do it again.

Jack Brayley

I always thought Gouzenko might have been an opportunist and I always felt sorry for some of the people involved in this thing because I think they might have been people carried away by this Friends of Russia idea. Some of them were real conspirators. But guys like Poland, I'm sure, had no motive but to help Russia win the war for us all.

Don Fast

We would come back off a trip and he was always hinting "Maybe we should go and see some girls." Jokingly. "What's the matter with you?" "Oh, I'm only joking." He'd arrive home and within two minutes he'd grab Anna by the arm and take her into the bedroom. Fine. Okay. Half an hour later he would take her into the bedroom again. Now she's starting to protest a little bit. Another half-hour would go by and into the bedroom again.

Roma Joy

Their personal life was quite active — sexually. Sometimes she never dressed all day. This was one of the things that upset me a little bit. It was going on in my home. And one time he beat her so badly. I would not tolerate this in my home. It was a bad influence for my children.

Herb Spanton

I think probably the biggest mistake — and there was nothing we could do about it — was that he was able to see Prime Minister Mackenzie King. He had little over half an hour with him with Norman Robertson sitting in. It was at that stage he was told about getting Canadian citizenship. There was a change. You couldn't blame him really. He had gotten to see the Prime Minister of Canada.

Mark McClung, *former chief of research for the RCMP Security Service*

The RCMP got him a false identity, a false birth certificate — everything. A complete new identity. It was done very well by the police, I must say. They were excellent.

Herb Spanton

After the meeting with the Prime Minister we were told we had to give him a positive identity. So I began to wonder about the kind of identity he should have. He can't be a Russian. At that time we wanted to get as far away from anything Russian that would still fit. He had to be something else. We had a discussion about what could we come up with. We stopped at a little hamburger joint on Queen Street and who should come up and serve us but a Ukrainian we knew very well. We hadn't seen him for a long time, so we shook hands. He was Ukrainian but born in southeastern Saskatchewan. [Later] we went outside. I said: "What do you think?" "I'm thinking the same thing you are. He's our man." We made Gouzenko into a Ukrainian. We were able to fit this man's identity into something that was suitable for Gouzenko. So we gave Gouzenko the same name and the same identity — the whole works except for the birth date and place of birth. This fellow was born near Estevan. We had Gouzenko born in Saskatchewan but closer to Saskatoon.

9 Money and Hollywood

Robert Keyserlingk

I was interested in publishing a book on Gouzenko and he was interested in writing one. I don't know whose idea it was first. It came out in our conversation and then we worked out the mechanics. He could write only in Russian. One of my jobs was to translate it for him. My problem was that I would get too interested in the philosophical side. When I wrote my first book, which was published by Robert Hale in London, Mr. Hale would say: "Mr. Keyserlingk, for goodness' sake cut out those metaphysics. Get to the story." I always wanted to explain. I thought this should really be a popular book, a bestseller type, and I knew my own shortcomings. Andy O'Brien was a sports writer and not as steeped in these things as I was and could jazz it up and leave out all the philosophy, which he did. For Andy the action was the important thing. Igor told me the story and then I wrote it and passed it on to Andy, and from that he wrote the book. He did a good popular job.

Andy O'Brien

It wasn't terribly readable, not the kind of thing you read into the wee hours of the night. There was an awful lot of stuff there but it was technical stuff and there wasn't enough excitement. It was a straight police report. They wanted to jazz it up, I guess, but that required interviews.

Svetlana Gouzenko

Igor of course was writing material for his first book. It was suggested that we could make a serialization out of the story and we had to think how we were going to live. The way we were planning of course was totally ridiculous. We thought that we would be free to live without fear.

Andy O'Brien

I could not interview him in the same city twice. I would be in my room in the Château Laurier they had reserved for me at seven o'clock. The phone would ring and I was told to go downstairs, where there were two policemen in civvies. They took me out the side door and into an unmarked car and a few blocks later [I] was told to get out of the car and into another one and ended up in the garage of the Justice Building and taken upstairs into the storeroom. Then Gouzenko would be brought in. The procedure was the same in the other cities. In Montreal I met him in the old post office building.

. . . At the Justice Building we went in a rear entrance. Four Mounties in civvies surrounded us and took us into a room that had only boxes. One Mountie took a position at the door and one Mountie at each window. I sat there and one Mountie held a watch and said: "You have so many minutes." When my time was up he said: "Time's up, Mr. O'Brien," and away I'd go.

The settings for the meetings were never in a comfortable place. Never in a hotel room. Never in the Mountie office. Never at my office. Always in some weird place. Usually in a storeroom.

Robert Keyserlingk

I got wind of the fact that he was talking to other people. I talked to him about that, but to him this is completely strange. What are rights? So I had to explain to him the basic facts of publishing rights: you can't plagiarize; if you sell an article here, you can't sell it somewhere else. This was a world he didn't understand.

Andy O'Brien

When he reviewed the manuscript he ripped out parts of the manuscript and threw them on the floor and walked over and looked out the window. The Mountie would shove him back from the window. We just kept on working. I remember on one occasion he picked up the rumpled pieces and pointed to the offending sentence and said: "I did not mean for you to do that, you understand. What I meant was this. What you mean is something else." And he'd explain it. I'd say: "All right, the next time we meet there will be a rewrite on this." As we progressed, he grew very, very friendly. I found him likeable in a suspicious way.

The thing that got me most was the mother angle. "When you defected, what happened to your mother back in Russia?" "She hasn't got long to live anyway." My trouble was that if I gave him the verbal lash over that, the thing would be censored. . . . I don't think he gave a damn if his mother was jailed. "What about your mother?" "Oh, she's old. But the kids are young." What a thing to say. It's a fact. But oh my God.

Robert Keyserlingk

At some point I figured I couldn't swing the thing. I didn't have the apparatus for trade books. So I went to Cecil Eustace at Dent and he bought the rights and sold them to Dutton in the United States. That was a deal between Dent and Dutton and they just paid me the down payment, which I turned over to Gouzenko minus my agent's fee. In the end the book was written by Andy and edited by Dent.

Andy O'Brien

He distrusted everybody. I finally got to him and got an autographed book from him with "Thanks for the honest writing" signed "my dear friend, Igor Gouzenko". It was the first time in all my time with him he showed any emotion. He was cold-fish suspicious until I got that autographed book. He seemed to be suspicious of almost everything — everything even I said.

John Picton

Lots of magazines were after him for interviews. I think it was *Cosmopolitan* that sent somebody up here to ask him for an interview and made him an initial offer of $5000. Gouzenko turned it down and *Cosmopolitan* kept coming back with more, and it just made the Mounties' mouths drop. Here were these Mounties making something like twenty dollars a week and they were offering this man the wealth of the Indies. Untold money. He could go and buy a car and a house and all those things. The Mounties kept urging him to accept and Gouzenko kept saying it was not enough and turning it down. On one occasion Gouzenko told me the Mounties were so furious that they refused to speak to him when they were driving him back. They were sitting beside him in the back of the car and they wouldn't talk to him, they were so furious. He was turning down these large sums of money. But Gouzenko knew exactly what he was doing. He knew what he was worth on the market and he ended up with a huge amount. I forget the amount but it was more than $50,000.

Svetlana Gouzenko

Fifty thousand dollars was signed on the twenty-third of November of '46. Then the first week of December here came *Life* magazine begging us. . . . They offered sixty thousand. Well, it's too late. We had already signed with *Cosmopolitan* for fifty thousand.

Robert Keyserlingk

I think Dutton was very angry about *Cosmopolitan*. They felt it was an infringement against their rights. The *Cosmopolitan* articles were a little different than the book. Actually, with the police raids on the apartments [of the spy suspects] and things of that kind, it was a story you couldn't copyright. Igor's statements of fact had been published in the newspapers anyway. So it was a very hard thing to copyright.

Roma Joy

If my memory serves me correctly, the first payment made to

him was $50,000. He wanted cash in his pocket so he could put his hands on it. Naturally they wouldn't let him have it. But they did give him $5000 cash so that he could have that in his pocket. When he came in he fanned them out in his hands and waved them under my nose and said: "That's money. There's lots more where that came from." Those were his very words.

Robert Keyserlingk

He got $75,000 [for the movie]. Fox [Films] paid that and I don't think they ever got their money back. Loew's Theatre showed it in Montreal and it lasted exactly three days. I know they paid $75,000 because it was done right in my office and I know that he got the full amount because I didn't take any agency fee. I remember both Fox and Igor came into my office to sign the deal. . . . It was the kind of money neither he nor I had ever seen.

Don Fast

When he got that $75,000, I said: "Look, do you know how much interest that could produce for you? You could live on that. You don't need any more money." He said: "There will always be money. There will always be opportunities." He was enthusiastic. He had himself convinced he could do almost anything.

Svetlana Gouzenko

There would not be enough interest to live on. It at maximum would pay back 3½ per cent only. If it would be $100,000, it would be $3500 a year. We could not live on $3500 a year.

Don McGillivray, *financial writer*

The average industrial worker was making $2500 a year between 1945 and 1950. The average wage was about $2000, but workers in industry got paid more than workers in the service sector. The buying power of $100,000 in the late 1940s would be worth about $600,000 of buying power in 1984. You couldn't get high interest rates for investments in those days, but you could get five per cent. Five per cent of $100,000 is $5000. So that would be about double the average wage-earner's income on the interest alone.

John Picton

Dana Andrews played Gouzenko in the movie, a most un-Gouzenko-looking man. He was advised by Gouzenko not to play the part with an accent — and he didn't. I think Gouzenko thought it would have been fake with an accent. He wanted to get the message across clearly, what they had been through.

Don Fast

When the movie *The Iron Curtain* was made starring Dana Andrews and Gene Tierney, he kept insisting and insisting he wanted to meet Gene Tierney. So it was arranged. They were invited to Judge Forsyth's home in Ottawa. John Dean, Mackay, and I, I think, went down with him. When we arrived at Judge Forsyth's home we were met at the front door and were taken into the kitchen. The big reception was in the living room. Gene Tierney didn't come but Dana Andrews came up. We were drinking in the kitchen, and after a couple of hours of no Gene Tierney, I guess the conversation had gotten pretty dull. Dana Andrews came into the kitchen and said: "Do any of you fellows speak any Russian?" I said: "Yeah, I speak Russian." He said: "How do you say prick in Russian?" I said: "Huok." He goes back to the living room and sat down on the chesterfield — we were wondering what he was going to do — and he was sitting there saying obviously to Gouzenko: "huok, huok, huok."

Then Dana Andrews came out to the kitchen and a few other people all came into the kitchen. There was more fun in the kitchen than in the party with this guy domineering the conversation. Gouzenko was holding court.

Peggy Blackstock

Gouzenko gave him [Forsyth] ten per cent of everything he got — from the magazine and the film. I saw the cheques. They amounted to $18,000. That was ten per cent of everything he earned. The total of everything Gouzenko earned was $180,000.*

---

*Mrs. Gouzenko disagrees with this figure. She says the gross figure is not much more than $125,000 and is considerably less when U.S. taxes and Mr. Forsyth's fee are deducted. *Maclean's* magazine in 1953 quoted Igor Gouzenko as saying the figure was nearly $150,000. Gouzenko never disputed that quote.

This was for the *Cosmopolitan* story, the movie, and the book. And the Americans took $16,000 in taxes and the Canadian government let them.

Don Fast

Forsyth did some negotiating on Gouzenko's book and some work on legal documents. I told Gouzenko he was stupid — why give him all this money? Gouzenko said: "If I give something to a real big man, he owes me something." It's the way the guy thought.

Svetlana Gouzenko

[Mackenzie King offered a pension of] $400 a month and Igor turned it down. He said "no thank you" because we just got it from *Cosmopolitan*, we just got the movie rights sold, and he had it in his mind to write another book.

. . . [RCMP Assistant Commissioner] Nicholson just gasped and flopped on the chair, surprised that this stupid young man refused a government pension. When he came home — I had already become a real good Canadian — I say: "Are you sure that you did a wise step? And you know when it is somebody offering you money you shouldn't really think of — " And he said there would be strings attached. It would be continuous. "They will dictate to us. And you move this way or that way. We will lose eventually more than we can gain from this pension."

Don Fast

Frank Ahearn gave Gouzenko a lifelong pension of $100 a month. It wasn't a living income but in those days it was a good chunk of money. I think Ahearn was honest in his efforts to try and help Gouzenko, believing that he had done a good job.

Svetlana Gouzenko

Ahearn learned that Igor refused the pension and Ahearn said you need a steady income from somewhere, so $50 for you, $50 for your wife. It's only $25,000 that he paid, but he paid gift tax on it. So it cost him $32,000 at the time. But he was a very kind man. He had a thick chequebook and he was always writing. Anybody who came to him he wrote a cheque.

Robert Keyserlingk

I remember his [Gouzenko's] paintings being displayed at Eaton's and I advised him very much against because I was afraid of it. The idea originated from Gouzenko, because he talked to me about it. I thought it was dangerous for exactly the reasons that the Mounties gave. But he was very insistent because he was proud of his paintings. How he got connected to Eaton's I don't know. Igor Gouzenko was a name that you could sell and I have a feeling he got on the telephone to Eaton's and that their merchandising manager thought this was a hell of a smart deal. I went and looked at the pictures and thought oh boy, if I really wanted to find out where he lived, which I didn't, I could probably do that. They were landscapes. They were not great art but he reproduced scenes so that they were recognizable.

Andy O'Brien

He wanted all superlatives. Superlatives only. You couldn't sit down and yak with him for long or kid him about his paintings. It had to be the greatest since Michelangelo.

Robert Keyserlingk

From the way he talked about his paintings, one would have thought that Rubens went to school under him or that Michelangelo learned to paint the Gioconda from him. He had an exaggerated feeling of his own importance. He did what I consider to be a very valuable service in exposing the spy situation in documented form and he was very conscious of merits on that. But when he also talked about his literary and artistic accomplishments he exaggerated.

Don Fast

He wanted a house in the suburb of Toronto something like my house. Which is what he got. He wanted to be a country gentleman with a home outside the city. So Spanton and Dean went out and started looking and when they found something good from a security point of view they took him down. In matter of fact I think they showed him only two or three houses.

Roma Joy

Right along the government was trying to find a home for him that would be out of the way and more or less safe. I wasn't told where he had moved. When I moved back west and opened my own fashion store, I had to make trips back east to Toronto and Montreal and also Ottawa. As it happened, I had some very close friends out in Mississauga and they gave a dinner for me and at this dinner they were talking about this house that was not too far from them that was a disgrace. They didn't know who had it, but it certainly didn't do the neighbourhood any good. And the more they talked, the more I began to wonder as to who it was. I didn't say anything because there were about twelve people at dinner that night. The next day I asked my host if he would like to take me for a drive. I said I would like to see this house. I did not tell him why. I was still under oath. When we got outside the house, I said: "You're a very good friend of mine. Will you trust me? I want you to park the car up the block. I want to go in here by myself." I went to the door and it was Igor.

10 The House

George Mackay

The original idea was to send him somewhere out in western Canada for at least long enough so he could be forgotten about. Unfortunately he wasn't quite capable at that time of hiding his light under a bushel. Secondly, I don't think he had a true appreciation of what there was in western Canada. He thought he was going out to a wilderness where he would be subject to the elements and animals. You couldn't explain this to him. He couldn't grasp it, or else he didn't want to. He was adamant he was not going, so they located a home for him.

John J. Robinette

I held Gouzenko's property as a trustee. The Mounted Police didn't want people to know where he was. I prosecuted a lot of federal government cases in O Division [RCMP's Ontario region] and got to know O Division exceedingly well during the war years. I guess they figured they could trust me. The Mounted Police provided the funds and I bought it in my name and it was conveyed to me. Then I signed a declaration of trust which was not registered. They didn't want anybody to know who was going into that house. Gouzenko had a cover name, but I think the Mounted Police felt it was safer if the property was not registered in that name in case there was a leak or something like that. A woman spotted my name in the records and phoned my wife and said: "I hear you're moving." My wife said: "Oh no, we're not moving there." Of course, I hadn't told her so she didn't know anything about it. I hadn't told anybody. Maybe the woman thought I had bought it for my mistress. I drove by the property once to see what the hell I owned out there. I couldn't resist that. Several years later I conveyed the property back to Gouzenko under his cover name. By that time I think they felt that any danger to him had pretty well passed. I think this arrangement had outlived its usefulness.

George Mackay

It was one of these places you had to buy the light fixtures for. It wasn't quite finished. So we had to go out and select the light fixtures. Then we had to get an electrician who Spanton knew and could trust. At that time it [the area] wasn't as built up as it is now. He chose quite well. It had an upstairs which gave her almost an apartment of her own.

George Burnett

In the summertime you couldn't see it from the road. There is a string of trees that covered it up. You had to know where it was or you would drive right by it.

G. B. Crysdale, *neighbour*

My neighbour told me: "I sold the house." This guy was a professional engineer. He did a lot of work on it. He said: "I just found out my wife has been running around with another guy all the time I was in the army and building a house for her. Now I don't need the house." I said: "I hope you sold it to nice people." He said: "I don't know who I sold to." He named the lawyer who handled it all and said: "Apparently it was sold to Mr. So-and-so, gentleman." Well, we knew from day one there was something strange there and before long we knew it was Mr. Gouzenko.

Minnie Crysdale, *wife of G. B. Crysdale*

My dad was the one who first solved everything. He was here and he knew it was the RCMP. He saw this man walking down the street briskly in front of the house and said: "That is not a chauffeur. That is a policeman." Dad had a military background. But we never talked about it for years and years until we started getting feedback, and then we figured everybody knew.

George Mackay

Then, of course, came the question of furnishing it. Yours truly got stuck with the job of taking them shopping. It was quite the thing to see them. They had quite good taste. It wasn't going to be garish or junk. They wanted good stuff. But the arguments they would get into over it. There you are standing in the department store warning them to be quiet. "You'll attract attention." They would forget and almost be shouting at one another and you'd be standing there embarrassed. Buying refrigerators, stoves, bedroom furniture, dining-room furniture. Then, of course, there was all that woodworking machinery. That was all bought. Never did I see him use it.

Del Maulsby, *retired RCMP officer who once handled Gouzenko's file at headquarters*

Gouzenko decided early on he would tackle woodworking as something to do and went to the store and bought everything — saws and all the tools that were needed. All this stuff then sat in his basement and collected dust. He never used it. Some of it he never even uncrated.

Elmer Driedger, *former Deputy Minister of Justice*

McClellan told me a story about Gouzenko's way of dealing with money. He had seen in somebody's basement some woodworking equipment and said: "That's for me." By golly, he went out and bought himself expensive lathes and God knows whatnot and had his basement loaded with stuff for a real wood craftsman and then never used it.

George Mackay

I don't know what happened to all that machinery. I don't know what it cost him but it was a complete and utter waste.

. . . We got him settled and then, by God, he had to have a car. Well, in 1946 cars were hard to come by. The war was over only in 1945 and you didn't just prance into a showroom. There had been no car production. Everything had gone military. He had to have a car. The tale that Herb [Spanton] told this poor dealer about how much he had to have a car. He gave him this sob story about how he had been in the north for many years and he decided to come down and settle and live on the wealth that he had accumulated and that this fellow had done him a favour and he would like to help him. He was a friend of Herb's and eventually he delivered. He gave us a car.

Herb Spanton

We could have got him small cars but he didn't want a small car. He wanted something for his family. He wanted a big car. There were no Buicks available. No Oldsmobiles. I scouted around and finally came up with a dealer on Yonge Street. A Hudson dealer. It was the biggest Hudson you could get and a nice car. Two-tone. Robin-egg blue. It attracted some attention. That was the one thing we didn't want but it worked out all right.

Willson Woodside

He told us at that time how he was living on a road, obviously in Mississauga, and he was living in the back of the house. The front of the house was full of cameras and he turned his movie camera on every car he saw a third or fourth time. He thought it was suspicious. He put his movie camera on them and developed the pictures. But at that time he hadn't seen anyone who was suspicious. He must have spent a lot of time watching. If they came by three or four times he thought that was too much, that they were looking for trouble.

Svetlana Gouzenko

We had the camera but that was once in a while. It was not all the time. But we were most of all concerned with the children's safety. . . . We had one babysitter that we paid an extra little bit of money. She was to keep an eye on school during recesses so no one would come and kidnap the kids. Oh, many things. We never mailed anything from here. We always drove to town and any mail from any publisher or anything came from Toronto and any reply we received in the lawyer's office. Well, many, many things. Small things but important. Particularly watched suspicious cars or anything. Licence numbers would be taken. It didn't do any good because a couple of times he asked the

Mounted Police, but it turned into too much work.

George Mackay

The baby was crawling and they were afraid of her falling downstairs. So I said: "Just get one of those gates and fasten it to the post and put a hook in the wall." The next time I went back he had put up this gate and was very proud of himself. You won't believe this. He took a two-by-six and with spikes drove that thing until he had the two-by-six level with the plaster so he could put the hook into it. Drove it right into the wall. There were cracks all up and down that wall. It practically destroyed the wall. If he'd ask any of us to do it we would have used an ordinary I-bolt and screwed it into the two-by-four that was alongside the doorjamb. It struck you as being funny at the time, but when you stopped to think back on it the boy had never had any experience with anything like that. His whole life had been regimented as a young communist and they weren't taught carpentry work or anything else. It was all ideology.

John Picton

He told me he had secretly bugged his own home. He told me he had an extension built onto his home in the early years and, according to him, the Mounties had insisted on putting in the lighting units. This, of course, made him highly suspicious. One day he said he wanted to go in and see at what stage they were and they said: "No, you can't go in today, they're putting in the lighting units." He was convinced his house was bugged by the Mounties. He said he in turn had put in a secret taping system that was voice-actuated apparently. I have no idea where the tape was kept. I never pursued that with him because he was so paranoid that would have made him nervous. He said he taped his own house so that if anything should happen to him he or his family would have a record on tape of what happened.

George Mackay

Some of us who were on the job were getting tired of the whole thing and he was becoming at times more difficult to handle. He wanted to go against the grain in doing certain things where we felt he was only endangering himself. He was very ready to accuse you of doing something to interfere with his life or his ambitions. Then I left and had nothing more to do with him and said: "I don't want to hear any more of him." I really wasn't interested. I had done the job they wanted me to do and had a clear conscience all the way through.

Don Fast

There were people who volunteered to be bodyguards and had no idea of what it was. I had all kinds of people who were going to take over from me and never did. They did and I said "Oh, hurray" but it didn't last very long and they called me back. I went so far as to even ask for a transfer to Vancouver to get out of it.

11 Conflict with the Mounties

Andy O'Brien

I had season's tickets for hockey in Montreal and Gouzenko was in town for a trial and I asked him: "Would you like to see a hockey game?" He said: "I would be delighted." I told my wife she had to stay at home. At about six o'clock of the night of the hockey game a phone call came and a very crisp military voice said: "We understand you're having a special guest at the Forum tonight." I said: "Yes." He said: "We regret he will not be there." Click.

Willson Woodside

My first contact with Gouzenko was in 1948 when he phoned *Saturday Night* over my review of his book. He astonished the RCMP by saying he would come at twelve o'clock the next day up the elevator to see me. Mr. McClellan of the RCMP phoned me that evening and said that Gouzenko had broken security. In fact the switchboard girl could have known who he was and have told others. The next day Gouzenko came up the elevator at twelve o'clock and I took him in to see B. K. Sandwell, who was the editor, and Mr. Sandwell said at once: "Well, let's go to lunch." So we went to the National Club and Mr. Sandwell signed in Mr. Gouzenko as Mr. Brown and we sat in the middle of the National Club wondering how many of the people around us would have loved to have known Gouzenko was amongst them. He was pretty big stuff at that time. He told us at great length his experiences with the RCMP, which were all bad of course.

Robert Keyserlingk

I think the Mounties had a little difficulty to understand him and he to understand them. I remember the Mounties once asked me to straighten him out on something. I can't remember specifically what it was but I thought he was not being very intelligent about it. I talked to him in Russian barrack-room language and that appealed to him immensely. His reaction to it was: "Bob, you are my only friend." I had really dressed him down. In a way I had a feeling he was being treated too kindly, with no understanding on the part of his Canadian contacts what a Soviet product is under the strict training they get down there, especially somebody like Gouzenko, who was trained as a KGB man.

This tremendous disparity between a man who is suddenly free — not only free but got himself quite a bit of money. Poor old Igor was completely lost by this.

. . . I discussed it with my Mountie friend at that time. I said: "I think he's an unhappy man because you people give him just too much liberty. Nobody steers him in any way and everything is left to him to decide in a world which is completely strange to him." I knew about the annuity that Frank Ahearn had left and about the movie money I had got for him. "Shouldn't there be some kind of control that would ration out the money to him to make it a little easier?" They said: "No, we can't do that. After all he's a free man." So there was already a certain conflict. How does a man from his background adjust to a free society so suddenly? It was just too fast. I was thinking if he could be broken in a little easier but there was no way of doing that. You couldn't restrain him. Either you gave him his salary or you didn't.

Willson Woodside

Gouzenko had no idea of saving money. He spent money on everything. He came into *Saturday Night* several times with bottles of Rémy Martin. One day he came to our house and wanted to take us out to dinner. He carried cash in his shirt pocket and would pull it out and it all tumbled onto the floor — twenties, fifties. He went through the first lot of money with some crazy scheme that failed. I can't remember what it was. He bought a farm and was going to raise pigs and this failed. This was early on. It's very Russian to spend money like water. His attitude was "it's only money". There was no reality to it.

Robert Keyserlingk

Gouzenko loved painting and he went out and was buying expensive brushes until the boys finally had to take him out of there because people would say: "Who the hell is that guy spending money like a drunken sailor?" He would not take an ordinary paintbrush but wanted a silk paintbrush which they obviously didn't have in that little store. So they would ask what did he want that for. And he went and bought himself refrigerators and things of that kind and that's why he was always short of money because he was buying things. It was a reaction to the lack of things in Russia.

Svetlana Gouzenko

I didn't have the slightest idea how to run the farm when he bought for me all this in one beautiful spring drive. Two hundred geese, four hundred ducklings — how many chickens did we have? — probably four hundred chickens. Twenty-five piglets. I will never forget. We were taking the cream out and selling it but the skim milk was going to the pigs. They were beautiful pigs, milk-fed pigs. They couldn't even drink so much milk because it was milk out of fifteen cows.

Don Fast

He had absolutely no money sense at all. And yet he was always sloppy in his dress. He lived well. He'd go into a liquor store and buy the best booze. He didn't know what it was but he got what had the most expensive price tag on it. He'd say: "I want two of those." We thought that ordering three meals in a restaurant was actually a pretty low trick until we found out it was actually his style. When he had his own money, that's how he spent it.

Svetlana Gouzenko

It [the farm] was not a bad investment, just that had we a milk quota right away we would be making [money]. But we were selling cream to a cheese factory because we could not get a milk quota for the farm. And that takes three years. I could not take three years' losses and keep employed people hoping three years from now I will get a milk market.

George Mackay

We had brought him up from Toronto for a meeting with Rivett-Carnac to ask him to move to western Canada where he'd lose his identity. I spent the whole morning outside Rivett-Carnac's office waiting for him. They were both in there. I was fed up. I had been just sitting there over four hours. The stenographer had already gone to lunch. He refused to go. He was just adamant. Rivett-Carnac said to me afterwards that there was no way he would move. Whether he was afraid to move out or didn't want to come out and lose his identity, I don't know. I said: "If he stays where he is, it won't be very long before everybody around him knows who he is, whether he's got a security man with him or not. He's not that tied in. He's too flushed with success with having done a great thing for Canada."

You could get a sense of feeling from him from the way he would talk when he went into that courtroom with policemen escorting him that "I'm monarch of all I see." That would never lessen. That Canada owed him a debt for the rest of his life, and that he wanted people to know the great man that he was. I heard the remark one time that when he was going to write his memoirs that he thought he should get as much as Churchill got from *Life*. He put himself on that level. Now I was orderly to Churchill during the first Quebec conference and the difference was night and day. This was the pedestal he had put himself onto and there was no way he was coming down. And if you feel that way, everybody has got to know who you are. This is where I could see the problems coming. And if he wasn't getting the attention he would force it somewhere.

Don Fast

He would give interviews against the advice of the RCMP. I was careful with him. We insisted he tell us where he was. He didn't drive, so either his guard or his wife drove him. That's why he wanted a guard, not for security but as a chauffeur. His guard would take him downtown or somewhere and he would tell the guard to stay in the pub all day while he did his business. That way the Force wouldn't know what he was up to.

Robert Keyserlingk

The Mounties had difficulty with him when they said don't do this or don't do that. He would do it. It was mostly a matter of lack of obedience to their measures. He would make it more difficult for them to keep his identity under wraps. That was their main complaint.

Robert Reguly

The breakdown between Gouzenko and the Mounties was inevitable. There was this deep suspicion that McClellan obviously didn't have his best interests at heart and may be a Russian spy for all he knew. He always harped back to McClellan. He couldn't trust the Mounties. There were Russian spies all over the place.

Robert Keyserlingk

When he realized that this machine didn't have the severity and the discipline of the Russian machine, he felt we were just a bunch of slack people. Down there they would have said: "Igor, if you don't do this, we'll shoot you." Here they were arguing with him. He was like a spoiled brat in the end. You will find a mother talking for two hours to her three- or four-year-old and the child will do whatever it wants. I gave him some barrack-room talk and cast aspersions on the chastity of his mother. That he understood. I spoke with a loud voice and yelled at him. That he appreciated. I told my Mountie friend: "You'll get further with him if you stop explaining to him." He said: "Yes, but he's got a right to his own mind if he wants to. We can't do that." I think this is where a lot of the friction came. He had been a cog in the machine and he wasn't used to this kind of freedom. There was too much slack in the machine. Where he came from you were told and that was that. If you didn't do it you were punished. The Mounties couldn't punish him and he knew it.

Don Fast

I told him. I took him aside and said: "Look, I'm a staff sergeant, here's the amount of money I'm making. Out of that I'm paying my mortgage and doing this and this and this. Why can't you on the money you had live within a range like that? Double it if you like but make yourself a range. You've got to have a plan." He said, "I don't understand that." Well, he just didn't even want to listen to it.

Robert Keyserlingk

He couldn't understand that at all because this is the arithmetic of capitalism, which he never grasped. To him the state was everything. Since he had served our state, he was constantly clamouring for more money from the state because he just couldn't understand why he couldn't get a dacha like the commissars did in Russia. If they served the state and the state didn't shoot them, they fed them. But this idea of putting money into an account and living off the interest is a concept he never had. I tried to discuss financial matters with him for his own interest and got exactly nowhere.

Svetlana Gouzenko

I had a little tractor and I go furrowing in between the rows of strawberries, all plants pushed into the row and I have a little tractor that I have to go and do it. Imagine the situation. Meanwhile our Mountie is here in the lounge chair in the front, reading the newspaper, throwing a stick for the dog and the dog will fetch the stick back, and Mr. Bridge [neighbour] looks on this scene and thinks and says: "You've got an easy life for some handyman. The lady of the house is there on a tractor and you are here tanning on a lounge chair." And my Mountie got insulted and said: "I am not a handyman. I am a Mountie." That's what Mr. Bridge told us. I don't remember which Mountie but all of them were in the lawn chair in the front.

George Mackay

He made allegations about members of the force in various areas. As far as I was concerned they were untrue. It's just the way he wanted to present things. He had the ability to question your statements and if you listened to him long enough it became a totally different thing from the way you said it. He could take your own words and manipulate them. All in all I'd had enough.

Robert Reguly

He claimed that one of the Mounties was making money off him, that his bodyguards were claiming expenses when in fact they were not spending money. So they were supposedly making money off him indirectly. Many years later there was a Mountie who committed suicide in Winnipeg. Gouzenko claimed he was the Mountie in charge of the money for him and he wondered whether it was suicide over the discovery that he had been robbing his account or holding back money from him or something like that. That Mountie was a very good guy from what I hear. Gouzenko named him — after the guy was dead. It was always after.

Don Fast

He always tried to play one man against the other. Very soon after I got to know him, when he was in my protection, he made trouble by making a complaint and saying I would support him on it. I forget what the incident was. The Mounted Police started an inquiry as to what is this all about and questioned me as to my position. I didn't know what the hell he was talking about. Then I had to go and categorically deny that I had said it. Now you can take something out of context. After listening to him for two or three hours you're nodding your head to everything he says — when you're not even listening. He would consider that consent and approval. He was always playing games that way.

Andy O'Brien

He was antagonistic toward any police. That's the way it was in the Soviet Union. In Toronto, Harvison, the Assistant Commissioner, told me once: "The guy is driving us crazy. He will phone us up in the middle of the night and want the complete guard changed. 'Change them all.'" He was suspicious of all policemen. If you were standing near a corner looking at him, that was enough for him to figure there was a spy.

Robert Keyserlingk

I tried to be a mediator between him and the Mounties but I wasn't always successful. As I left him I had to go and listen to the Mounties crying on my shoulder about what a son-of-a-bitch he was. Finally I decided maybe I could help both sides to deal with each other. There were some very apt expressions which I had learned when I was a sailor on a Russian ship which came in very handy. He was stubborn. He was conscious of what he had done, of the risks he had taken in the service of Canada, and he always felt that the country wasn't grateful enough to him, financially and in other ways. This was mainly because he didn't know our way of life at all.

George Mackay

I can always remember him reading the newspapers: "No. They shouldn't say that. They should tell them not to." I'd say: "My dear man, that's just what you've run away from. Don't you understand that?" He'd give no answer. No answer.

Peggy Blackstock

I remember when Gouzenko sued the *Toronto Star*. He arrived Friday afternoon with the story in the *Star* and asked me to help him write the letter to answer it. I thought: "Oh my goodness, he shouldn't answer this. This sounds like a very serious case of libel." . . . That was the only time I ever saw him frightened. He was afraid to go home.

Nelles Starr, *Gouzenko's lawyer*

Gouzenko always had a theory that before the Russians would kill him they had to destroy his credibility, because they never killed anybody unless they destroyed their credibility first — any person in the public eye. And so he was determined that they weren't going to destroy his credibility with an article in the *Star.* . . . Gouzenko thought it was perpetrated by the Russians but I don't think so.

Svetlana Gouzenko

High living! Buying thirty-two head of Holstein cows is high living? Buying a Massey-Harris tractor is high living? What they are doing, this bunch of useful idiots working for the Soviets, is discrediting a defector who did a valuable service to this country. And those who contemplate to come to the western side, each of them will say: "I can't bring half the documents Igor took with him. Look how they are treating him."

Jocko Thomas, Toronto Star *reporter*

My story was based on the fact that Igor Gouzenko was giving headaches to his official guardian. . . . We were all ready to go to trial over this story. We had had the examination for discovery in the King Edward Hotel, where we would meet on the corner of Victoria and King and wear a flower in our coat. Somebody — one of the court people — would come up to you and take you to the second floor, where you were introduced to somebody else who took you up to this room where the examination for discovery was held. This was the pre-trial stuff. It was the first and only time I saw Gouzenko. The examiner had a little table there with the shorthand reporter and he asked some questions.

Nelles Starr

They [the RCMP] put the heat on me, tried to make me settle. Oh, tried a lot of tricks. And we had an examination for discovery at the King Edward Hotel and you never saw so many guys with hats drawn over their heads and pockets bulging with guns and Lord knows what all. Well, they were afraid the Russians were going to kill him. And so eventually the RCMP put some more heat on me. They sent the commissioner down and it didn't work. They tried some tricks with Gouzenko and they didn't work and eventually the *Star* apologized and paid him some money.

Jocko Thomas

We hired the best libel lawyer in Canada at that time, Thomas Phelan, who's now dead, and he worked on the case quite a bit. We had witnesses coming from Chicago and had rooms reserved for them. We were all ready to go. We were going to photograph him going into the courtroom and all this sort of stuff. I think he was going to testify with a bag over his head. The trial was to start on Monday and the settlement came on the preceding Thursday or Friday. They approached us and the *Star* paid four thousand dollars for the cost of Gouzenko's lawyer and a front-page apology. I think at the last minute their side realized they would be very embarrassed and that's why, in my opinion, they sought a settlement before going to trial.

Nelles Starr

He was intelligent and knew the meaning of English words. When we were drafting the apology the *Star* printed, Gouzenko would spend half an hour on whether he knew one word or another.

Svetlana Gouzenko

Igor wasn't demanding money. We didn't get even half of what he spent. He was demanding it [the apology] be put in this same spot [in the newspaper] where the article was. Not somewhere in the back pages. The apology should be in the front of the newspaper.

12 Montebello

A. J. MacLeod, *Department of Justice lawyer*
Gouzenko's time had run. He was in hiding somewhere. There was a general feeling at that time in the Department of Justice that Gouzenko was of more nuisance than of value. This was the feeling on the legal side of the Department of Justice. Whether the RCMP considered him to be still of value I don't know.

Frank Rasky, *then editor of* Liberty *magazine*
The Toronto *Telegram* at one time picked Gouzenko up in a circulation drive and built him up as a hero. He exploited them and they exploited him. They were very careful to present him as a hero, masking any untoward things about him. I talked to one of the *Tely* reporters who wrote about him and he hated him.

J. D. MacFarlane, *the* Telegram's *managing editor in the 1950s*
I remember having a pleasant chat and telling him how I was very pleased he was making material available to the *Telegram*. It wouldn't be very sizable but we would pay money. And rightly so. We were regarded as right wing, conservative, loyal, true blue, and national in our views, which we were. There was never the suspicion as there was with the *Toronto Star*, our opposition, as the red rag. I don't know if it deserved it, but it was certainly a lot more leftist than we were. Gouzenko was right at home with the *Telegram*.

Peter Worthington
In those days I don't know if it was Gouzenko coming to the

Telegram or us going to him. For the first ten years Gouzenko was a find and he could command a bit of money. There's no question the *Telegram* paid him a fair buck in those days for articles and things. He stopped later, but even in the sixties he was still hoping for stories or to be asked for comment.

Eugene Griffin, *long-time Chicago* Tribune *correspondent in Ottawa*

After the trials, Gouzenko kind of faded out and we forgot about spies. I was always digging for something to write about. That was the occupational disease of any American correspondent. What do you write about? *Maclean's* came out with an article on Gouzenko by Blair Fraser. Somebody told me later that *Maclean's* was going to serialize his book, *The Fall of a Titan.* I thought the story was pretty dull and thought: "Well, if he wants to be interviewed, this looks like a possibility of reaching him." So through that article I contacted him. It mentioned his publisher. It was as easy as that. Anybody in the world could have done it. I mean anybody. There was a name in the article, so I wrote a letter. They didn't know me and Gouzenko didn't know me. If they were protecting him, why did they allow anything like that?

I got back a letter telling me Gouzenko will page me at 1 P.M. on Saturday October 24 — this is 1953 — at the Genosha Hotel in Oshawa. I was choked up with a head cold and feeling like hell and I had to go by train to this town. I didn't think very much about the security of it. Nobody came to see me and talk to me. It was just "Go to a hotel and be paged." It could have been a set-up. I sat around the lobby of this hotel and after a while a man came up to me — I was looking for Gouzenko — and said: "Mr. Griffin, come with me." I have no idea who he was. I went into his car and he took me for quite a ride to a luxurious home. We were met by a maid in a uniform and were ushered into this beautiful big room and there was Gouzenko, whom I knew from covering the spy trials, and his wife, who was very charming. Way off, it seemed miles away but was still in this big room, a library, was a man just sitting there — the owner apparently — just listening. We were never introduced and he never said a word. I could have been anybody if I had wanted to kidnap Gouzenko.

Gouzenko and I talked and talked. It seemed to go on forever on this Saturday afternoon and I wasn't getting anywhere. My sinuses were plugged and his accent was very, very thick. I was thinking: "How did I get into this?" And there was no lead to the story. He was very ideological and strong but it wasn't news. Towards the end, I was ready to collapse. I said: "Do you think it would do any good if you met Senator Jenner or one of those committees in Washington?" He said: "If they have any loose ends, I may be able to help." It seemed very innocent. So the thing broke up and I got back to the train station and back to Toronto. I filed the story that night, wanting to get it into the Sunday paper, and the only lead I had was that he felt it would be useful to go before the committee.

Svetlana Gouzenko

He felt that he had some good suggestions to give to western intelligence. And that was the five-point program.* He did not say he had new information. What the newspapers and the reporters did [was to say] that he has got new information.

Eugene Griffin

This thing got totally out of hand. Before I knew it there was a press conference and External Affairs and I think it was Sid Freifeld, the press officer. By this time the thing was quite a story and immediately was going to get much bigger. He read this denial from External Affairs. "Mr. Gouzenko denies he told the *Tribune* or Griffin this or that" and then listed a number of items. I was going wild saying "I never said that. I never said that." And he said: "That's our policy." So all the papers came out that "Gouzenko denies the whole thing." So I phoned a

*Gouzenko's five points are:
1. Friendly protection;
2. Immediate citizenship;
3. Financial support from the state;
4. Work according to abilities;
5. State recognition and gratitude.

Mountie, an inspector in charge of something or other, and I said: "What do you mean he denies these things? The paper doesn't say he said that." I said: "Did you read the paper? I could get fired for this." He said: "Well, that's too bad." And I said: "Well, that's a good quotation." "You can't quote that." So he got all excited.

Svetlana Gouzenko

Whatever [report] went into the Department of External Affairs we don't know. It started with the Department of External Affairs making the statement that Igor already had been interrogated and he said then he was misquoted and he had no new information. He never said in the first place that he had new information.

Eugene Griffin

I had to find Gouzenko again. I was flapping all around and made phone calls letting it be known I wanted the guy. Somehow somebody — I forget who — told me to go to the Royal York Hotel in Toronto and be there. I was given a key to an apartment and I've forgotten how I got that key. Anyway, I ended up in a hotel in Toronto with a key to an apartment which would be empty and I would go in and Gouzenko would arrive. The apartment was a long cab ride from downtown Toronto but I was flying blind. The *Tribune* was on my back, the government was on my back, everybody was on my back. I went in and sat around for a while and soon the door opened and in comes Gouzenko. Gouzenko was as mad as I was about these denials and I got his statement reaffirming what he had said and he signed it.

Gary Marcuse

He then told the *Tribune* that he had some special understandings and special information which prompted the Senators McCarron and Jenner to make repeated appeals to the government, including some veiled threats that they would give out some information about Canadians if Gouzenko's information wasn't forthcoming and if he wasn't allowed to testify.

Robert Morris, *counsel to the U.S. Senate Subcommittee on Internal Security*

We were having hearings on interlocking subversion in government. I had learned from a source that Gouzenko had all these secrets up there and that the Canadian government was not allowing any access to them. So we had to build up some kind of a demand from the press to allow it.

Walter Goodman, *author of* The Committee

It was the Cold War period and the Senate committee was thrashing about to get whatever it could get for use in nefarious ways. And if they hear Gouzenko was testifying on anything to do with communists in this country or spying, they would go any place — much further than Canada — to get it.

William A. Reuben, *author of* The Atom Spy Hoax

This is right around the time that McCarthy started coming under attack by his own colleagues in the Senate. So the colleagues and supporters and the right-wing champions of that whole witch-hunt Cold War atmosphere needed something to keep the fire going. When the Rosenbergs died without giving them any more names, they almost came to a dead end of names. These inquisitors fed on names. This is the thing they need to keep the thing going. So I think they had come to the end of a trail, and with McCarthy under attack and in the shadows and the Rosenbergs executed they needed a new threat somewhere to start a bonfire going.

Robert Morris

I had been having a great deal of difficulty dealing with the Canadian government while acting on behalf of the committee. They kept throwing roadblock after roadblock in front of us and then, of course, we had to build up a demand to see him. It was a public relations thing. "Why shouldn't we be allowed access to a man who has secrets about the Soviet Union which is working to overthrow us?"

Arnold Smith, *Canadian diplomat and then special assistant to External Affairs Minister Lester Pearson*

The American committee acted as if they had the right to have a meeting in Canada and to question this guy under oath. Gouzenko had just written a book and I think his publishers had put him up to this so as to get publicity for Gouzenko to help sell his book, which was slick and smart and probably not his idea but an American advertising man's idea. Anyway, this was an affront to Canadian self-respect as a sovereign country and there was humming and hawing about what to do. They finally decided there would be a Canadian hearing under a Canadian judge. Pearson asked me to go down to this meeting. It was in the Seigniory Club in the Papineau Lodge. It was very comfortable and we had that place to ourselves for that occasion.

Gary Marcuse

As a result, the two senators came up to Canada and had a secret meeting in Montebello presided over by Mr. Justice McRuer of the High Court of Ontario under Canadian ground rules, which meant the Americans couldn't go on a fishing expedition about Canadians.

A. J. MacLeod

I recall it was the time of the McCarthy hearings. I think that bothered the Canadian contingent a little bit. Canadians in Ottawa circles didn't like what was happening at the McCarthy hearings and thought this was merely an extension of that. They were prepared to fulfil friendly international obligations to a neighbouring country.

Hon. E. Davie Fulton

My recollection is that Gouzenko was embarrassing the government, and while the Opposition was always looking for areas to properly criticize the government, my recollection is that we felt this is an area we should keep our hands off because Gouzenko was just being damn difficult and that in fact he didn't have much new to say. It is unfortunate that this became a matter of controversy between us and the United States. We felt we should co-operate with the United States if it wanted information on security matters from Gouzenko if it could be done without prejudice to our own interests and without prejudice to Gouzenko's cover but that really Gouzenko didn't have much new to say and that this thing was being blown out of all proportion. Gouzenko was taking the position it was most important that he should give evidence, whereas it wasn't, because he had nothing really new to say. The whole thing was a tempest in a teapot.

A. J. MacLeod

As the legal advisor to the Mounted Police, advising them on a day-to-day basis concerning their legal problems, I was appointed to be with the Canadian delegation to go to Montebello for this interview by the two visiting American senators with Igor Gouzenko. I was in the company of David Mundell, a lawyer in the Department of Justice who was a few years senior to me, who was to represent the Attorney General of Canada.

There was a good deal of cloak-and-dagger element on the evening before the meeting. We were picked up at our respective residences. It was after dark when a Mounted Police vehicle came. I got into the vehicle and we sped off into the dark in what seemed to me to be an unnatural air of secrecy. We went up in kind of a convoy. There were three or four cars in one group.

... We arrived in Montebello and got established in rooms in the hotel and David Mundell and I were summoned to a meeting with the Chief Justice in his room. The Chief Justice felt that above all that Canadian integrity had to be maintained. I sensed a feeling that in his mind there was something not quite appropriate about two American senators coming onto Canadian soil to interview someone who was under the protection of Canada about something that had happened in Canada. The Chief Justice, I'm sure, did not profit by anything Mundell and I had to say. He seemed to have made his mind up rather firmly as to what course would be followed in the morning.

Mark McClung

The meeting was held in this marvellous residence, the Papineau House on the Montebello grounds. Beyond the hotel there's a hill and Papineau House is up there. It's a beautiful eighteenth-century house. Magnificent. I've never been in a place like it in Canada. Gouzenko was escorted by a police sergeant who almost literally slept with him. Never let him out of his sight. The meeting was set to start at ten o'clock in the morning. We're all there. Ten o'clock came and no Gouzenko. 10:05 and you could see people getting restless.

Philip Baker, *then an articling law student*
I was a law student living in an apartment in a home in Toronto in which a friend of his lived. He asked me as a friend to accompany him to this meeting. All the necessary arrangements were made and I went with him in the car. After a sixteen- to eighteen-hour trip we arrived at the meeting site well after midnight the night before the meeting. We were taken to a room which was extremely hot. No windows could be opened. They had either been painted closed through age or closed for security reasons. We were never told why, but they just couldn't be opened. It was well over eighty degrees in the room and we were expected to sleep in there — with a guard outside the door. On retiring some time between 1:30 and 2 o'clock in the morning, we asked the guard and the sergeant in charge to make sure to awaken us at 7:30 in the morning. The first call came either fifteen or twenty minutes prior to the scheduled meeting time when Mr. Gouzenko was told to hurry and not keep the senators waiting. Mr. Gouzenko was extremely worried about the fact we were late getting there and I told him he would require a shave, a shower and some breakfast before we went for such an important meeting. I also told him to inform the senators and his honour Chief Justice McRuer that we had been roused late by our guards. He subsequently went to the meeting, where I was refused admittance and waited outside the door.

A. J. MacLeod
The Chief Justice presided with an iron hand and with certainly an iron will, maintaining that no questions would be permitted that would impugn in any way on the Government of Canada,

its conduct, or the conduct of any of its agents. I don't recall anything of importance that Gouzenko said. This may be faulty memory on my part or — and I strongly suspected this — that he had nothing of any great importance to offer.

Mark McClung
Chief Justice McRuer put on an outstanding performance. The visitors had with them the counsel for the committee, a very shrewd, hard lawyer. He examined Gouzenko. And as soon as he started and asked his first question, McRuer said something to the effect: "I don't like to limit your freedom of asking questions of this witness but I have to remind you that in some ways the Canadian law of evidence is different from yours." And then read him a little lecture on observing Canadian judicial standards rather than American. It was done in a very calm way. But he put the guy down. It was a beautiful job. Very dramatic. No voices were raised. "You don't ask hearsay questions" — and so on. This was one of the men who had torn strips off these helpless witnesses before this godawful committee in Washington. I was very proud of our system that day.

A. J. MacLeod
I recall there was a certain frustration on the part of Americans that they weren't allowed by the Chief Justice to pursue every line of questioning they wanted to to the length they wanted to. You could feel it. My recollection is that the Chief Justice was very much in command and the American senators knew it. The impression I got at the end is that they didn't get what they came for, whatever that may have been.

Gary Marcuse
It emerged that all Gouzenko really had to say was that he had the suggestion that Americans ought to offer any future spy who wished to defect a new identity and lots of money, which was hardly something which the Security Service had not thought of on their own; that he had no other information really and that he had shared it with them before. So it was an enormous charade.

Peter Worthington

I think his five-point program, which he spent his life dedicated to, is very good. It hasn't got a flaw in it. It's perfectly reasonable. I do think that without defectors coming to us we're mostly in the dark. Those have been the exposures [the defectors who exposed the Soviet system] and you would think we'd have a system of encouraging such people. But I don't think we want them. I think this was a real shock to him all his life that we're not really an anti-communist society. The Soviet propaganda creates the West as a seething mass of anti-communism and everybody in the Soviet system is in danger when basically even somebody like myself who doesn't think much of the system doesn't spend much time brooding about how I can fight the system. None of us are anti-Soviet the way the Soviet propaganda machine works against the West, which I don't think he ever really understood.

A. J. MacLeod

We were just anxious to break up and get home, largely thinking it had been a great nuisance and waste of time from Canada's point of view. There was nothing earthshaking that came out of it. . . . It was one of those one-day wonders.

Arnold Smith

Gouzenko had no new information. It was a publicity stunt. One of the American senators realized it and he said: "You know, this is one of the slickest public relations operators I've ever met." Well, this was Gouzenko eight or nine years later, obviously under the coaching of an advisor to his American publisher of this novel. It was a very slick piece. His name was in the headlines again.

J. G. Sourwine, *counsel to the U.S. committee*

I think this whole great production could have been avoided if everybody had been a little less on tenterhooks. The Canadians immediately burst into this hard line "You're not going to ask questions about Canadians; you're not going to question Canadians." If we had been a little less pushy, we might have got more in total than we did in the end. But that's looking at it in retrospect.

Eugene Griffin

This incident was voted the top news story of 1953 in Canada in a vote of editors taken by Canadian Press. The Canadian federal election held that year was the fourth news story. That struck me as kind of funny.

John Picton

Gouzenko told a story that when the two U.S. senators came up to interview him he insisted that this lawyer come with him as they were being driven to Montebello. There were two cars. He was in the second car with the lawyer and the Mounties were with him and in the front car. Suddenly on a quiet Quebec road as they were approaching Montebello the two cars stopped in the middle of nowhere and the Mounties wanted to separate Gouzenko from this lawyer. They said: "You ride in this front car and the man will ride in the back." And Gouzenko said: "Why?" and they said: "For security." Gouzenko made the point: "What could that security have meant?" So he refused and insisted that he and the lawyer ride together. He always claimed to me that was a set-up.

Don Fast

On this trip to Montebello we took a roundabout route and near Montebello we circled around some town and did some manoeuvres. He was a little suspicious of what we were doing. He said: "You don't have to do it that way. Why go around town?" "We want to go around the town and come back to the highway to see if we're being followed." We came back and sat on the road to see if any car was coming from behind. There was nothing. But we didn't have to because there was a lot of security on the road. We tried to explain to him what we were doing so there wouldn't be any alarm.

James Dubro, *who knew and interviewed Gouzenko in his later years*
Gouzenko insisted that the Mounties had planned to assassinate

him on that Montebello trip. Frankly, I never understood how
he arrived at that conclusion.

Peter Worthington

I think he's in print in one of the Ukrainian papers as saying
that George McClellan was a Soviet agent. He hated George
McClellan. He thought he was trying to kill him on that trip to
testify before the Americans. He brought a witness along and
insisted much to their dismay so that if they tried to make it a
car accident with him they would also involve somebody else.
It's fairly shrewd thinking if indeed there is an attempt. But he
was convinced he was supposed to travel alone in a car and that
there would be a car accident and that he would be killed in it. It
taxes the credibility somewhat. But there is no question in my
mind that Lester Pearson was doing all he could to prevent
Gouzenko from testifying and the reasons seemed very strange.
There are three or four lies that Pearson made to the effect that
Gouzenko didn't say this and that.

Eugene Griffin

He always told me he was more frightened of the Mounties than
anybody else. He thought they were going to push him out a
window or something. He said: "Remember, if I get pushed out
a window it will be the Mounties."

Peter Worthington

He was convinced the RCMP was filled with Philbys and he
judged them a lot, I think, by their reactions to him. He had
really close to a photographic memory and he would recall
innuendo and slights and that sort of thing and would come out
with some damaging stuff against some individual he didn't
know but he knew would have been a spy in the Privy Council
Office simply by the way he treated him. He was convinced that
Norman Robertson was a Soviet agent. Absolutely convinced.
And he even told a tale of when he went there. He claimed at
one point Robertson's bags were packed ready to do a flight
because he felt that Gouzenko might have known and had his
name on the list.

Eugene Griffin

I met him at the Royal York a few years after the Montebello incident. He had a big new article with all kinds of things in it and I'd ask what. He wanted quite a bit of money and I asked the *Tribune* and they asked: "What's he got?" I said: "He wouldn't tell me. If he told me I'd have it for free." So we agreed to pay him a thousand or a couple of thousand dollars, which was a pretty good price. We took a chance on him. So I was all set to get a story and the office phoned very angrily. The damn thing had already appeared. The guy was reading it in a magazine. Gouzenko was selling us what he had sold somebody else. So that fell through.

Don Fast

We got rid of this guard who was living in Gouzenko's house. The guard was a drunk. This guard locked himself into his room and was brooding. I had to climb through the window to take his gun and haul him out. The guard was an Englishman and wound up in hospital for three or four years. The Force gave him a medical discharge. I don't think Gouzenko drove him to this. He was already into the booze pretty heavily. My recommendation was that the guard should not be replaced. Gouzenko insisted he needed a guard but he only wanted a chauffeur. It was better to have nobody. A guard only attracted attention. I did casual contact after that.

Several guards said they would quit if not relieved from Gouzenko. There was a constant turnover of personnel. Some volunteered to be guards and soon regretted it and couldn't take it. One guy lasted three or four years — this was the alcoholic — and was quite content as long as you left him with his bottle. Most would last only months. Gouzenko wouldn't want to keep some because they wanted to do the job properly and clashed with him.

Mark McClung

Gouzenko continually broke security and endangered his own life. The police got very worried and decided: "We must prepare a speech for the Minister of Justice to deliver in the House of

Commons in the event that Gouzenko disappears — to protect the government." If he disappeared, we could only assume that the KGB did get him. Then the government would be criticized: "This helpless little man; why did you let the KGB get him?" The assignment came down and eventually was given to me. I was given access to all the Gouzenko files. It was a fascinating story. So we drafted a speech which exposed him for what he was. The speech was going to pour it all out. It never had to be used.

13 The Fall of a Titan

Robert Keyserlingk

Judging by his name, Gouzenko, and also by his Russian accent a little bit, there was no question about it that he was Ukrainian. His speech had a slight Ukrainian sound. In English and in Russian you can almost tell from the drawl which region the man comes from. With Igor you could definitely say he was from the people. He was very well trained but not very educated. He had read very little at that time. When I tried to involve him in conversation about the details of the ideology, I found that was not his cup of tea. That's why I was so surprised to find him dealing quite a bit with it in *The Fall of a Titan*. He must have read it up since.

J. D. MacFarlane

I read with a great deal of admiration his book *The Fall of a Titan*. I thought it was remarkable for a man who is a cipher clerk with a limited educational background to produce that excellent book. I must say I was envious of the man's ability to produce with such a grace a document of that type.

Herb Spanton

I remember this very well. I told him once: "Igor, instead of writing like Tolstoy, why don't you take a more journalistic approach? I'm sure it would sell much better." He listened, then turned around and asked me where did I ever learn to write. I said: "I couldn't even write my own name at one time. I wouldn't even know where to start. But I do know what people in this country appreciate." This created some friction. I forget what words he used but he more or less told me to mind my own business. He kind of said: "If I want to know something, I'll ask you."

Robert Keyserlingk

When he began working on *The Titan* he asked me whether I would be interested in publishing it. Frankly I didn't think he had it in him. I found he just didn't have enough material. Then all of a sudden he came out with the book. As a matter of fact he sent me a copy. The first thing I said was: "What the hell does he know about it?" Then I read it over and found it was a fairly good yarn, but I couldn't recognize my Igor in it at all. His wife was a much more intelligent person. She was more educated than he was. My theory at the time was that she might have helped him with *Titan*, at least a certain amount of it.

Don Fast

I have about twenty classical volumes in my library including Tolstoy and whatnot. And during this time he would sit down and start to write and then would stop and grab a book and read it for two-three hours and then suddenly he'd have a brilliant flash and would say: "Ah, I've got something." And off he would go to write. He did a lot of his research in the books that I had.

Robert Keyserlingk

He goes into the psychology of Maxim Gorki, who was poisoned by Stalin. I don't know whether it's true or not but that was the yarn. I had quite a number of discussions with him at various times and I found he was getting into profundities of Maxim Gorki's attitudes which made me think, where did he get it from? He must have read a lot of books on Maxim Gorki. He didn't come out of Russia with all these things. Because when I talked to him of Maxim Gorki and so on, I would say he was almost a little ignorant of these things. It's like somebody coming out of Russia and writing on Solzhenitsyn, because Solzhenitsyn isn't known in Russia half as much as he is known abroad. If I remember rightly he writes about Maxim Gorki on his visits to Italy and things like that. Now, I don't think that was part of the curriculum of a KGB agent being trained as a cipher clerk. So I think it was something he caught outside.

Don Fast

When he was writing *Fall of a Titan* I would say he had enough material there for five or ten novels like that. It was sorted out and brought down to proper length by Black, who worked on it. In matter of fact I would say that Black wrote the book.

Mervyn was constantly talking about the amount of time he had to spend on the book. I believe in some cases he must have worked on it all night. He indicated it was a hell of a job. Black was a very patient man, a very quiet man and a very nice guy. He certainly sweated blood on it. He was very slow, and after a short while would come a chapter which he would give to Gouzenko, and Gouzenko would then tear it apart and then go off on another long writing session on that particular chapter. And that's how it was written, just by a hell of a lot of labour. There was endless hours of discussion. I read some of the chapters and would say: "Oh boy, nice." But he wasn't satisfied and would tackle them again. Then he'd end up with enough for five more chapters and poor old Black would have to whittle them down again. I think in the end Black just did his own work and finished a chapter, then just stopped. There was some dispute as to whether or not this thing should be concluded and Black finally put it into final form and said this is it.

Lydia Black

My husband put it in the right form so it could be presented properly. I think that's why it became a first selection of the Book-of-the-Month Club. My husband was a talented writer. He wanted to write but he was very busy with the RCMP and didn't have much time for himself at all. He translated the book after work and on holidays. Saturdays and Sundays. He would stick his nose in the book and write and write. It took two years or so.

Don Fast

Black was a long-suffering guy. He spent endless hours with Gouzenko. Mervyn Black was a slow, patient, nice guy who was used to the Russian style because he lived in Russia for so many years. With his Scotch background and Russian experiences he could sit for hours with Gouzenko. I think he shut him out but he was there smiling. He had this tedious job of writing the book from the notes Gouzenko prepared and I'm certain that a great deal of it was Merv Black and not Gouzenko — certainly in translation and interpretation.

Robert Keyserlingk

I would definitely think it was ghost-written because it read smoothly. I've seen some of Black's work for Gouzenko which was accurate but a little like a police report. It was accurate but didn't have any writing sparkle. So I would imagine somebody must have done that job for him and did a job which, I think, is beyond the Gouzenko I knew.

Don Fast

He certainly added a great deal to the book. Black had been in Russia and was there during the revolution. He made his way out of Russia. He came out to the prairies and tried to homestead and failed at that and then went to work for the Mounted Police in Saskatoon as an agent.

Frank Rasky

I heard from my managing editor, John Dalrymple, that John was ghost-writing his book, *The Fall of a Titan*. Gouzenko was a short little fellow coming into my office. I had a big set of newspaper-like offices with my managing editor and assistant editors and the art department all in one huge room at 73 Richmond Street and he was using my office as a mail drop. He would come in at lunchtime, pick up his mail addressed to him care of Mr. Brown. Then he'd get together with John Dalrymple and John would arrange on his own time to ghost-write this book for him. John was a very accomplished guy.

John Dalrymple

My work with him must have extended at least over a year. I spent most of my time trying to make sense of his material. It was one of these Russian novels which wanders over the panoramic landscape and I kept trying to get him to thread the story together a little bit stronger. I'd say: "You can say this so much shorter this way." Being a magazine-type writer naturally I was all for the short, direct wordings and, of course, Igor with his Russian circumlocutions considered these to be an essential part of the fabric of the novel. We used to have dandy arguments. He was quite difficult to convince on certain matters and in some cases quite unconvincible. So once you found you couldn't convince him, you just shrugged your shoulders and did it his way. In the final analysis he would always win because he was the client. He paid me as work progressed — an exceedingly modest rate, I might add. It was fair enough.

. . . It was my understanding that one of his kids was doing the translating. I thought he said it was practice for one of his kids. But that was just an understanding. I'm quite sure he had just about everybody involved with him in any way taking part in the book in one way or another.

Alla Dalrymple, *wife of John Dalrymple*
Igor was writing a book and my husband was editing and helping with his English and everything. Co-writing it really, I suppose. He had it written down and my husband would rewrite it.

So they used to come around and I would give his wife a cup of coffee and cookies and sit and John and Igor would go into the den and go over the next instalment. Or Igor would come and pick it up after my husband revised it. He was a peasant-stock type of man who got a bit educated. But they were very pleasant. She only brought one or two kids to the house. I understand they had more. But I only saw two, a boy and a girl.

We were about the fourth or fifth house from the corner and they would park around the corner and walk to the house, which I tried to tell him was more conspicuous in suburbia than it would have been to drive into the driveway. There was nothing as conspicuous in that neighbourhood as anybody parking their car five houses away and walking, but I could never convince them they would be less noticeable if they just

drove into the driveway. They thought they were fooling everybody by parking around the corner.

John Dalrymple

He had a vivid imagination. That is certain. His imagination
overrode into his daily life because he saw assassins behind every
bus stop. I think he could have very well produced the theme of
the story. I don't believe his command of English was ever sufficient to get it into semi-readable form. In my opinion the final
form, even as it was, was only semi-readable, and that was despite my best efforts. Frankly I was surprised the book did so
well, because I didn't think it was that good. I was not happy
with the results of my participation in it. I felt that something I
had participated in ought to have read better. That's the way I
felt about it.

Peggy Blackstock

He brought in the first nineteen chapters of *The Fall of a Titan*.
It was translated and he had insisted it be a literal translation by
Black. Dents in Canada and Dents in London were interested
and I was trying to find an American publisher. I knew Annie
Laurie Williams, who was one of the best agents in New York,
and sent her the manuscript. She did the theatres and her husband did the magazines and the books. Annie Laurie's husband
submitted it to six of the top American publishers and they all
turned it down. So her husband wrote back saying Gouzenko
might as well realize he couldn't write a novel.

So at that point I said to Gouzenko that it isn't good style and
I think you've got to tighten this up and I'm willing to do it if
you agree. If you will let me, I will take the first chapter and
rewrite it the way I think it should be done. I said: "You've read
War and Peace in Russian, haven't you?" He said yes. I said:
"Okay, I'll give you the Constance Garnett translation of *War
and Peace* and some Kipling short stories. While I do this, you
read those." I just couldn't think of any other way of getting
across to him what was necessary. And he came back and said, "I
see what you mean." In Russian in order to make a greater
impression you keep adding phrases. He said: "In English you

just strip it all away to the bare bones, don't you?" I said: "That's right." So he said: "Go ahead." So we did it chapter by chapter by chapter. I spent about nine months doing it.

Robert Glasgow

Gouzenko [came to me and] said: "I've written a book and I would like to offer it to *Life* magazine for first rights." I thought: "Oh Christ." I said: "Well, what kind of book is it?" "It's a novel." Well, that's even worse. If he had had a real-life account about "how I screwed the Russians", that was one thing. But here's a guy with a novel. . . . We talked and talked and I said: "Look, I'm busy as hell and I don't really know how to resolve this. I'll tell you what. I'll call *Life* and will talk to the articles editor" — a guy named Jay Gold. I said: "I'll talk to him and see if he has an interest in it."

Peggy Blackstock

There was one chapter where he was describing this great big beautiful home with its terraces going down to the river. With the way he described it I said: "I can't visualize it. I don't quite understand how you get down to the river." He said: "You don't?" So he just sat down and did an architectural drawing and said: "You see, you just come down the steps here, and here are the pillars and the gardens and so on." It made it perfectly clear. So I rewrote it to make it clear. It was so verbose in Russian and the sentences got confused.

Robert Glasgow

I sent some of the manuscript down to Gold. . . . [Later] I called Jay Gold. Gold said: "Christ, are you calling me about that goddamned shit you sent me?" I said: "Well yes, I am. I gather you're not infatuated with the possibilities." He said: "Holy Christ." I said: "Well, can you send that stuff back?" He said: "I'll be very glad to."

. . . Finally Gouzenko called and he said: "What's the news?" I said: "Well, I'm afraid the news is bad." "What is it?" I didn't tell him what Gold said. I said: "Mr. Gold just said he's not interested." He said: "This man Gold, what kind of a man is he?" I said: "What do you mean?" He said: "Do you know anything about his background?" I said: "I haven't the slightest idea. I know him casually and know that he's worked for *Life* for a long time." He said: "Well, you know, there are a lot of communists on publications in New York City, in matter of fact all over the world." I said: "Well, I don't know if he's a communist or not." The funny thing about it was that the American Newspaper Guild unit at *Time* at one point had a lot of communists, some of whom I knew. I didn't know anything about Gold but I saw the direction this was going in. So I said: "If I understand what I think you're implying, believe me there have been no ideological considerations involved in this matter at all. It has nothing to do with whether this was by the Russians or by a Russian defector. It has nothing to do with anything. Gold simply said he does not feel it is suitable for *Life*." Then he wanted to know what the hell that meant. I tried to explain. I said: "Why don't you try *Harper's*." He said: "No, *Life* has a circulation of six million. I want this message to get the greatest dissemination possible." I said: "Well, it's out of the question, at least as far as I know. He's sending it back." It hadn't come back yet. He said: "What's *Life*'s telephone number in New York?" I gave him the telephone number. He said: "Well, I'll get back to you."

I didn't hear from him for about two days. About two days later I got a call from Gold. He said: "Goddammit, will you get that son-of-a-bitch off my back." I said: "What's the matter?" And he said: "Christ, that bastard has driven me crazy. He's called me several times each day. He's called me at home at night. He has catechized me in every way and he thinks I'm a Soviet agent or something." I didn't know what the hell to do. So I said: "This is between you and him. I'm trying to get rid of him myself. I hope this is the last I hear of him." Well, I knew it wouldn't.

Peggy Blackstock

We were absolutely desperate because we just had to find somebody to publish it. I had finished most of the work on it. There was a Canadian Authors' meeting at Hart House and this agent came up from the States. I've forgotten his name — his brother was the editor of *Saturday Evening Post*, a famous fellow. We collared him at this meeting and said: "You just have to take this manuscript. It's a great book." We gave him the manuscript and all the press clippings about Gouzenko and said he was famous. He took it away and somebody in his office sent it to Brockway of Nortons without telling him who Gouzenko was, and he snapped it up right there and published it in the States. Cassell published it in England and Canada and it won the Governor General's Award here and it was a Book-of-the-Month Club in the States.

Robert Glasgow

I didn't hear from Gouzenko for two or three weeks and I had hoped that he had gone away. Christ, he calls and tells me the Book-of-the-Month Club had chosen this book. I thought: "This shows how much I know about his book and it shows that Gold doesn't know much either." . . . Then I knew immediately I would have to do a story on it now for *Time* which would get me more deeply involved in Gouzenko. The fact that the Book-of-the-Month Club had selected his book automatically made it a story of some interest for the Canadian section of *Time*.

Don Fast

I knew that when I visited him there [at his home] that people came and went quite freely. The neighbours knew the situation. He had his books all lined up on the table and when I walked in he was sitting there and signing autographs for the neighbours — openly. I said to him: "Look, what the hell are you doing? You're going to let all the neighbours know who you are." He said: "Oh, don't worry. These are good friends of mine." When the neighbours knew, you had a complete breach of security.

John Dalrymple

He felt quite happy about the marketing success of the book and he felt, naturally, it was a deserved success. He was very hopeful that Hollywood would waft us all away and there were great but generalized promises of big things that would be coming to me as soon as Hollywood scribbled its name at the bottom of a contract. He was very disappointed the movies didn't pick it up. That was his heartbreak.

Lydia Black

My husband had finished translating the book and then had a heart attack and died not very long after when the book was completed and published. Gouzenko was paying him little by little and eight hundred dollars was left when he died. Gouzenko went to his lawyer and told him he had no money. The lawyer said: "The man you owe the money to is dead, so you don't need to pay." I suppose he had already spent the money he got from the book. My husband should have gone to a lawyer, but he was very loose that way. He would never go after people for anything like that. He thought: "Oh well, maybe he'll pay." Incidentally, he was sick. I said: "Are you still translating? Why don't you tell him to pay the money before you finish it?" He kept on translating and the book was published and everything and the money was still not paid. He said: "He will do it later." Afterwards he got sick and he passed away and that was that. I was too worried about my husband at the time to pursue the matter. And we had moved into a new place. And when my husband died we didn't have any pension from the RCMP, even though he was there twenty-seven years — because he was a civilian. Everything piled up at once. I didn't know what I could do. I went to a lawyer and he said: "Well, you go sue him." I said: "Oh no, you don't. I haven't got money to pay. He has the best lawyer, paid by the government, and I am a poor widow. If I lose the case, I will have to pay the costs." Gouzenko had the best and most expensive lawyers.*

John Dalrymple

He seemed to think that what he'd done was exceedingly important and figured he had proved himself to be a fairly sizeable

*Mrs. Gouzenko maintains that Black was paid fairly and fully for his translation and does not believe any amount was left owing at the time of Black's death.

literary figure rather than just a cipher clerk.

Don Fast

He said this is one of the books that will go down in history. When he got the Governor General's Award he said: "This is just a minor prize. There should be more."

Willson Woodside

After *The Fall of a Titan* was published, a *New York Times* editorial called him another Tolstoy and Dostoyevsky. That ruined him for life. He wanted the Nobel prize for the book and went through some considerable effort to get it. To get nominated for a Nobel prize you have to be sponsored by certain types of people, and he was approaching people to do this. He made photocopies of his material at great expense and bound them and sent them off to well-known people. I knew the outside world and he tried to get me to make the introductions. I kept telling him he should write another book for the Nobel prize but he didn't like that idea. He talked of writing another novel and had a plot for it. I'm not aware that it ever came out.

Don Fast

He thought he was a Tolstoy and always referred to him. And his wife would say: "You're not Tolstoy. You just get down to business and write the stuff that's needed." She was a little critical of him.

John Picton

He told me that a group of three U.S. professors of English and two Canadian professors of English had nominated him for a Nobel literature prize for *Fall of a Titan*.

Willson Woodside

I remember going up with him one Sunday to a nearby drugstore and telephoning from there to a man who had been in the CIA or FBI who was with a senator in Washington. I can't tell you who it was. The purpose of the call was to get a nomination for the Nobel prize. Gouzenko sent him by special delivery a copy of all his photocopies. It was a beautiful binding. He had a lot of packages of material. He spent a lot of money on those. He worked hard to get the Nobel prize and he never got anywhere near.

Peter Worthington

There were allegations when Laurie McKechnie died that Laurie McKechnie of the *Telegram* had ghost-written it. I remember that day so clearly when Gouzenko came charging into the *Telegram* threatening to sue. He came to me saying he didn't want to sue but they had mentioned that McKechnie had ghost-written it. Gouzenko came in with a suitcase with his manuscripts in it and spent an hour showing me how he wrote the book.

Gouzenko was trained as an architect at school and could draw, so he did the book as an architect would do it. He sketched a house with rooms in it and he had all the rooms which would be chapters where various characters would meet. So Gorki would be in this room and he would come over to this room, so you have the house leading up to whatever happens with all the characters along the way. You meet this character in this room and two chapters later there he is. So he has filled the rooms and then wrote the book according to his plan.

Svetlana Gouzenko

Laurie McKechnie didn't write anything except articles for the newspaper. Writing articles in the newspaper is one thing. Writing a literary opus is entirely different.

J. D. MacFarlane

It was another case of Gouzenko threatening to sue. He was always threatening to sue somebody. McKechnie helped him with the book. McKechnie, as I recall it, edited his manuscript as I've done in a number of cases with colleagues who thought it would be helpful. Somebody moved it a little bit farther into the realm of ghost-writing, which was crap. I don't blame Gouzenko for complaining, but he wouldn't just complain. He'd call his lawyer and start an action.

Leslie McKechnie, *Laurie McKechnie's widow*
That was a mistake. Laurie didn't write the book. But Gouzenko did have Laurie check over the manuscript. I know that. I remember seeing a manuscript with Laurie's notes in the margins. I also remember seeing a piece of paper separate from the manuscript with a whole list of things on it.

Bill McKechnie, *son*
My father died in 1965. I was going through his papers and there were file folders full of notes and chapters for the Gouzenko book, some of which were Gouzenko's handwriting and some of which were my father's. I had already known that my father was helping Gouzenko with the book.

Leslie McKechnie
Gouzenko visited Laurie at our house a few times. They probably went straight up to the den because I don't remember having more than two words with him. He was always Mr. Brown. In fact he wore a brown suit. And it was always the same suit. He had glasses and thinning hair. He was a person who wouldn't stand out. As a matter of fact I always wondered how he had the courage to defect. Because he didn't look the type. So he must have really wanted to very badly.

Peter Worthington
The Mounted Policeman who did the translation must have been a very unusual guy to get along with Gouzenko. In those days he could have known no English, but Gouzenko wouldn't let him get away with anything. He had pages of the stuff, and without knowing the language — and I don't know how he would do this — Gouzenko would say: "I don't think that word is right. I don't quite know what it means, but are you sure that's the one?" He would pick out the thing and they would worry about the phrase or the way of putting something. So Gouzenko, who didn't really know English, made the English better by getting the precise word. If you read the book, it doesn't read like a translation. It reads like a novel, a very good novel.

Peggy Blackstock

He was wonderful to work with. He was so curious about the English language and getting it right. I sat there with a great big Oxford dictionary. You really think you know how to define a word but you find it isn't as easy as you thought it was when you go to do it. So the two of us would be sitting there with the Oxford dictionary. It was a very exhilarating experience. The only thing he was furious about is that I wouldn't let him pay me. He paid everybody else who ever did anything for him, from Keyserlingk to Black to everybody else. But I said I'm being paid by Dents, so you can't pay me twice.

Ann Orford, *then a publisher's representative*

Some years after *The Fall of a Titan* he told me he was writing another book or had another one planned. I said: "Well, what is it going to be?" He was going to write a Canadian novel and it was going to move around a Canadian girl. I just laughed and said: "I don't think you're the person to involve a Canadian heroine." I didn't see how a Russian mind could understand a Canadian gal's mind. Oh, he was quite serious, but I never heard any more about it.

Robert Glasgow

He called me one day and said: "Mr. Glasgow, I'm going away. You will not be hearing from me for some time. But don't worry." I said: "Okay, I'm glad you let me know. I won't worry." Every once in a while I would get a postcard. He wrote a beautiful script. I don't know where he learned how to do that. He could have been an illustrator. Matter of fact, in the dedication to me in the book he did a drawing of the characters. He was a very talented guy. Anyway, he would write me these postcards and the postcards would have a picture of either Lake Louise or Banff or something like that. Obviously it had a postmark of where it had been mailed but he would always write on the top of it: "Somewhere in Canada." He would write me and say he was having a good time. "Hope to see you some time in the future." I got quite a number of those cards from him and they would always say: "Somewhere in Canada." If he was located in one place, and I think he was, it was probably outside of Vancouver some place. There are a lot of woodsy places around there. I had a feeling he had a car and was doing a lot of sightseeing.

Charles Chaplin, *then Canadian general manager of United Artists*
I hosted a dinner party for Gouzenko and for various representatives of the press at a suite in the Royal York Hotel. The hotel was instructed not to give out any information about the suite. The people from New York were C. R. Smith, president of American Airlines, Bob Considine, John McCarten from the *New Yorker*, [John] Tracy from Canadian Press. We waited and waited and Gouzenko didn't show up. I went down to the lobby and found him wandering around with his wife — I had met him before — because he had forgotten the suite number. Of course he couldn't find out the suite number. I brought him upstairs and the first thing he said was, "The radio is bugged." The dinner was set up in such a way that I had arranged for Igor Gouzenko's wife to sit at the head of the table and at that end of the table I placed the representatives of the press so that they could talk to Igor during dinner.

Alex Barris, *broadcaster*
There was a movie done in the 1950s and the people who were releasing the film were United Artists. They invited John McCarten, who was then the film critic of the *New Yorker* magazine, to come to Toronto for a private screening of the film and also a chance to meet Gouzenko. McCarten flew to Toronto with columnist Bob Considine. As it happens it was the very night of Hurricane Hazel, so that places it in the fall of 1954. Now McCarten had been drinking anyway and proceeded to get further drunk.

Charles Chaplin
Shortly after the dinner started, McCarten, who was drunk and sitting across from Gouzenko, suddenly said: "Igor, I was paid to come here and kill you." And with that he reached into his

inside pocket and Gouzenko stood up and opened up his jacket and said: "Go ahead," and McCarten pulled out a notebook and said: "Yeah, I've got it written down here." And Bob Considine looked at McCarten and said: "McCarten, I've never met you until this morning when we left New York. I've read your writing for many years and always admired it. But you're nothing but a drunken shit. And if you don't keep your mouth shut, I'll shove my fist right down your throat." With that McCarten kept quiet and never said another word.

14 Broke Again

Willson Woodside

There was a proposal made to move Gouzenko to a rural setting in Nova Scotia. I know about it because I was involved. It would be around 1956-57. St. Laurent was the Prime Minister and Nicholson the Commissioner [of the RCMP]. The RCMP was still willing to make one last effort. Gouzenko's documentation would be changed, which involved a lot of work because someone would have to go through the old records and change them to show that he immigrated at a certain time and location. Gouzenko was supposed to be completely cut off and give no more interviews. His only contact with the outside world was to be through the retired Inspector down the road. Gouzenko suspected the RCMP was infiltrated and wouldn't be put into the Force's hands. He turned down the proposal for, I suspect, both money and ego reasons. I can't remember who put me onto that proposal. I was supposed to arrange it. I was in Ottawa at the time and was to go to the Minister of Justice, the Commissioner, and Gouzenko, and get agreement from all three. Certainly Gouzenko didn't propose it to me.

Hon. E. Davie Fulton

My recollection is that not too much longer after I became minister of justice the Commissioner of the RCMP advised me they were having difficulty in maintaining Gouzenko's cover, and that they really couldn't tell me that his whereabouts and identity were not known but that they were not widely known, and that it was still desirable that his whereabouts and identity be kept a secret. They were not taking the position that they should establish a new cover for him, but that they should maintain the existing cover in so far as was possible, and that he was constantly making that difficult. They were doing their best to maintain his cover, but they wanted me to know it was partly shot. Gouzenko was a Canadian citizen and had the rights of a Canadian citizen, so his cover could be maintained only on the basis of his co-operation. They wanted me to know they were having these difficulties, so that if anything came of it that I wouldn't be taken by surprise.

I wondered sometimes if I should meet Gouzenko and try to reason with him myself, but I came to the conclusion that it wouldn't be wise. It is my recollection he was the kind of man, according to the facts that were disclosed to me, who would simply try to capitalize on it.

Stanley Frolick, *Gouzenko's lawyer*
Soviet citizens don't have any knowledge of the operation of a free market, of a capitalist system, of investment, of savings, of how financial things work in this kind of a country. Therefore he was a real victim and an easy mark for all kinds of speculators and unconscionable people who took advantage of him. And, as they say, a fool and his money are soon parted. He was a brilliant man but a fool in financial matters. He was a babe in the woods. He had no idea how to structure his financial affairs. So that money was badly invested. He lost money in all kinds of bad investments and screwy schemes and that sort of thing. So in no time at all he was worse off than ever.

Don Fast
Gouzenko was broke within two years of receiving money from his novel *The Fall of a Titan*. The fact that the option on the movie was not picked up was his fault. He was making all kinds of demands. I met the director of the movie of his first book in the kitchen with Dana Andrews at the party at Judge Forsyth's. I had sent him a copy of *The Fall of a Titan* on behalf of Gouzenko. He told me in the kitchen that it was the third copy of that book he had received from Gouzenko. He farmed out the movie rights for *The Fall of a Titan*. It was too costly. It was like

War and Peace. There were too many characters. They wanted to do a portion, but Gouzenko made unreasonable demands and was obnoxious about it. I gather he wanted complete and total say on the running of the movie.

Franc Joubin, *an acquaintance*

He was not a show-off, but money went through his hands like water. It was difficult to know where the money went, because it was not spent ostentatiously. His home was modestly furnished. There was no evidence of extravagant living. He sold the publication rights for his first book and I asked him where that substantial sum went — either he or some other knowledgeable person told me he had realized some $50,000 — and he dismissed that with just the wave of his hand. He said it was ridiculous, it was nothing. "It's nothing. Nothing. It's all gone." So I said: "Where?" "I don't know. I don't know. Canada is not a cheap country to live in."

Svetlana Gouzenko

Not one cent was spent wrongly. Of course, we shouldn't have bought the farm, but then we wouldn't have an income. No, I don't think we made many mistakes. We made a mistake. We made one big mistake. He signed this $100,000 [option] for the movie rights to *The Fall of a Titan* and got an advance and we didn't know they could drop the option. We thought the option was already in. So therefore we bought a little piece of land. Because it was a very, very wise purchase. Eventually it proved to be a very wise purchase, but that's about eight-ten years later that it proved it is a wise purchase. Meanwhile we were out of money, running around like mad, borrowing here, paying there. Then borrowing from one when the loan comes due, borrow from somebody else, pay to that one just to keep it on until we sell something. Well, this is the type of life when there is no steady income. That's the life. But we never spent money anywhere wrongly. Actually what threw us out of balance was believing that this option is already the agreement.

Stanley Frolick

I never handled any of his so-called investments. I do know, for example, that he bought into either a butcher shop or a chain of butcher shops or meat shops or something. That was a disaster, because they apparently were on the verge of bankruptcy. He grossly overpaid and, of course, they couldn't be salvaged, so all the money went down the drain. He bought some other stocks or something. I don't know what they were. To be as charitable as possible, they were highly speculative.

Don Fast

When he was broke I got him a job at Malton Airport for Avro working on that plane that was scrapped [the Arrow]. We had a connection with Avro. We did a little bit of security screening for them, and as a return for favours we said: "We have a man here that we want to get a job for." They didn't know who it was. They said: "Sure, no problem." So that's how we got him in there. It was a nice job with good pay but he didn't want to get up in the morning. He was squawking all the time he couldn't write because he was too tired after working. At first she drove him. Then he got a ride from someone else, but he would miss the ride half the time and she would have to rush him to work while looking after the kids. I remember one time I watched for the car pool to come in, bring him home, to see who was in it — because I wanted to know just how he was travelling. There were two or three other people in the car and they dropped him off. But when he slept in, they would wait for a couple of minutes and drive away. He never drove, so she had to drive him. He was absent a lot. He stuck to it for five-six months but he got tired from the grind of getting up in the morning. I'm surprised he stuck at it that long. His claim of not being able to take a job because of security is a lot of crap. In fact it was more secure if he did work because people would wonder if he is lying around all day.

Nelles Starr

I knew he was broke because I got a call from his bank manager one day wanting $3000 or something. And I said: "Phone Gouzenko. Don't bother me about it."

Eddie Goodman

I saw him just a couple of times. The only purpose Gouzenko wanted to see me was not for any legal reason nor any political reason but straight to see if he could get any money from me. And eventually I did end up loaning him some dough, either once or twice. In total it couldn't have been more than $4000. It might have been less, so it wasn't any big money.

. . . When he came to me he just needed this loan to tide him over until he got this great fortune from the movie rights. He had an inordinately high view of what he was entitled to for the movie rights. And, I believe, as a result he didn't get anything.

Floyd S. Chalmers, *publisher*

He came in to see me when I was president of Maclean-Hunter. He said: "I want $3500 from you." I said: "Why?" "Well," he said, "because of what I've done for this country. I think I'm entitled to some little reward." Well, I didn't give him the $3500. I found he was going around to all sorts of people and asking for money because of what he had done for Canada. I didn't give him the money, of course. It was ridiculous.

Fergus Cronin, *retired journalist*

He would ask me to help him borrow money. I wrote a letter once to one of the founders of Imperial Oil, who was still living. The reply I got from him sort of cured me of doing this. I don't think I did it any more because this guy was rather upset. He was very polite but he said: "You do yourself no favour, Mr. Cronin, by interceding on his behalf." So that kind of made my ears burn.

Willson Woodside

He went through Bay Street and then he started borrowing from the Ukrainians. He became a Ukrainian nationalist to satisfy them. He never paid them back. He figured he had done a great service to the western world and that it owed him a living and therefore it had to pay.

Don Fast

He ran out of money completely. He had exhausted everybody and his dog. I knew he was running around all over the place looking for money, and Mrs. Gouzenko finally came to me asking for some money for groceries. I refused her. I knew if I gave her money once, she would be around on almost a regular basis. It was one of the hardest decisions to make and I knew I had to make it, otherwise my own life would be full of problems. She came knocking on my door one day. I believe she asked me for $50 and I didn't even have $50. In those days you carried only two bucks in your pocket. I immediately got in touch with Ottawa and told them: "This man is broke. We're going to have some problems here. We better get him some money."

Peggy Blackstock

The last time I saw him would be around 1959. He and his wife came in and were so hard up they didn't have enough money to buy groceries. I gave them $40.

Willson Woodside

What finally turned me off about Gouzenko was his attempt to borrow money from me. Gouzenko had traded in his car and when he went to pick up his new one the dealer told him he hadn't paid for the old one. So he needed more money. At the time I was free-lancing. I had no job and five kids to support. The car he was trading in was better than the old car I was driving. He came to me. Imagine that. I was penniless. That really burned me up. I was really strapped for funds. I don't know if he knew or cared. He showed no embarrassment over it. I have never seen him embarrassed. I was very definite about it. I just didn't have the money.

Franc Joubin

In all subjects relating to money he had this obsession he was above normal business. Canada owed him. It amazed me and turned me completely off this man. He showed no gratitude for anything. Publishers had robbed him and there was nothing good he could say about various political mandarins in Ottawa. He had done so much and they double-crossed him. It got quite tiresome.

Frank Rasky, *author of* Gay Canadian Rogues, *which contained two complimentary chapters about Gouzenko*

I was quite amazed one day in my function as editor-in-chief of *Liberty* magazine to get notice in 1959 from his lawyer saying he was suing me for $1 million and that he wanted copies of the book taken off the newsstands. In the list of sins committed apparently the main one was the title itself: *Gay Canadian Rogues*. In those days the word gay had an utterly different connotation. I was surprised because in the very first chapter I presented myself as a Gay Canadian Rogue. I had a chapter called "My Cowardly Career as a Gangster" in which I did an exposé for the *Vancouver Sun* as a cub reporter. All these chapters are written in a light-hearted fashion. They are really a collection of magazine pieces that I've written.

Lloyd Tataryn, *journalist*

I found it incredible as I talked to Rasky that the reason that Gouzenko sued was over the title of the book. That was one of the key reasons. He objected to the word rogue. The word gay hadn't fallen into disrepute but the word rogue, he thought, tainted his image and consequently Gouzenko thought this was good and just reason for suing. It was amazing.

Frank Rasky

I was very astonished but not so astonished were the lawyers for Harlequin and Thomas Nelson. We had a little get-together at the office of the lawyers — I forget the name of the lawyer, he was a very dramatic lawyer and a very good one. One of the first things he said really frightened the heck out of me. He turned to me and asked if I had the money to fight this in court. I said no, I didn't have that kind of money. After a lot of questioning on the part of the lawyer, they decided to regard it as a nuisance suit, because their opinion was that Gouzenko went around making his living, apparently, by suing people and collecting nuisance suit money. The notion of the lawyer and myself was that he didn't give a damn what you said, he just wanted to sue you and collect some cash and make his living thereby. In any case, that was the last of it, because they settled out of court. I believe they settled for something like $10,000. The publisher, Harlequin, did indeed remove the book from the bookstands. I was sore as all hell that they didn't put up a fight about this. Here's a guy who comes along, obviously a scoundrel, and merely because he makes a threat they turn tail and pay up. I talked to them about justice, freedom of the press, and so on. These were just gibberish words to them.

Fergus Cronin

He said he got a final settlement against Rasky et al. for $10,000 plus apologies which were to be put into all three Toronto papers. He told me not to tell anyone about the amount because he said all his creditors would be down on him and he was going to tell them he only got about $100 out of it. That's what he said.

Svetlana Gouzenko

I only know that we went happily, that we have it settled. We were passing a Simpsons window and [saw] those grey coats there and my muskrat fur coat was already fifteen years old or something. And we say when we will make the next big money I will buy myself a coat like that. Well, you have never met my husband. He was most wonderful. Any wife would say he was a wonderful husband. And I say I will buy the coat when we will make the next big money. He say: "Let's go and try it." I say: "No way, the salesgirl will be trying on — I will be trying out coats and when I am not buying she will be serving me and then she will have nothing. No way." And he say: "No, no, no, I want to see how the grey collar looks on you." So we went. I can't really start a fight with my husband on Simpsons' third floor, so I say okay. "Ahhh," and he say, "I like it." Of course I walk out with the coat on my back because that's my husband. I cannot fight him. It's over my dead body, believe me. But he bought the coat for me. He spoiled me.

Alan Harris, *who later became Gouzenko's lawyer*
I believe a library had copies of a book Frank Rasky had written and which was libellous of Gouzenko and which Nelles Starr had been successful in having taken right off the shelves. All copies had been retracted. But somehow a particular library had a copy that Mr. Gouzenko had found out was being circulated. So he had me write to them to retract that copy.

Frank Rasky
One of my writers was Hugh Garner, the novelist, who recognized Gouzenko. Hugh told me that he saw Gouzenko over at Simpsons' book department going through books apparently with the idea of seeing who he could sue next, and Garner, who had a nice sense of mischief, yelled out at the top of his lungs: "Hey Gouzenko, Mr. Gouzenko, I see you. I know you. What are you doing over there?" Gouzey, as he called him, then turned tail and scuttled like a scared rabbit down the corridors of Simpsons.

15 Front Page Challenge

Peter Gzowski, *writer and broadcaster*

I remember when I was a very naive magazine editor with *Maclean's*. This would be around 1958 or '59. We had a story meeting in which Gouzenko's name came up and it really astonished me that you could find him. I was asking: "Would it be possible to get him?" I remember Ralph Allen saying: "All you do is run a cheque for $500 up the flagpole on the Maclean-Hunter building and he'll be there."

Jim Guthro, *producer*

I was producing *Front Page Challenge* and we had a twice-a-week meeting to try to get somebody on the program who represented a story where all the facts hadn't come out. In other words, we wanted a lot of old stories with new material. I decided that Gouzenko was such a story. So we set out to get Gouzenko.

. . . We talked about the show and he said he would like to be on it. And he talked about money. The whole conversation was based on money and how we would disguise him. It turned out he wanted quite a bit of money and we eventually agreed to pay it, which was $1000. Which was more than normal. We used to pay $200. I thought it was worth it because no one had ever seen him. I gambled that I could present him without the pillowcase and I lost that gamble. He said he would be shot in the studio. He said they were out after him. I said: "How will they know you're going to be there?" He said: "The newspapers will be there. They'll find out." I said: "No, no. We'll put the thing through as just another story. Even the script won't have it."

He said he was having trouble getting along financially. But I didn't get the impression he wanted the money to help him out financially. I felt that he thought he was a marketable commodity and that it was his ego. That seemed to be equally important to him. In fact he was very annoying. He annoyed the hell out of me. Even after we agreed to the $1000 he tried to bump it up after we made the deal. I thought to myself: "I'm going to have trouble with this as it is. All of a sudden he wants 1250." I think I just told him: "We've already made the deal. A deal is a deal."

John Dalrymple

He got the word they were going to have him as a guest on *Front Page Challenge*, complete with black bag over his head. That was terrific. I don't recall the sum, but as Igor was almost invariably broke he was allured by the prospect but very, very nervous about appearing. So with one of his friends who used to work at Massey-Ferguson, who would supply the car and drive it, he decided that I would be the one who would ride shotgun for him, the payment for which was supposed to be a lobster dinner at the King Edward Hotel afterwards. So on the evening he handed me a nice .38-calibre gun. As far as I was concerned it was strictly for yuks, because I could not believe that the KGB was still after him as hard as he always used to think. So I did the old trench coat thing with the collar turned up and met him at some pre-arranged spot downtown. Mr. Prychodko was driving the car and we went up to the CBC studio on Yonge Street north of Dupont. The *Front Page Challenge* folks had taken great, great precautions. The place was literally ringed with shoulder-to-shoulder cops who were keeping everybody out and that, of course, included us.

Fred Davis, *host*

Some fairly elaborate arrangements had been made about spiriting him out in a car through one of the stage-set scenery-loading doors where the trucks come in. Because in those days the program was live and he was afraid if somebody who was after him — he really believed this — and was near enough to the studio and knew that Gouzenko was there live, even though he would be disguised with a hood over his head, that they might get down to the studio in time to kill him. So that was all arranged.

John Dalrymple

We drove around the block about three times and couldn't get in. The cops kept moving us along. Finally I got out, in spite of the fact the cops tried to keep the door shut and move us along, and insisted on seeing who was in charge there and finally got myself ushered in and pointed out to them that their massive security arrangement was keeping their guest of honour outside. So the word passed and the car was allowed into a little back lane behind the studio on our next tour of the block and into a basement garage. So I escorted Igor to the dressing room, where he donned his bag over the head. When it was time for him to go on, I did my bit going down the hall ahead of him which had been all cleared by security people and appearing around the corner at each intersection — really hamming it up.

Fred Davis

On the night of the show somebody — I assumed he was his bodyguard — literally searched the studio. Gouzenko figured if somebody heard about it they might put a bomb in the studio. So the studio was searched to make sure it was secure.

Gordon Sinclair, *longtime panelist*

We [the panel] sit around and guess who we are likely to have — and we're usually wrong. Sometimes they pop up years into the future. I remember we had anticipated him right from the beginning. This was when the show was reasonably young and we had gone over a list of people we thought for sure would come up. Now on the date that he did come up I think we missed him.

Lucio Agostini, *orchestra leader*

All the musicians, of course, knew that he was coming. When we rehearsed the music in the morning, the title on the music said Igor Gouzenko. So they knew he was coming.

Bernard Cowan, *announcer*

You can probably count on the fingers of one hand the number of occasions where we did not have an opportunity to talk to the guests in an informal way in the afternoon. This was one of those occasions. Even the Prime Minister was easier to get to. I'm quite serious. When Trudeau appeared, they drove him right into the studio. We had an opportunity to talk to him. But the security for Gouzenko was quite different.

Gordon Sinclair

I was a little irritated by some special sort of snoopy goings-on backstage. It's so long ago I really don't remember what they were but there was some security there that annoyed me. I remember I was followed into a dressing room where I kept a spare jacket. I didn't say anything to the man who followed me. I just wondered who he was and what he was doing there.

Fred Davis

Just before going on the air it suddenly occurred to Gouzenko that his voice might be recognized by the people in his local community where he had another identity. He demanded that the engineers in some way disguise his voice. And if this wasn't done he wouldn't go on. The audio people came up with some kind of neck mike which was clamped on over his throat which certainly distorted the voice. What went out on the air was no normal-sounding voice. The problem was we were live and had no chance to check this out.

Gordon Sinclair

When Igor Gouzenko came on, I kind of thought he was a phony. I can't tell you why but I didn't trust what he was telling us and I didn't trust the make-up deal.

Jim Guthro

We had a lot of difficulty with him on the program because he would not answer questions directly. He turned every question around to a different question and it was infuriating. It was not a good interview. He didn't answer the questions. Furthermore, the pillowcase over his head gave us an audio problem that we didn't anticipate, namely the microphone was muffled.

Fred Davis

I forget whether the panel got the story or not. We get the mystery man into the hot seat — he's sitting there with the hood over his face, a very dramatic picture. The hood is muffling his voice. We've got this gizmo on his neck which is further muffling it, and apparently as he got more nervous his Russian accent got more pronounced. And to this day I still can't remember what he said.

Jim Guthro

The technicians didn't know what was causing all the problems. "Why can't we hear all his words?" I remember in the control room we didn't know whether it was the pillowcase over his head or whether we had altered the mike too much. We're sweating in the control room. I'm yelling at the audio man saying: "Do something." You can't. It's a live show.

Fred Davis

I could hear the panel asking him questions but I'm not sure they were too sure of what he said because the muffled, disguised voice with the thick Russian accent got thicker as the moments went on. And we had allowed a long period of time because this was quite a news scoop to get Gouzenko because he was definitely the man of mystery in those days. So here we were with eight to ten minutes to fill and I'm thinking this is a disaster because we don't have a back-up guest and I can't understand what he's saying. I was hoping the audience could. As it turned out, because he was getting a direct feed to air, he was more intelligible to the home audience. But in the studio I'm sweating, thinking this is a disaster and we're filling the air with twelve minutes of gibberish. So I was a little upset, but the panel manfully did the questioning.

Jim Guthro

The muffled audio plus his heavily accented English — a very Slavonic way of speaking English — and the fact he indulged in this odd way of answering questions made it, in my opinion, one of the worst interviews we ever had. But it created a sensation. The hood gave mystery to him and increased the impact of having him on. Of course it made the newspapers. It was a big deal. After we had him on, newspaper reporters were after him and it gave the story another run. I don't know how many interviews he gave after that but I know business picked up for him. It was an immensely successful item for the show even though we had the problem.

John Dalrymple

When it was over, we were to leave instantly. As soon as he was off-stage, whoosh, down into the basement and into the car, and a CBC man whips up the garage door and the car makes a right-angle turn out the door at high speed and bursting down this narrow lane all lined with garbage cans so that we can't be followed. All of a sudden, as the headlights bounced up and down the lane, out from behind a garbage can leaps this wild figure waving something in his hand which, by God, looked to me like a gun. I thought: "Oh my God, this can't be for real." I pushed Igor down and, believe it or not, out came my gun and I got it out the window and I'm trying to point it in this bouncing car at this shadowy figure which had leapt up from behind the garbage can. Just a fraction of a second before I am ready to tighten the trigger, we've come up to him and the headlights catch him and I recognized by weird coincidence who it was: a guy who went by the nickname Kayo. He was the undisputed autograph king of the Toronto cocktail-party circuit. Nobody knew who he was or what he did for a living, but whenever there was a celebrity in town Kayo was there to get the autograph. He crashed the weirdest places and I had seen him so many times I recognized him instantly. I said: "Oh my God," and shoved the gun back into my pocket and we spun out into the street and went zipping down Yonge Street and did the usual thing through the side streets. I think Igor, despite what I told him, thought Kayo might still be a KGB man. Poor old Kayo did not get an autograph. He nearly got a hole in the head.

Fred Davis

Happily for us, he got off the air without incident and he got into his car and screeched out of the studio. But of all the stories we've done, that one stands out because of the great cloak-and-dagger build-up.

Ray McConnell, *current producer*

Years later he wanted to know if I'd be interested in another appearance on *Front Page Challenge.* . . . He wanted quite a bit of money to appear on the show. When I said to him: "Gee, we don't pay that kind of money," he said: "Well, the last time I was on the show I got that kind of money." I said: "Yeah, things have changed. We just don't have that kind of money to pay." I added: "Although if you're willing to come on in the flesh I could probably get permission to give you that kind of money." Then he went to great pains to tell me why he couldn't possibly do that. I tried to lighten the conversation and suggested: "Why don't you come on the show and we'll have everybody on the panel wear bags over their heads." This went above his head and I felt badly after having said it. We talked all around it for the next half-hour or so and came to the conclusion that I wasn't going to do him any good and quite frankly a repeat appearance with a bag over his head wouldn't do me any good. So we let it drop. What was interesting was how desperately he needed the money.

Lorraine Thomson, Front Page Challenge *co-ordinator*

We thought at that point there wasn't really anything that he could have said beyond what he had said already behind the hood. Although subsequently we found out from things that came out close to his death that there may indeed have been something. He also wanted a lot of money. He wanted $1500 to

$2000 and our top fee really was $500. And we pay less than that now because nobody pays anybody any more. We just decided not to go with the story.

Fred Davis

I got the impression he was fairly hungry. Whether he needed the money or just thought he was worth more than the market price allowed, I don't know. I think for the kind of audience we could have delivered it would have been wiser for him to take what he was offered, if he was looking for publicity, or do it for nóthing, rather than hold out for a big chunk of money. But I guess he was looking for anything he could get.

16 Pension

Del Maulsby

I went through the files and was amazed at the stuff I came onto where Gouzenko borrowed money and nobody would know. In case he dropped dead, these things would have had to be dealt with. It's amazing how many people loaned him money just on his signature. These included a lot of private individuals doing their patriotic duty, but there were also banks and trust companies.

Stanley Frolick

I was his lawyer for a long while. I was the one who represented him in negotiating with the government in procuring his first stipend that was ever given to him by the Canadian government. That was under Prime Minister Diefenbaker. . . . I remember I contacted him and I think Mr. Gouzenko did as well, on his own, [contact] Mr. Starr, who was the Minister of Labour. And he, of course, was a rather close confidant and friend of the Prime Minister, so he was able to do his part in convincing the Prime Minister that there ought to be a pension given to the Gouzenkos.

Hon. Michael Starr, *former Minister of Labour*

When I was Minister of Labour he came to see me one Sunday at my home in Oshawa and spent a couple of hours with me. Originally a friend of his from Toronto acted as go-between. I was supposed to meet him at the bus station in Oshawa at two o'clock one Sunday afternoon. It was sort of cloak-and-dagger stuff. I waited at the bus station for half an hour and nobody showed up, so I went home. Then I got a phone call to say he changed his mind because the circumstances weren't right. Then a couple of weeks later he came right to the house. After that he seemed to come about every second Sunday. Eventually I found out he was keeping his car a couple of blocks away with his wife in it, so I asked him to bring her to the house. His problem was he was broke. As I understood it, he had unwisely invested the money from his book, *The Fall of a Titan*, and he was hard up. He had a batch of children, too. So I spoke to Mr. Diefenbaker, the Prime Minister, and he agreed with me that we as a country owed him something. So we decided on a pension of $500 a month. We decided that his financial know-how wasn't worth a hoot, so we gave the pension in her name. That pension, I understand, grew over the years.

Stanley Frolick
It was, like most of those things, an arbitrary figure. It was compromise. His needs were greater. I must confess I forgot now what we asked for, but it was more than that. Our government used to be very parsimonious and tight with public funds. The strings of the public purse were drawn very tightly. And now it seems they spend their money like drunken sailors for everything. But really and truly twenty and thirty years ago it was entirely different.

Willson Woodside
It was good money at the time. I knew about this action through Mike Starr, who was in the Diefenbaker cabinet. The Conservatives were more sympathetic to Gouzenko because presumably they had some affinity for the Ukrainians. The Liberals seemed to want better relations with Russia.

Del Maulsby
Gouzenko was paid his monthly stipend from the defectors' fund, which was controlled by the RCMP. We sent the monthly tax-free cheque to the trust company and it would pay Gouzenko. The cheque we issued was made out to the trust company

and not to Gouzenko. If additional money was paid to Gouzenko, and often there was, it would not come from the defectors'
budget but would come straight from Treasury Board, which
first had to approve the sum. I seem to recall that he had eight
kids. He used his kids as reasons for needing more money. In
fact, two of them were married and living away from home and
he was still citing them as financial burdens.

Stanley Frolick
It was pitiful. I remember when one of the babies had just been
born. It was still an infant, whether it was the last or the second
last I don't know. And she came crying to my office, alone, not
with her husband. And she said: "Look, please help me. We're
freezing. It's cold. It's winter. We have no heat in the house. And
the oil company — I went and cried and said: 'Look, we'll pay
you somehow. Will you put in oil?' They said: 'No, we won't get
you any more oil until you pay us what you owe us or you pay
cash.'" So that's how bad it was. For lack of $30-$35. . . .
    He owed money all over the place and they were all after him.
One of the things I dealt with [was that] they were suing him.
For debts. Actions were going on against him to correct debts.
Banks were after him and mortgagees to foreclose — to get a
judgment against him. There were all kinds of problems. I was
involved in some of them in the legal sense in the courts. It was
a most unusual experience anybody who practises law has ever
run across. Where for security reasons the defendant in an action
cannot be produced and legitimately can be hidden. And the
other side uses everything possible to get the legal system to
disgorge this person so they can get their hands around his
throat.

J. W. Temple, *lawyer*
We had two clients with claims against Gouzenko. I forget the
other one, but one was [William] Hultay. If I remember correctly,
Hultay owned a hotel in Toronto. Gouzenko had years ago
blown his cover and the net result was that everybody over there
knew him. And Hultay from time to time loaned him money. I

can't remember the amount. In those days you couldn't get hold of him to have him served, so we had to drop it [an affadavit] on the RCMP.

. . . Then we had to go up and wait our half-hour in the special examiner's office. He didn't appear, and then we served an oath of motion that we're going to apply for an order for contempt of court to have him jailed. It's long ago, but I think probably what happened was that when we got to the deadline of putting him away we got a call from the solicitor involved saying they were going to raise the funds and they needed thirty days. And we all know in this business that thirty days often stretches into ninety or a hundred and twenty. But somewhere along the line somebody paid us and we were rid of it.

B. B. Osler, *lawyer*

One evening around 1961 a man my wife knew through helping central European immigrants — his name was Prychodko — brought a man whom he introduced as Mr. Brown. Mr. Brown was Igor Gouzenko. I congratulated him on what I thought he had done for our country in 1945. He was very pleased and told me he was living under an assumed name. He had to appear in court in Brampton the next morning as a defendant in a claim by a fairly well-known Canadian company and he was afraid that if he did appear in court his identity would become known and he would be killed by the Russians. The claim was for about $2000. I think he had bought a car on a conditional sale agreement.

Gouzenko said: "I need $2000. I've got to have it first thing in the morning." I said: "Well, I simply haven't got $2000 in my house." He looked around and said: "I don't believe you." "Well," I said, "I don't carry my money. I use banks." He still looked as if he's saying "I wonder why." He didn't believe me. A most extraordinary thing. In any event, I said I would raise the money probably by the next afternoon between myself and some of my friends that I would hit for him. In the meantime I had to get him off the hook for his court appearance the next morning. So I called the president of the company — it wouldn't be fair to name him or the company — and told him the story as I'd had it from Gouzenko. I said would he mind instructing his solicitors to ask for an adjournment in court the next morning because I believed that I was going to be able to raise the money between myself, my family, and my friends. Well, this chap very kindly said he would instruct his solicitors to ask for an adjournment and that was done.

I spoke to my sister and my brother, several of my friends, and some of my partners. Between us we raised two thousand-odd dollars to pay off that debt. Within ten days he was back in my house in great trouble. He had a lot of creditors and they were all hounding him and he was afraid he was going to be killed. Could I possibly help him? I said: "Well, how much do you owe?" He said he didn't really know — but quite a lot. I said: "Gouzenko, if you give me a list of every creditor you have, precisely what you owe him, when you borrowed the money or otherwise came to owe it to him, I'll look at the list and see what I can do." He brought me that list and disclosed that he had 114 creditors to whom he owed a total of $153,104.46.

Svetlana Gouzenko

Mr. Osler asked my husband to give him a list of all the debts he had — the dozens of Ukrainian names that he owes $300 or $200. When he was going to an interview he would ask for $500, but he got three men who have to take off Saturday — Friday night if they come from Kingston or Niagara Falls. So they will take the day off and come here. That was from the Ukrainian organization. They know the men that they can trust as anti-communist. And ninety per cent of the time there was not enough money from the interview to pay the expenses when they come here — transportation, rent of hotel, their day off, that they have to take the time. So he would give them an IOU note because we have got this $100,000 [movie option] offer just about to come [and] the book that he is going to place in the hands of a publisher. . . .

Now that was quite a list. Maybe it came out to $1000 or $2000 only, but it's a big list of Ukrainian names that were indebted. Then when the mortgage came due and we hadn't any cash money from anywhere we would drive to the same people who were guards — maybe went with him to interviews some few years ago — and borrowed $100 or $200, $300, and paid the mortgage to meet the mortgage payments. But he could write it always: this is a loan without security. So he would always give a large bonus. If it is $500, he would write $750.

B. B. Osler

One reason for the debts in that amount is he went around buying properties, being sure they would increase in value, and he would make money that way. But he didn't have the cash to pay for them, so he put big mortgages on them. Then he couldn't pay the mortgages. So these people were demanding payment and threatening to sue him. I think that's what brought it to a head really.

Stanley Frolick

Some [of the debts] were large. Because he had made these investments, given back these mortgages, put down payments, and owed money, and then, of course, he couldn't come up with the money. So some of the sums were very large . . . from $30 maybe to $3000 to $30,000.

B. B. Osler

I looked at the list. It included several banks, including six branches of one bank and many people. He had gone to them, nearly all of them, with the story that within thirty days he would have money from our government to compensate him for what he had done for the country. It wasn't true, but they believed him. And because they felt he had been useful to the country, they would lend him in some cases all the money they had. But he got scared at the end because there were so many of them. I discovered all of this only later. This took me about a year and a half to a year and three-quarters to clean up. I had to go and see every one of these 114 people and then go back to my office and decide how much each was going to be paid and how much I was going to make each give up and how much I'd try to make each postpone. I had to go over that pretty carefully. And, having decided that, I had to draft the agreements that they

"Here is the Government award for you", said Malenkov.
(page 418)

With best wishes,
July 6th, 54.   Igor Gouzenko.

Phil Eustace
My father had been very helpful to Gouzenko in a number of ways, and when Gouzenko gave him a copy of his second book he took a little extra time and drew this caricature of a fat, plump little man handing out a document across a desk. It was a scene from the book. That's how he autographed the book for my father.

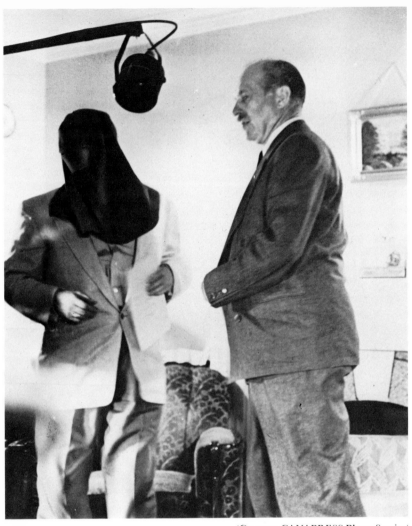

Gouzenko dons hood for television interview with the late American journalist Drew Pearson.

Willson Woodside

I remember very clearly the day he gave the television interview to Drew Pearson. It was the first time he ever used the hood on his head. It was a black hood and I have it here at home. He came to me on Sunday morning and the interview was all set up in East York, but I didn't know anything about it at all until Gouzenko came to my door. Gouzenko said he wanted to get out of it. I said: "Did you sign anything?" He said he had. I said: "You can't get out of it then because he'll sue you for non-appearance." So he went through with it and insisted I go with him. I remember going over in the evening and finding a house in East York all fixed up for television with electrical cables coming into the house from the outside. He didn't have anything to say actually. This is why the Russians hadn't killed him. If he had had anything new, they would have killed him.

Peter Worthington
You had to meet him on his terms. He would never keep an appointment. He was so security-conscious that you couldn't make a date or an appointment over the phone. He had a very distinctive voice. The minute he said hello you knew it was Gouzenko, and yet I swear he thought he had no accent. And he wouldn't want any mention of his name or any suggestion of where you would meet him or that he would come by car or whatever. The next two or three days you would have to be free for lunch and he might call any moment. Which wasn't so bad in those days. It got harder later on when I got tied down into the *Sun*. You just couldn't drop everything. Except I did mostly.

Richard Jackson
He did a lot of crying about how tight-fisted the government was; how it refused to understand his difficulty with finances. He told us a couple of stories that led me to believe he was very careless about his money.

IGOR GOUZENKO

MEMORANDUM

TRUDEAU, A POTENTIAL CANADIAN CASTRO

Because Canadian and U.S. press, radio and television largely ignored the past activities and writings of Trudeau, the public is not aware of a real possibility that on the 6th of April, 1968, the next Prime Minister of Canada might be a self-admitted radical socialist, and Canada might with ever increasing pace turn into a second Cuba. The situation is already pregnant with a multiple threat to Canadian freedom.

The present Minister of Justice, Pierre Elliot Trudeau, was elected to Parliament only in 1965. Before this he was professor at the University of Montreal; he was the founder of a radical left magazine, Cite Libre. He is careful not to call himself a communist, but as a matter of record, he was once barred from the United States as a communist. Below is the clipping from the Toronto Daily Star, dated February 16, 1968:

In another revelation, he admitted he was once blacklisted by U.S. immigration authorities because they suspected he was a Communist.

Yet in spite of this background, shortly after Trudeau was elected to Parliament in 1965, Prime Minister Pearson appointed him his Parliamentary Secretary, and then made him, of all things, the Minister of Justice.

Pearson now supports Trudeau in the leadership race in obvious preference to other candidates. Press, radio and television are giving Trudeau unprecedented publicity, building him up as an intellectual, ignoring the fact that many of his so-called new ideas are borrowed from the outworn, reactionary writings of Lenin and Mao.

The Liberal Convention will choose not just a new leader, but a new Prime Minister. The next Prime Minister, therefore, would be elected not by the Canadian people at a general election but by several hundred delegates at the convention. The responsibility of the delegates, therefore, takes truly a historic proportion.

Page one of a pamphlet written and distributed by Igor Gouzenko.

Lloyd Tataryn
In 1968 Gouzenko, under his signature, published a squalid pamphlet during the 1968 Liberal leadership race. The pamphlet called Pierre Trudeau "a new Castro" who would turn Canada into a "radical socialist state". In the pamphlet Gouzenko said: "Castro at first stages of his climb to power has made more efforts to hide his communist nature than Trudeau is doing now. Still Trudeau is very successful at it: he is posing as an intellectual, throwing clouds of words presenting old, out-worn communist ideas as if they were new and progressive." I found this interesting.

(Courtesy *Maclean's* and Duncan Macpherson)

Duncan Macpherson

I was looking for some sort of military attitude in the man and he didn't
have it. He was just another guy off the street when he was in the
courtroom in terms of demeanour, manner, and poise. When he spoke he
raised one eyebrow, which is unusual. If you watch you will notice that
most people raise both. He almost had no lower lip. It seemed to slide out
to a definite chin. He certainly had a very well developed neck. That can
sometimes be an illusion. If there is a round head it sometimes sits
differently than a long skull. If I was cartooning him it would be quite
simple. I would start at the base of the neck and sweep up into the chin
and back into the mouth under the nose fairly well — like a French
wood-carving, those little sailors they used to whittle along the St.
Lawrence.

(Courtesy *The Toronto Star*)

Duncan Macpherson
I went over to do some sketches of Gouzenko when he appeared in the courtroom. I took an educated guess as to how he was going to leave the building. I phoned a *Star* photographer, Bob Olsen, and he took the west entrance.

Bob Olsen
I just followed him out with a camera under my arm, and I just walked out the same door being as nonchalant as I possibly could. And then

(Courtesy *The Toronto Star*)

when he stepped out the door — and I sort of had to feel how far away he was from me — I suddenly just turned around and took a couple of photographs. But as soon as he saw the camera he, of course, went berserk.

Duncan Macpherson
His wife was outraged and was swinging a handbag at Bob. Bob was pretty quick on his feet, I must say. He moved around like a quarterback.

Gouzenko in 1975, seven years before his death.

Robert Reguly
He was square. Square in the sense he had an angular, square build. He looked like something out of Central Casting when they'd say: "Send me over a Russian." You'd pick Gouzenko. Particularly the way he wore his hat straight across his head. He had a stolid walk. He was chunky square. He looked like old photographs of heavies out of the 1930s movies.

would sign to do this if they got paid so much by a certain date. And then, having got all these papers drawn up, I had to go back to each of them and get them to sign the damn thing.

There were all sorts of small bills. He owed the South Peel Hospital $5. A doctor with a central European name had come and treated him and had a bill for $7. He owed one person $27, another $23.25, another $28.63, and so on. There were a number in the seventies. The highest individual was for $10,000. There were some credit unions, mostly run by new Canadians who formed their own credit unions. I listed all these people and made up my mind that there was no hope that I could raise $153,000, but I might be able to raise somewhere around sixty or seventy thousand.

Some of these people were desperately hard up. They had lent him all their savings. These were the people from central Europe who were out here as new Canadians. I decided they had to get paid in full. So I said to the banks — to anybody who was well off or who I thought might be willing to do it — that I was trying to arrange to pay off those that need the money at once and get the others to postpone the amount of payment until he came into funds. All the banks agreed to postpone everything he owed them and to cancel entirely about half of the figure. I went through the whole list that way. I decided who would get paid in full, who would get paid in part, who would be asked to cancel. Most people were very co-operative. I put together a list of people who had agreed. All the small people would be paid in full, others agreed to postpone either the whole or a sub-stantial part of it, and others agreed to cancel everything. I ended up having to pay $67,282.03 promptly, allow him to postpone $61,578.00, and to cancel $24,244.43. Those figures add up to $153,104.46.

Stanley Frolick

This new plan was put in to him to accumulate all these vast debts and other expenses — make it all into one, pay it off, start with a clean slate, and provide enough money for their liveli-hood so they would not have to immediately go back into debt. That was the whole purpose of the arrangement.

B. B. Osler

In order to be sure that these things were tied up properly and that the creditors were secured for the amounts which they had agreed to take, I had to work out an agreement between the Gouzenkos and a trustee in accordance with which the trustee would act for the protection of the creditors who had agreed to a postponement of payment of their claims; so I asked National Trust Company, Limited — the senior officers of which were my close friends — if it would undertake the responsibility. I told them it would probably be a time-consuming and frustrating job for their company but that I hoped that they would undertake it, and, of course, I told them all the facts. They very kindly said they would do it and with no charge except for their out-of-pocket expenses, so I drew up the required agreement, which I insisted should be signed by Mrs. Gouzenko as well as by him and the trust company. The agreement required that the Gouzenkos should convey to the trust company, to be held in trust, all of the real property which they owned and anything else of value which could be discovered, including any rights they had or might later have with respect to any book or books which Gouzenko had written or intended to write. The agreement also provided that the trust company should be entitled, in its discretion as to time of sale and price, to sell any of the real property — except the Gouzenkos' own residence property — which had been conveyed to it and to apply the proceeds for the benefit of those creditors who had postponed a part of the amounts owing to them. In the negotiations with Gouzenko he tried to insist that he and his wife should have the right to veto a sale of any such property if they thought they should receive a higher price. I rejected this demand and required that as a condition of raising such money as I was able to obtain he must give the trust company the absolute right of decision. He was not required to pay interest on the amounts of the debts which were to be postponed, so it would be in his interest to delay payment of the debts until after he was dead.

Gouzenko and his wife were in my office one day about lunchtime. When they realized that I could not be persuaded to include in the agreement a condition entitling them to veto a sale by the trust company of property other than their own residence whenever and at such price as the trust company thought appropriate, Mrs. Gouzenko suddenly began to scream. I never heard screams like it. You would have thought she was being cut up. This happened on the twenty-fourth floor of my office in the old Canadian Bank of Commerce building on King Street. So I went to my door and opened it and said: "Get out, I'm finished with you." I said: "If you change your mind you can come back. But I'll have no more of this kind of behaviour." And I took them to the elevator and could hear her screaming the whole way down twenty-four storeys in the elevator. Gouzenko went with her like a lamb. I think it was a put-up job. I think they had agreed they should do this if I didn't give on this point. They had come determined to get it and I wouldn't give.*

They spoke to a partner of mine and tried to get him to change my mind. The next day he spoke to me and said: "I'd been told this. Do you have to be as rough with them?" I said to him: "If you want to look after it for them, take it over. It's all yours." He said: "No, you go ahead." I said: "I go ahead only on the terms I've told them." So he called them and told them that and they came back that day and signed the agreement.

Don Beavis, *former security official in the Privy Council Office*
One of the things about the Gouzenko file was that it was very closely centralized. It would come over to us only when it was absolutely crucial. And then the thing would go back to the RCMP. And it would be edited. The RCMP would take the names and locations out, because that sort of thing wasn't anything that we had any need to know. What we needed to know was how we were going to pay for this god-damn excess.

The first time I saw the file was when he was looking for another hundred grand — cash — to get himself squared up on a business he had run into the ground and other debts he had contracted that were such that he couldn't possibly bail himself out. I was astounded. It was being handled at another level — between the Assistant Secretary to the Cabinet, the Secretary to

---

*Svetlana Gouzenko recalls no incident of this nature.

the Cabinet, and the Prime Minister, and then the cabinet itself was given a selected briefing to spring funds. It was just grief all over.

B. B. Osler

The poor people appreciated it immensely. The wealthy ones were glad to have it, but it didn't matter so much. But it did matter to those owed $100 and $75. It mattered like hell to them. I'll never forget one poor old chap from Hungary or Romania or maybe Yugoslavia. He was to get a small cheque for perhaps $75 or $80. He came into my room and said: "Mr. Osler, I can't tell you how much I appreciate this. I know your secretary must have had a lot to do. And she'll get nothing from it. Would you let me give her this little present?" He produced a perfectly lovely embroidered hanky — very fine linen hanky. Maybe cotton, but very fine. With coloured embroidery at some of the corners. It was really beautiful and not the kind of thing you would expect someone not well off to have. "Well," I said, "Mr. So-and-so, there's no need to do that." He said: "I would like to." I called her in and he gave it to her. She burst into tears. It was really touching.

I thought I had done a good job for a fellow who deserved it because he had done a good job for the country. Of course, I never charged him anything. I paid some of the expenses myself. I don't believe in charging people who can't pay or who can't pay without hurting themselves. And I wouldn't dream of charging for this sort of thing. If Gouzenko had been a client who was well off he would have had a bill for about twenty-five or thirty thousand dollars. You see, lawyers have to do things often for people who can't afford to pay. They shouldn't withhold their services just because they can't get paid.

Don Beavis

They put in an audit on one occasion that I recall to try and find out whether what he said his indebtedness was was in fact true. It turned out it wasn't. He was claiming he was farther in the hole than he actually was and at that stage of the game — and this would be probably back in Diefenbaker's time — they put the funds in the control of an element of the Force. There was just no way he wasn't going to blow it again. What they were concerned with was to see if they could dole out the stuff in such a way that he would gradually get acclimatized to living within what are substantial means. The guy was wily as hell. Even with that audit, much to the confusion of one of the RCMP commissioners and certainly to the people who received the file, he managed to overspend under even those circumstances. They thought they had him clamped in but he managed to contract debts that they had no idea about, and it wasn't a failure of vigilance on their part. It's just that this guy was about as easy to deal with as standing an eel on its tail. He was something else.

B. B. Osler

The news that I had done this got around among other people who were his creditors who I didn't know about. And I would get telephone calls from A, B, C, and D. "Uh, Mr. Osler, I understand you're raising money to pay Mr. Gouzenko's liabilities." I said: "No, no. I've raised some money to pay those liabilities of which I knew, which he disclosed to me." They said: "Oh well, we're so-and-so. He owes us X dollars or Y dollars." It might be some large amount. And I would say: "Well, I'm sorry, but you weren't on the list he gave me. I can't do anything for you."

Some months after I had helped him settle his affairs I received a complaint about something he had promised to do or promised not to do, I forget which. In those days he was being very friendly to me because I had done a lot for him. I called him and he came to see me. When he came in I said: "Gouzenko, I've been told this," and told him about the complaint. "Well yes, Mr. Osler." "Well," I said, "how do you justify what you've said to these people that you're not going to do what you've promised?" "Oh well, when I promised that, it was convenient to get you to do what I wanted. And so I promised it. Now it's not convenient. I'm not going to do it." I told him that in my opinion he was a rat, he behaved disgracefully, and I'd have no more to do with him. He tried to dissuade me from being so rough but I said: "You may leave my office. I don't want to see you again. I won't help you any more."

Don Beavis

It had always been a consideration as to whether we should just leave him sink — and indicate why. I do recall that on both occasions when I was involved with one of Gouzenko's petitions for a financial bail-out there was a strong impetus, not only in the RCMP but elsewhere, to say: "All right, let's not just dry up the funds but let's dry them up and lay it on the line." Then you start wondering not about his safety from the KGB but what the political consequences that that sort of action would provoke.

B. B. Osler

He asked me if I would have his book *The Fall of a Titan* produced for TV or a movie. This was before we had our difference of opinion. I happened to have a friend who was a lawyer who worked for people in Hollywood who produced movies and TV and so I said I would see what I could do. And this friend made inquiries with his clients and they said yes, they would be interested. I asked how much would they pay for the movie or TV rights. That was a different matter. They said they would have to think about that. I said he wanted a half-million dollars. They finally came back and said they would pay, I think, $300,000 — I forget the figure. And they were doing it, I think, because they knew he really needed their help. Gouzenko turned it down. Now that $300,000 would have more than paid off his debts with $150,000 left over. He was just as greedy as anybody you would ever know. He was a plain son-of-a-bitch. A cheat from the word go. I discovered this only after I had helped him.

Don Beavis

His point of view was that he did his work when he went over the fence — that's it; we owed him. And if we didn't cough up, bang, he'd make this ill treatment of this dedicated and noble chap public in block letters. This is what always tipped the balance in grudging accession to his crazy demands. Plus the fact there was always the residual doubt — this is something the RCMP would never say categorically — that he was no longer a target of the Soviets. The cannier heads in the RCMP had come to the view that they expressed privately — never put into the files — that the KGB was aware of the difficulty the son-of-a-bitch was causing us and didn't want to wipe him out. I sort of subscribed to that theory. The Soviets were just sitting back and laughing. How could Gouzenko be a more disruptive influence than being alive and being a charge on the parish? Dead he was just another piece of meat to stick in a box and plant.

B. B. Osler

All these creditors were people to whom he owed money. Different people for different reasons. Some because he bought something from them. Some because they lent him money. But they were all simply creditors and, as far as I know, none cared much about him. I can tell you one thing: some hated his guts, if you'll excuse the term. He owed a couple of thousand dollars to one man, a foreigner, and I decided that man should postpone half of what was owed and take half as part of the cash I was to raise. I went to him to get him to sign the agreement and he said no, he didn't want to. I pressed him. I said we hadn't enough to pay him in full and I couldn't get enough and wasn't going to try. That it wouldn't be fair. One day this man's wife came in to see me. She was a strikingly good-looking woman. Really unusually good-looking woman. She sat across from me at my desk and tried to butter me up. Then, when she thought she had me in a pliant mood, she said now, they really had to get more than I was offering to pay and wouldn't I please consider increasing the amount. She was looking at me with what I can only call loving eyes. I said no, I wouldn't. If you could have seen that woman's eyes change! In one instant she was looking as if she loved me, the next she was hating me. Her look could have poisoned me. And her voice changed too — dramatically. Frightfully. I said: "I'm sorry. Whichever way you look, I'm still going to give the same answer. This is all you're going to get. Do you want it or not?" And they took it.

17 Late Sixties

Eugene Griffin

For years my desk was back to back in the Parliamentary Press Gallery with the Tass desk right against the window. So the Russians would come and go. One day in the late fifties I was sitting at my desk and several of the Russians were there and I looked up and there came Gouzenko walking into the gallery. He was all alone. How he got in I don't know, and he came walking directly toward my desk. I immediately thought: "What's going to happen when he walks into all these Russians?" He had this thick accent. So I didn't introduce anybody. I just said: "Let's go up and have some coffee." Later I didn't tell him he was standing next to the Russians because I didn't know what he'd do. He might hide. He might fight. I didn't know what he'd do.

Ray Argyle, *former Toronto* Telegram *staffer*

One of my first assignments when I joined the Toronto *Telegram* from United Press was to work with Laurie McKechnie in the planning for the coverage of the 1959 Royal Tour. I went to Laurie's office one day and he had a gentleman there who seemed to perceive shadows over his shoulder. I remember he had a rather tattered raincoat on and a worried look on his face. You could see he was a troubled man. His face was lined and he seemed ill at ease. He was there only for a minute or two and then left. I asked Laurie who that was and Laurie said: "Oh, that was Igor Gouzenko." I said: "He looked rather worried." Laurie said he was, because he believed the KGB had made an attempt on his life a couple of nights ago. Laurie explained that when the matter was investigated it wasn't an attempt on his life. It was Halloween, and the neighbourhood children had been setting off firecrackers in his driveway.

Andy MacFarlane, Telegram *managing editor in the sixties*
He used to come in, I gather, to see Peter Worthington in the newsroom at the *Telegram* and one day a tall guy with a handlebar mustache walked in and very obviously looked around the room. He did an exaggerated version of casing the place, and then he beckoned by jerking his head and a blonde woman of reasonable size in a raincoat came in, and then she looked around and beckoned and a rather small man came in. They made this parade right across the newsroom. I had never seen Gouzenko before, but this entrance was so overdone that it was obvious it was Igor. No one would put on a show like that. So a few minutes later I came back to my office and the same little guy was standing in my office. He said: "You don't know who I am." I said: "Sure, you're Igor Gouzenko." He said: "I haven't been here," and left. That's exactly what happened.

Peter Worthington, *who later became Gouzenko's contact at the* Telegram
We would always have to go through the charade of Mr. Brown coming in. And I would be working at my desk in the newsroom and I would get a very hushed call from somebody in the reception area saying, "Mr. Brown is here to see you," and I would say immediately, "Who's Mr. Brown?" and they would say, "Mr. Brown — Gouzenko." Everybody knew who it was, but everybody pretended they didn't. And I guess Gouzenko to the end of his days thought that nobody recognized him. Everybody in the business knew who he was. And it carried over into the *Sun* too.

You had to meet him on his terms. He would never keep an appointment. He was so security-conscious that you couldn't make a date or an appointment over the phone. He had a very distinctive voice. The minute he said hello you knew it was Gouzenko, and yet I swear he thought he had no accent. And he wouldn't want any mention of his name or any suggestion of where you would meet him or that he would come by car or whatever. The next two or three days you would have to be free for lunch and he might call any moment. Which wasn't so bad in those days. It got harder later on when I got tied down into the *Sun*. You just couldn't drop everything. Except I did mostly.

Karen Milne, *lawyer*

He actually had a couple of first names for Brown. When we called up asking for such-and-such Brown, he knew the nature of the person calling by the first name that they used. For lawyers I forget what it was, but it wasn't Peter. Somebody once told me it was because he categorized people. If they called him such-and-such Brown, he would know it was a restaurant. If it was another name, he'd know it was a reporter. He had different identities for Brown.

Fergus Cronin

He'd sometimes arrive at my home with this lawyer and I'd say to him: "Why did you bring him along? It's expensive to carry a lawyer with you." "Well, just so there won't be any misunderstanding." He didn't like to be at any particular place predictably. If there was an appointment, he would deliberately break it. He would either get there early or late or a day late or not at all. He made quite a fetish of being unpredictable. I think this was partly for effect.

Richard Jackson

One afternoon outside the House of Commons front lobby a strange woman came up to me and introduced herself as Mrs. Gouzenko. I said: "What can I do for you, Mrs. Gouzenko?" She said: "I want you to see Mr. Diefenbaker for me." I said: "What about?" She said: "We're starving on the pension they gave Igor for his great service to your country. All our pleadings and representations to the Liberal government were in vain. Can you take me up to Mr. Diefenbaker's office and introduce me?" She was crying. I thought it over and said: "All right, I'll do that." If I had known what kind of character Gouzenko was, I wouldn't have done it. So up we went into Dief's office and his secretary took us in without any delay and I introduced her to

Dief. Dief was very courteous and asked what he could do for her, and at that moment I left. I didn't make a point to seeking her out afterwards but I was still around the Commons about twenty minutes later when she came back down and thanked me. So I took it that Dief had been accommodating.

Greg Guthrie, *then an assistant to former Prime Minister Diefenbaker*

I had an office down the hall at the time and I remember Dief called me in and asked me if I would take Mrs. Gouzenko and talk to her. So I did and tried to placate her. From what she told me she had a genuine beef, because apparently Gouzenko just let money slip through his fingers. I gather he had gotten into some rather doubtful business ventures. She was worried about the children. She gave me the impression that Gouzenko was a feckless husband. She didn't show any animosity toward him. She just said: "Look, he's not going to provide for us. Can the government do something for us?" I had no reason to doubt that her need was real.

Del Maulsby

I can't remember when Gouzenko started getting his monthly tax-free stipend from the government. It was before the time I was handling his file at [RCMP] headquarters. However, it was during my time, which was about 1968 to approximately 1971, that he started getting regular increases. He was always agitating for more money, so we decided to come up with a formula that tied his increases to the rise in the annual industrial wage. We didn't tell him what it was so he wouldn't come back to us complaining.

Richard Jackson

I string for the London *Daily Express* and have for about thirty years now. I got a call from Rene McColl, chief foreign correspondent for the *Daily Express*, a famous figure on Fleet Street. He called from Portland, Oregon, saying: "I'm flying into Ottawa tomorrow and we're going down to Toronto to see Gouzenko. I want an interview." I said: "You can't do that. I don't how the hell to get hold of Gouzenko. He's living under-cover and under constant police guard. God knows how to get his address." He says: "Well, you better do it because I'm going to be there and I don't want to waste any time."

I came in the next morning bemoaning my fate about this impossible *Daily Express* that will not accept the word can't. I was telling Tommy Van Dusen about this. I said: "How's a guy supposed to find out where Gouzenko is? I know he's in Toronto some place but you can't go knocking on every door in To-ronto." He said: "Why don't you try Mike Starr?" He was an MP and later Minister of Labour in the Diefenbaker cabinet. He was very close to the ethnic community. So I went up to see Mike and I told him that I was right up to my knees in blood and I'm going to bleed to death unless I get this story, that my very life is at stake with the *Express*. Mike says: "You call this number." So right in Mike's office I called the number. He said: "Who is it? What do you want?" I told them. He said: "We'll call you back." I said: "Is that Mr. Gouzenko?" "No, it isn't. It's an interme-diary." About five minutes later the phone rang and the man said: "Yes, we'll see you, but it will cost $500." We were to be at an address in Etobicoke at 2:30 that afternoon.

We flew down and checked into the Royal York. And I said: "Just to make sure everything is on the level I will call that number again." So from one of the lobby phones in the Royal York I called and the guy answered and said: "Oh yes, the price is up. A thousand." "Wait a minute. We've come down here. You've got us by the hair." So I turned to Rene and said: "They want a thousand now." Rene says: "I haven't got a thousand, but tell them we'll take it and we'll be out there not at 2:30 but at 5. We'll have to raise the dough."

Rene says: "Where will we get the money?" I said: "Why don't we try the CNR telegraph office? They can cable New York or London and get a credit on it." So we went across Front Street and sent off a cable and got back the okay in cable form. So I took this to the manager of the Royal York Hotel and he gave us the extra $500, which I thought was pretty decent of him. We went out to this place and went from house to house and in about four transfers got to Gouzenko.

I don't know whose place it was. And Rene got nothing new from this interview — nothing that hadn't been printed a hundred times before, but he was able to write that he had talked to Gouzenko face to face and this is what he looked like and sounded like. He did a lot of crying about how tight-fisted the government was; how it refused to understand his difficulty with finances. He told us a couple of stories that led me to believe he was very careless about his money. He had a bestseller and blew the money. He told us that. It was gone. He bought a big oversized, overpriced, luxury car. He didn't go into details about how he'd blown it. He just said it had vanished and he'd got rid of it. So we thanked him and got into our cab and got back to the Royal York. And Rene say: "Jesus Christ, we've forgotten to get a receipt. We'll have to get a receipt. We'll have to pay for it out of our own pocket unless we can prove we paid the money." He said: "You pop into a cab and go out there again and pick it up." So I did.

Gouzenko hadn't left the house, so he gave me the receipt for $1000 and he says: "I want to go downtown with you, is it okay?" I said: "Sure, but what about your cover? Aren't you afraid of Soviet agents knocking you off?" He says: "Aw, they don't know me. They haven't seen me in years now." So he got into the cab with me and went back to the Royal York and up to the room. I brought him in. Rene said: "What are you going to do with him?" I said: "I don't know." So Gouzenko said: "You're going to buy me a drink." And Rene said: "We've only got the end of a bottle here." So we poured him that. And that wasn't enough. So Gouzenko said: "Why don't we go down to the bar?" Rene said: "Christ, if you go down to the bar everybody in the Royal York is going to see you and know. Every reporter will be down to the bar in ten minutes." He says: "Nobody knows me but the police and my immediate family and my close friends. I can go down with safety." I said: "All right, we'll go." So we went down and had two or three rounds of gin and tonics at the old bar, which is just off the Imperial Room. And I said: "Now what are you going to do?" He said: "I'll just go back home." So he bummed cab fare off Rene and away he went.

He was short, ugly, blond, and still spoke — quite understandably — broken English. And, I felt, he was thoroughly unlikeable. I couldn't warm to him at all. Maybe I didn't like the idea of having a guy on the phone say half an hour before we were due "The price has gone from $500 to a thousand." That kind of poisons your mind against the guy. You think of him as a chiseller. And I went out thinking: "What a dirty trick. He knew he had us, so he squeezed." He was lucky it was the *Express*, which at that time didn't give a damn about money. I'm not a fashion plate but I'm conscious of a person's appearance. He wore very baggy trousers and a very baggy jacket, unmatched, even at the Royal York, which I thought would make him more of a standout than he was. I had forgotten that the years would dim people's memories and their awareness and alertness. It was true by that time he could walk almost anywhere and the only people who would know him were his police bodyguards and close friends.

Fergus Cronin

I wrote an article about him for *Weekend* magazine and in it quoted him about some Russian disappearing from the embassy in Ottawa and he said: "The following day there was a smell of burning flesh in the vicinity." The implication was that they had murdered him and burned him in the furnace at the embassy. Well, I didn't believe that, but I used it simply because I was quoting him. When I questioned him on it, I could tell almost from the way he answered it. He was rather evasive about it and he didn't really want to make too strong a point of it because it was a lie. It was far-fetched.

Peter Worthington

I never paid Gouzenko anything. He wanted money whenever he could get it and often other papers or the BBC would call me for some reason to get Gouzenko and I would always tell them that Gouzenko really wants money. They would say: "Well, we could give him $500 if he will go for that," and I would say: "I suspect he will." So when I told Gouzenko that they wanted to speak to him, he would say: "How much will they give me?" I would say: "You can probably get $500 from them." I was kind of pimping for him in a way, or being his agent, which I really didn't mind. They're just mutually using one another anyway. But Gouzenko never asked me for any money. I never gave him any.

Fergus Cronin

If you wrote a story about him, he would ask for money before he let you do it. For the story I wrote for *Weekend* magazine they paid me their usual fee, but they also had to agree to give him $500.

Doug Fisher, *columnist*

It was a weekend in the winter just before or after Christmas. I think it was '66. It was certainly before Trudeau became prime minister. I was no longer an MP and had been writing my column for the *Telegram* for about two years. It turned out that it was as a columnist that he came to see me.

One day I get this phone call asking me if I was going to be in and who's at home. I said my wife and kids. Who are your kids? He wanted to know their ages, so I explained their ages. Then he said: "I want to talk to you. What I have to say is important and must be kept secret. Are you willing to talk to me on those terms?" I had dealt with people like that before, so I said fine. The next thing I know my wife says there is a car parked up the street at the corner. These two people came down. They were both cruiser-weights — big square-shouldered people. The woman took the initiative in the social exchanges and introduced themselves as Mr. and Mrs. Gouzenko. On top of that they were bearing gifts and they had some gifts for the kids. I've forgotten what they were but I know there was a teddy bear there. This European penchant for giving gifts is always embarrassing for Canadians and North Americans. What do you do? Complete strangers walk in with gifts for the kids. The kids were wondering who were these two big people with the strange voices and accents with the gifts?

Mark Fisher, *son of Doug Fisher*

I was probably about sixteen years old. I was interested principally because I knew Igor Gouzenko had figured prominently in an early time and I was titillated by the fact he was out visiting with my parents. I didn't know when he arrived that he was Igor Gouzenko. It was Mr. Brown, except he had a very heavy accent. It struck me as funny.

Doug Fisher

The reason he had picked me was very clear: my columns had been critical of the RCMP. My articles had convinced him I was not only critical of the RCMP but that I wasn't afraid to write about them. His story was the bad deal he had had from the RCMP and the government. He wanted more money and better treatment. He felt the RCMP had treated him very badly and wanted some attention drawn to this. He felt that if the RCMP had been more understanding of his needs, the case to the politicians would have been made better. He had been very hopeful during the Diefenbaker regime and there had been a modest improvement, but it was not nearly enough. Since the Liberals had returned, he had the feeling the chill was back and that he was considered both by the government and the RCMP as supernumerary and a nuisance.

Barbara Fisher, *wife of Doug Fisher*

I know I was very apprehensive about them being here. I almost had a fit. Not about them as people, but I thought: "Oh my God, what's going on? We'll all end up in jail. Spies and all that thing."

Doug Fisher

I remember I did try to find out from him why it was necessary for all the secrecy. One of the points I made to him was that I had never seen any real communist threat in this country of any significance — not at the heart of things but out across the country. My feeling was that there were all kinds of communities in which he could live and be known for what he was and it would be fine. The answer, as I remember it, was that I didn't really understand how diabolical the KGB was. I know he mentioned what happened to Trotsky. That was that.

Robert Reguly

When you would mention he was ultra-cautious, he would say: "Well, we're still alive, aren't we?" The answer is irrefutable. You haven't been hit by lightning yet, that proves this keeps away lightning. May this house be free from elephants. You say what kind of blessing is that. Well, have you seen the elephants in the house? It's the same thought process.

Fergus Cronin

He used to latch onto members of the media at regular intervals. After he died I thought it was amazing the number of reporters who came forward and said: "I knew Gouzenko well." He would latch onto him and get whatever publicity he could get from them and then have them go to work for him. At least he'd try. I just got fed up with being used. I once accused him. I said: "Listen" — Stan, I think I used to call him. When I first met him, people used to call him Stan. I said: "You're just using me." He said: "Oh, don't we all use one another." I got kind of annoyed. I just got fed up with it. It became a nuisance.

Peter Worthington

He was always in search of allies, thinking of people who could help, partly because he had a feeling of desperation half the time. He would get panicky if there was no income or if the mortgage wasn't paid. He would have none of the sources somebody born in this country might have. His umbilical cord was to the government, a government which didn't much like him and which he distrusted, and a security force which he was very suspicious of and which was often openly hostile to him. The basis was not a very firm one and yet these are the ones he relied upon. He had to. He had nothing else. So I think he was always searching for a life raft, and often the life raft was a financial one.

Doug Fisher

Some time within the next year I got the phone call again and they dropped in. They were still very friendly and easygoing, but this time the mission was different. He wanted recognition, something like the Order of Canada, some kind of reappraisal within the Canadian context of the literary achievement of *The Fall of a Titan*. Beyond the money and so on, he felt that Igor had not been given proper recognition. That's when I began to see a little bit more clearly that both of them shared an obsession about the contribution and achievements of Gouzenko in Canadian terms. In some ways he almost felt he had put Canada on the map and saved Canada. Their terms of reference on the novel was really putting them in the league with Hemingway and Dostoyevsky. She gave me to understand there really wasn't a Canadian novel to compare with *The Fall of a Titan*. They had some propaganda stuff and reviews of *The Fall of a Titan* and I said I would see what I could do.

Peter Worthington

What Gouzenko wanted more than, I would say, any single thing was the Order of Canada. The government would never give it to him. I jumped into this one too, I guess. I thought it was outrageous that he couldn't get a Canada Council grant for his book, for his second novel which was never published. When they were giving it out to these screwballs and guys who wrote poems without commas or whatever, they were getting all these grants and here's a guy who had won the Governor General's Award for fiction.

William McMurtry

The Order of Canada would have been a tremendous thing for him. He felt again they made a mistake. As much as he would have loved it for personal reasons, he said: "What does it look like for somebody in my position who's thinking of defecting if you make me look like some mercenary and neurotic?"

Gary Marcuse

Warren Davis once interviewed Gouzenko on the [CBC] television program *The Day It Is* and asked him if he felt the KGB knew where he was, and Gouzenko said: "Well yes, I assume they knew." Davis then asked him: "Are you in any danger? Has the KGB made any attempts on you?" He said: "Well, yes, they have," and then wouldn't elaborate, leaving an air about it that he had been attacked or an assassination attempt had been made. When subsequent interviewers would ask him the same kind of question he would say something to the effect "Well, they made an attempt to smear my name; they were trying to do character assassination," as if that had something to do with his physical safety. Without this sense that there was some kind of physical danger attached to his existence a lot of the glamour surrounding him would have disappeared and he would have become like other defectors who, whether in art or science, were not as well known as Gouzenko and would live out fairly unremarkable lives.

Peter Worthington

The *Telegram* in the old days was having trouble with an Indian named Kahn-Tineta Horn. Beautiful Indian woman. She's still around. A reporter by the name of Robert McBain who sat directly behind me at the *Telegram* had gone and interviewed her and written about her — this would be around 1970 I suppose — and she was angry at him. She was on the warpath. She was coming into the *Telegram* to see him and orders had been given not to let Kahn-Tineta Horn into the building because she had blood in her eye for McBain.

In the meantime Miss Butterfield was coming in for a job interview with Andy MacFarlane, who was the managing editor. So down in the lobby Miss Butterfield is being held by the security guy and she is saying: "My name is Butterfield and I have a job interview," and the security guard is saying: "A likely story, Miss Horn. Out the door you go." And she's being given the bum's rush out of the building. Meanwhile, beautiful Kahn-Tineta Horn walks past the scene and goes up to the newsroom. Also in the meantime, Gouzenko had been in to see me and I would go into somebody's office to talk to him and we were coming out as Kahn-Tineta Horn was coming into the newsroom. McBain is sitting at the desk, sees Kahn-Tineta Horn, and very quickly grabs the phone and goes into a phony conversation with some prime minister or something, trying to make it sound important. And Kahn-Tineta Horn, who stormed over to him, is standing in front of him waiting for him to finish. He can't go on any longer, so he hangs up the phone, whereupon Kahn-Tineta Horn reaches over and sinks her talons into his face and rips down. Arnold Agnew, editor-in-chief at that time, is looking down there and all he sees is Kahn-Tineta Horn bent over McBain and says: "Isn't it strange? That woman is kissing McBain."

Just at that time Gouzenko and I are coming out there and Gouzenko is looking with absolutely square eyes at this woman sinking her nails into McBain's face and ripping down and blood spurting everywhere. He's terrified. He says: "Even the Soviets didn't do that to me." And he wonders whether it's a KGB plot to catch him. Pandemonium is breaking loose now and phone calls are going off and everybody is scrambling around trying to get rid of her and Gouzenko is very uneasy about his own security, thinking it may be a diversion to knock him off. We go dashing into a room where he can be hidden out of sight under a desk or whatever. And Gouzenko left thinking he's very fortunate only to be a Soviet defector and doesn't have to go through life in a newspaper factory. I'll never forget the look of shock that went over him when he saw this attack and immediately related it to him.

Del Maulsby

One year he entered the Royal Bank's Man of the Year contest. To enter you had to pay in $1500. Gouzenko didn't have the money, so borrowed it from the trust company that handled his affairs.

George Burnett

He had to have the résumé of the application for the Royal Bank Award bound in book form and there was a prescribed manner to submit it. The book had to present your credentials and everything else. That's what he told me. So he needed money for that.

Del Maulsby

It was the year Wilder Penfield won it. The manager of the trust company was aware of Gouzenko's money problems before he made the loan and was quite embarrassed about it later. The Force wouldn't cover it. He did it without telling us and the company couldn't deduct it from his monthly cheque.

Peter Worthington

Gouzenko would come in suggesting articles for every anniversary he had. And as the years went by there were more of them. Half the articles I did on him were his suggestions. There was a reason to do it, but I didn't remember the anniversary of his defection, the anniversary of how long he's been in Canada, his birthday, he's now been in Canada longer than he's been in Russia — you go through the year and there's nine or ten. And he would come and remind me. So you'd start off and say: "Gouzenko has now been thirty years in Canada" and go into the usual five-point program for defectors.

Gary Marcuse

I was doing research for a CBC documentary-drama and went to the CBC to gather archival material for use in the documentary and discovered maybe six-eight-ten entries in the Gouzenko card file.

. . . It would be evident that the interviewer thought that Gouzenko was going to make some important pronouncement. They would say something like: "Well, Mr. Gouzenko, what new information do you have?" Gouzenko's English wasn't all that clear for a radio audience, so in a heavily accented English he would start to explain that in fact he didn't have any new information but that what he wanted to tell them was — and then he would go on to make a kind of statement that was evident that he had come into the studio to make to begin with and it usually consisted of either a warning of the activities of the KGB or a suggestion that there was some kind of clues that he had given out that were never followed but which he couldn't outline in any more detail because he didn't know anything more about them but was sure that these things hadn't been pursued. And if that sounds confusing, that's exactly the way it was presented on the radio time and again.

18 Libel Suits

John Dalrymple

He found it quite profitable to become litigious. I think he found libel suits an excellent fringe benefit, but inside he really felt that these things should not be said about him and that he was a national figure and felt that no doubt should be cast upon his status. I think he really felt that way. But his cash was running short, too. I used to twit him: "Don't worry, somebody else will write a story about you and you can sue them too."

Peter Worthington

I disagree with the view that Gouzenko went around looking for people to sue, because I would mention to him: "Did you hear or read so-and-so?" And he would laugh — and this is where his sense of humour comes in — and say: "I don't want to know. If I see it I'll have to sue. I don't want to sue. Better I don't see it." But he was leech-like. He'd hold on and you couldn't shake him.

Lloyd Tataryn

On February 24, 1964, *Newsweek* published an article entitled "The Debriefing Process for the USSR's Defectors". The word defector was used many times in the article and the word traitor also appeared. At one point the article stated that "defecting intelligence officers tend to be a psychologically troubled lot" and then at another point stated: "Since they are firmly convinced that an automatic order for their assassination went out the moment they deserted the Soviet service, they are often reduced to behaving more like frightened animals than human beings." The article then gave three examples, one of which was Gouzenko. . . . Gouzenko felt he was obviously libelled by the contents of the article and retained a lawyer to sue *Newsweek.*

John Picton

He hated the word defector. "I didn't defect. I escaped," he would say. He used the word escaper. He thought there was something demeaning about the word defector.

Alan Harris

Defector was a pejorative word and he felt that was one of the allegations you use in a libel case. It was bringing him into contempt and ridicule and disfavour with the Canadian public, that it was not proper for Canada or the United States to be calling him a traitor, etc. That from our eyes he should not be such a thing. Indeed, I think he has good reason for alleging that. He was helping us.

Nelles Starr

By this time I was getting a little fed up with Gouzenko because I thought he was using these things to make money and I didn't approve of that. . . . My conclusion eventually was he couldn't handle democracy. He was very anxious to take all the benefits of a democracy and not very anxious to assume the responsibilities.

Alan Eagleson, *lawyer whom Gouzenko consulted about suing* Newsweek

He came to my office when I was a young lawyer and we talked for a couple of hours. I found him a very quiet, worried man. Maybe worried is not the correct word. Nervous is probably better. He was very cautious in any of his comments to me. I found him very slow. Methodical, careful. I think almost well-rehearsed. In my opinion he knew exactly what he was going to say and how he was going to say it and did it slowly.

Peter Worthington

Newsweek said he was cowering in fear somewhere. This would get him terribly upset. He was not a cowering, frightened man. He didn't cower. And he sued them.

Alan Eagleson

I felt that after the first few meetings that we were going to be involved in a very long process and a very expensive process, and it was obvious to me I couldn't afford to give him the time for nothing and he couldn't afford to pay me except on a contingent-fee basis. I was not in a position to review that type of thing because of the position of the Law Society and because of my own financial position. It would be different in today's times when you can devote a little time like that to a cause. But I wasn't in that position at the time.

Lloyd Tataryn

In 1964 Gouzenko sued *Maclean's* magazine over an article by Blair Fraser in which Fraser said several things about him. Gouzenko took exception to the piece because he felt it demeaned him.

Ken Lefolii, *editor of* Maclean's *at the time*

The article wasn't about Gouzenko in the first instance. It was a masthead article in a special edition of the magazine about the 1940s. Blair Fraser had done an overview of political life in the 1940s. It was one of those attempts to create instant nostalgia that periodicals go through from time to time. Blair had done a survey piece about what political life had been in the 1940s, and in the course of doing that piece, which touched most major events of that period, he raised the Gouzenko defection and recalled Churchill's coinage of the Iron Curtain metaphor after Gouzenko's defection and then dropped it. But in the course of doing that, which didn't account for more than a few paragraphs, he said a couple of things that seemed to Gouzenko to have disparaged his courage and contribution and to have implied that he had somehow or other profited in ways that people would not find admirable if they were to sit down and think about it. It was really that general.

Graham Fraser, *son of the late Blair Fraser*

I understand the basis of the libel suit was the suggestion that the Mounties noticed that Gouzenko's fear for his own safety became particularly acute when it came time to put on the storm windows. . . . I just remember Dad being kind of ruefully amused at how this confirmed precisely the kind of points he was trying to make in the article. It was an indication of not only Gouzenko's bitterness but his sensitivity.

The article said it was no secret that Gouzenko felt he had been rather shabbily treated by his adopted country. I think what really outraged Gouzenko was that this article in rather tongue-and-cheek fashion didn't take him as seriously as he felt he deserved to be taken. It's been at least ten or fifteen years since I last read the piece, but when I went down to look for it, what I remembered is the suggestion that he wanted Mountie bodyguards especially when he needed his storm windows changed. It's a very graphic image and it would just enrage somebody who took himself as seriously as Gouzenko apparently did.

Alan Harris

One of the libels, by Blair Fraser in that *Maclean's* case, was that it was an open secret as to where he lived. And, of course, *that* Mr. Gouzenko was extremely perturbed about, because if he didn't attack that article he felt that everybody would say: "Oh well, there's no secret where he lives any more." And anyone who did know or found out where he lived would give out his address and make it public knowledge.

Ken Lefolii

Blair and I felt that Gouzenko's complaint followed his standard operating procedure. Most reporters working in politics in Canada at that time felt that Gouzenko lodged an intention to sue virtually every time his name appeared in public. Most reporters working in national politics generally assumed that the sort of thing Blair Fraser said was pretty accurate and I think that grew as much out of Gouzenko's barrage of writs as it did from direct knowledge. The guy was just suing everything that moved when his name was mentioned.

Peter Worthington

His view on this was that if he doesn't protect his name, nobody will. And if it's wrong, he's got to sue. I really do think that clearing the name was more important to him than the money.

Alan Harris

He was trying to protect his reputation. That was what they always wanted to do. To this day the family is still trying to look to protect his reputation. They have always felt that the Russians had two tactics. One was simply to kill people they did not like. And the other was that they would try to ruin them. Ruin their reputation. Ruin them economically to the point where, if nothing else, no one would care about their safety and therefore they could then be eliminated physically if necessary. But if you ruin somebody from the point of view of their reputation to the point of ridicule and where everybody just doesn't care about them, I suppose that's as good as killing them physically. And that's what they've always been conscious of, that they had to protect the reputation at all costs. And it was costly to protect it. Extremely costly.

J. D. MacFarlane

He was supersensitive to his position and to anybody casting the slightest aspersions on his motives or his character or suggesting he had inadequacies or whatever. I think this is because he had made such a major move when he left the embassy in Ottawa that having done that he was looking somehow to maintain and add to stature that wasn't forthcoming. He wasn't given the recognition which he felt he deserved and which I think he deserved. I'm not prepared to discuss his motives for what he did. Whatever his motives were, they certainly proved valuable. He took these terrible risks and made this very daring move and I'm afraid the Canadian authorities were inclined to look upon him as a kind of turncoat, a man who betrayed his own country. He was supersensitive to anything he felt cast the slightest aspersions on his motives. So he always had libel actions on the go.

Lloyd Tataryn

Harris at one time had negotiated with *Newsweek*, which had agreed to give Gouzenko a settlement of $1000. Gouzenko wanted more money and rejected the out-of-court offer. In the examination for discovery, according to a judge's findings later on, Harris became leery about Gouzenko's chances of winning against *Newsweek* in court and therefore decided, with Gouzenko's approval, it would be wiser strategically to pursue the *Maclean's* case at that time.

Alan Harris

He asked me what case was best. The reason for that was about this time in '65 not only did we have the *Newsweek* case and the *Maclean's* case going but in addition there were two articles in the *Globe and Mail* and in the *Telegram* that he felt were libellous and we served notices under the Libel and Slander Act on those papers. At least one of them retracted. Maybe both of them. I think they both published retractions. . . . I wasn't really in a position to finance four lawsuits. Because lawsuits are expensive and libel cases are particularly expensive and complicated. The law is extremely complicated. So I at one point in time pointed out to him he better push on the best case. He asked me what was best and I indicated to him I thought the *Maclean's* case was best from the point of view of they wanted to get on to trial. They hadn't been stalling as such — I felt that *Newsweek* was stalling — and consequently I recommended that we press on the *Maclean's* case. So we did, leaving the *Newsweek* case in abeyance.

Lloyd Tataryn

Gouzenko won in court but was awarded the grand sum of one dollar from the jury. Evidently the jury didn't think Gouzenko's reputation had been damaged very much.

Ken Lefolii

I suppose the outcome was more or less fair. There was some technical fault on the side of *Maclean's* but that the fault really was technical. I don't think there was the kind of defamation that provided substantial injury to Gouzenko. So it would seem like a reasonable judgment on both sides.

Lloyd Tataryn

Gouzenko's lawyer successfully argued an appeal, however, that the jury had been unfairly influenced to arrive at the small damage decision when the judge incorrectly expressed doubts as to whether some of the statements in the article could be considered defamatory. A new trial was ordered, but *Maclean's* decided not to go through with it. By then it had had enough and washed its hands of it and gave Gouzenko $7500.

Floyd S. Chalmers

The lawyer representing us said it was a lot simpler to settle this thing and stop spending money. I was opposed to it at the time but they decided to settle.

Peter Worthington

It was a big mistake to settle, in my view. *Maclean's* settled. They settled because they thought it would be cheaper than the legal fees if they followed through and won. But the principle of not letting him win is fairly important if you're in the right.

Alan Harris

It was after that, which took four to six years to get up to that point where we finally settled *Maclean's*, that the *Newsweek* case came alive again. Because after we won and settled the *Maclean's* case, he then said: "Okay, let's do the same thing with *Newsweek*." And I said to him: "Oh no, once was fun and it was reputation-building and just a learning experience. But the second time is for money." And since he had money, because I got him a good settlement, I wanted him to properly retain me for the *Newsweek* case. And he didn't do it. In fact one day he simply had a new set of lawyers serve me with a notice of change of solicitors, saying that he now had new lawyers.

. . . He did find a very young lawyer again who worked for nominal money. Maybe he was spoiled by young lawyers working for a pittance. There's no question a young lawyer will work for a lot less than an experienced lawyer will. And he didn't give very much money to the other lawyer.

Peter Worthington

He must have gone through every lawyer in town. Every time he heard of a new anti-communist lawyer he would flood over. The lawyer would get intrigued. It was interesting, and he saw it as a kind of challenge. And they'd get hooked onto it. They'd want an advance and he'd give them $500 or something. Then the troubles would begin.

Alan Harris

He was a generous man in his way. He enjoyed good living. We used to go out from time to time and we would eat and drink on a fine or grand scale. I recall that he took me to the Franz Josef Room of the old Walker House Hotel, which was quite a swanky restaurant in its day. It was down at the foot of University Avenue. It's gone now. It's torn down and a very large building has gone up in its place. My wife is Austrian and I had been in the Ratskeller at that hotel but I had never been in the Franz Josef Room, which was a very expensive restaurant. To celebrate the *Maclean's* case we went to the Franz Josef Room and I recall he had nothing but French champagne and we had a great time. He picked me up in the brand-new station wagon to take me down there with my wife and his wife to the Franz Josef Room. He was very proud of this new station wagon. I, of course, at the time was still driving a Volkswagen beetle, which I drove for many, many years.

Peter Worthington

I would take him out to lunch all the time and I would pay for it, or the *Sun* or the *Telegram* would pay for it. But whenever he got in a bonanza he just couldn't wait to blow it. He would insist he was going to take me or somebody out and buy the lunch. In those days he would want champagne — a very lavish lunch in the Imperial Room at the Royal York. The very best. He wouldn't know the best if it hit him in the face, but by the

price he would know it was the best. And I would berate him
and wonder why in God's name he didn't save it — don't waste
it on me. So he wasn't niggardly in the sense of being a tight-
wad. If he had it, he spent it.

Lloyd Tataryn

After eight years, the courts tossed the *Newsweek* case out, saying
that Gouzenko had had plenty of time to push the case. They
said by waiting so long Gouzenko had prejudiced the ability of
the defendant, *Newsweek*, to defend itself, since it was so long
ago. So Gouzenko sued his lawyers, both sets of them.

Alan Harris

I was dumbfounded [when he issued a writ against me]. . . . We
really felt aggrieved because we really felt we had done an awful
lot for Mr. Gouzenko. So we were hurt by the lawsuit. We were
really shocked and felt poorly done by.

Alan Eagleson

I'm always surprised when somebody winds up suing a lawyer
who has tried to help. In these times it seems to be more common
than not.

Lloyd Tataryn

At the examination for discovery Gouzenko tabled his notes,
which said he thought Harris's inactivity on the *Newsweek* case
was (1) coloured by Gouzenko's failure to accept a $1000 settle-
ment offered by *Newsweek*; (2) that *Newsweek* had bribed Harris
so that he wouldn't pursue the case; or (3) that some persons
connected with the secret Soviet police were influencing Harris
to delay the case. The judge said all these theories were completely unsupported by the evidence.

Alan Harris

You've got to remember in the middle of that lawsuit he came to
me and asked me if I would act as his lawyer again. . . . I was
running a political campaign for Dennis Flynn. He's the Mayor
of Etobicoke now but was running provincially at the time. I

had a campaign office up the street in Etobicoke and he came and took me to lunch over at the Constellation. We had champagne and everything. He wanted me to be his lawyer. He said we've always gotten along well together. I forget the exact conversation. He had high praise for me even then, I guess. I, of course, couldn't do anything at that stage. He shouldn't have done it, I suppose. It worked against him in the case. But there was no real ill will. Certainly on his part there was no ill will at all. On my part I suppose I sure wasn't very pleased at being sued. . . . Everything I owned was on the line because I was being sued for $2 million. It would have wiped me out if he had won. But later on when the case was over I had no ill will at that point in time.

Duncan Macpherson, *cartoonist,* Toronto Star

I went over to do some sketches of Gouzenko when he appeared in the courtroom. I took an educated guess as to how he was going to leave the building. I phoned a *Star* photographer, Bob Olsen, and he took the west entrance. It was a small entrance that goes out to a little patio. Gouzenko was with his wife and son. Bob anticipated him at the western entrance and took his picture, which he didn't particularly like. His wife was outraged and was swinging a handbag at Bob. Bob was pretty quick on his feet, I must say. He moved around like a quarterback. He got a couple of clunks on the side of his head but got in quite a few snaps.

Bob Olsen, *photographer*

He didn't know where to go. It was actually quite funny when you think about it because he was like a caged animal and had nowhere to go. But his wife — she was a different scene. She just came at me like a bull. I had to be like a little halfback for about twenty minutes, or ten minutes, there. If she could have killed me I'm telling you she would have. And I don't blame her. I think she had every right to try to knock my head off.

Svetlana Gouzenko

No, he was too far away. He was jumping. I was just trying to shade the faces so that the camera would not take the faces.

Duncan Macpherson

At the time I took a change of heart. I thought: "My God, I don't want to cause so much upset personally." So I went back up to the sheriff of the court is I guess who he was. The Gouzenkos went back there too and they were laying a complaint about the photographer. I in the meantime phoned the *Star* and said: "There's a big ruckus going on here." And I advised them not to use the photographs. And they didn't. And, by the way, they didn't use my drawings either. I was introduced to Mrs. Gouzenko and the son in the sheriff's room and told them I was with the *Star* and that I had phoned the paper and there was nothing to worry about, that we weren't going to use them. Well, that calmed them down a bit. I didn't go so far as to admit that I had gotten Olsen over there in the first place because I figured I'd get belted too.

Peter Robertson, Toronto Star *picture editor*

The day the picture was taken we knew indeed we had something very special. But because at that time he was still unknown to the public we decided we would not publish it and we put the negatives and the prints into our vaults, not to be used until he died. . . . We really didn't have any reason other than to have exposed the man, who wasn't a criminal. And he might well have been right [that his life was in danger]. Something might have happened to him and we would have felt pretty awful if it had happened. So we didn't publish.

Lloyd Tataryn

In dismissing Gouzenko's suit against Harris the judge concluded: "I find the advice given by the lawyers was sound advice and the plaintiff refused to accept the advice. Under the circumstances, I am of the view he is the author of his own misfortune with regards to the costs and is not entitled to recover them."

Alan Harris

When we won the case and we got our costs awarded to us, we

then had to collect. And at that point in time I had to get a hold of him. A judgment against Igor Gouzenko might not have been very good, bearing in mind there were other executions — or there had been in the past. I had to find him. Correspondence and things were sent. My partner found out somehow roughly where he lived. Roughly. And told me. . . . I went out and dug around and I found out where he lived and I knocked on his door one day.

Svetlana Gouzenko

He found us through one of his secretaries who was working in his office. I don't know whether she was working at that time or not. And she really staked the connection through one of our neighbours. Who heard rumours.

Alan Harris

He said: "Oh, come in." I went in and explained what I was up to, I wanted my costs and I had found him. He, of course, was extremely concerned that I had managed to find him. We just talked and he said: "Don't worry about the costs, you'll be paid." We slowly struck up conversations and a friendship again. And over the years we got to be fast friends. I used to go over there with my wife a lot and talk to them.

Svetlana Gouzenko

We were supposed to pay Harris $16,000 and there were three days left to pay the $16,000. So one of my daughters took the mortgage on the house and we paid the $16,000. . . . We didn't even know that there were three days left. He found us and told us . . . to pay the money or they will put a lien against the property. Then it would be disclosed. It would be registered, our identity would be disclosed, which was the most important thing that we cared about.

Alan Harris

In later conversations after this lawsuit was over Mr. Gouzenko said to me: "Why didn't you pay off?" And I said to him (a) I wasn't covered by insurance and (b) even if I had been I would never have paid a penny because I didn't believe I was liable. I'm just the type of guy, as he should have known, that would never pay just to settle a case. I'm the kind of guy who would just fight to doomsday. And certainly in this particular case I felt, as I think the judgment revealed when it came down in my favour, I always felt I had acted over and above and beyond the call of duty with Mr. Gouzenko. But I don't know if he ever truly realized I wasn't insured and that in fact all my personal assets were at stake, which probably made me fight even harder than if I had been insured. . . . I got the impression that either it had never been fully explained to him or he couldn't comprehend that fact. Never got a straight answer. Never pressed him on the point. He won the case against the other law firm.* In fact, what happened was that anything he won against the other law firm was lost in paying my court costs.

*While Gouzenko lost to Harris's firm, he won against the law firm that handled the *Newsweek* case after Harris. Although he found the second firm negligent, Mr. Justice Goodman in the Supreme Court of Ontario said he was satisfied that Gouzenko's libel claim against *Newsweek* was bound to fail and awarded Gouzenko only $1, plus the recovery of the fees and expenses he paid out to the negligent lawyer.

19 Trudeau

Gary Marcuse

Gouzenko went on the [CBC] television program *This Hour Has Seven Days* back in 1966 and was interviewed by Laurier LaPierre, who made reference to him having a special experience because he was a spy in Ottawa like the other ones. Gouzenko became extremely indignant — in another case he actually sued somebody for the same reference — and made a heated disclaimer to having been a spy.

Ken Lefolii, *then producer of* This Hour Has Seven Days

After the taping, but before the interview went to air, Gouzenko said he was going to sue for defamation. Gouzenko's lawyers were jumping up and down and the CBC's lawyers were jumping up and down and everybody was in a frenzy and nothing was getting on the air. What struck me as ironic and amusing at the time, I remember, was that the threats to sue were happening before the material had been put on the air.

Lloyd Tataryn

In 1968 Gouzenko, under his signature, published a squalid pamphlet during the 1968 Liberal leadership race. The pamphlet called Pierre Trudeau "a new Castro" who would turn Canada into a "radical socialist state". In the pamphlet Gouzenko said: "Castro at first stages of his climb to power has made more efforts to hide his communist nature than Trudeau is doing now. Still Trudeau is very successful at it: he is posing as an intellectual, throwing clouds of words presenting old,

out-worn communist ideas as if they were new and progressive."
I found this interesting.

Ian Adams, *writer*

He called Trudeau and Pearson communist agents. To make
that kind of leap I thought the man had unmasked himself. You
would think (a) he was incredibly stupid and obsessed that he
would be so naive and provincially-minded to write something
like that; or (b) he had lent his name to equally stupid and
virulent right-wing organizations who didn't like Trudeau and
didn't want to see the Liberals in power.

Peter Worthington

He was up in Ottawa at that convention hanging around the
Château Laurier. He was there delivering it himself in the corridors of the thing. Passing out the pamphlets. I sat with him in
the Château Laurier and said: "You've got to be nuts." He said:
"Well, I've got to take the chance. I've got to stop him before he
gets in there. Canada's future is at stake." He was up there. Half
the people didn't know who they were getting it from.

Lloyd Tataryn

Gouzenko went as far as to suggest "that there was a suspicion
that Trudeau was a Soviet spy." He used very circumstantial
evidence to arrive at that conclusion. Gouzenko noted that Elizabeth Bentley, one of the people who had testified about Soviet
spy rings in the United States, said she had met a young, rich
student from Montreal who had participated in Soviet spying in
the United States. On that flimsy basis Gouzenko suggested that
this Soviet spy was Pierre Trudeau. If you examine the records
you will find that the rich student with the millionaire background Elizabeth Bentley named was somebody totally different.
But Gouzenko was willing to suggest it was Trudeau.

Svetlana Gouzenko

He didn't invent anything. He just stated that it could be. He
didn't write then that Elizabeth Bentley said it was Trudeau,

but, by description of the man, that it could be Trudeau. Therefore, when he believed it to be true he is right; even that he is
wrong, this is right.

Peter Worthington
He acknowledged that there were some things he didn't know
but he said his basic thesis was right. He began to joke about it
at the end because it was so apparent to him that Trudeau was
working for the Soviet side. He would kid about it and laugh
about the latest antic of Trudeau. It would be the sort of laugh
that he would never understand Canadians.

Doug Fisher
When the Liberal leadership convention of 1968 was coming
into the home stretch, Gouzenko stopped into the press building
with those pamphlets he was distributing.
   . . . It had absolutely no impact. For that kind of stuff to be
effective it has to be gotten out well ahead of time and it has to
become widely and publicly known. Nobody was willing to
publish it. I can just see editors saying: "That's pretty libellous
stuff." For the majority of people in 1968 Igor Gouzenko was
the guy with the bag over his head. The program that gave him
the greatest reach across the country and had everybody talking
was the television show *This Hour Has Seven Days*. But he had
no stature. I can't remember anybody who was talking about it
other than a few press people. What I can remember is that the
leadership candidates or their people who I talked to almost had
a baby when I was trying to figure out who distributed it. "Oh,
not us."

Lloyd Tataryn
The *Toronto Star* wrote an editorial on June 7, 1968, entitled
"Hate Flows in Canada Too". It was written by Val Sears. The
editorial concluded that these sorts of pamphlets "should be
stamped on and exposed as vicious frauds by ethnic community
leaders wherever it appears. It is sick literature and if it touches
a sick mind it could produce a national tragedy." The tragedy

the article referred to was the kind of hate that would produce the kind of assassinations in the United States that led to the murder of Kennedy. It was published a couple of days after Robert Kennedy was shot. Sears' view was that when you foment hate in the population, some sick mind will use that as rationalization for doing something idiotic like bumping off a political leader who they feel are part of the international communist conspiracy.

Val Sears, *writer of the* Star *editorial*

Gouzenko's material showed up in the office. The atmosphere of the time was one of assassinations and sick minds and paranoia and it was also a time of considerable East European immigration and a lot of people were saying strange things about our leaders. Out of that grew this editorial, which we thought would be a useful contribution to the debate because there was nothing practical we could do to stop such literature without interfering with free speech. But I thought it would be useful to point out this poisonous material could not be entirely ignored because of the effect it would have on the minds that had been tortured by communist perversion or any other kind of perversion for a period of time.

Alan Harris

The interesting thing was that while the *Star* wrote that editorial there were a lot of people, both Liberals and Conservatives, very high-ranking, as I recall, on both sides, came to Mr. Gouzenko and asked for permission to reprint that pamphlet. And they did. And I know the names that Mr. Gouzenko told me. I guess that's as far as it goes and I'm not even [going to] repeat those names anyways. But certainly they were right at the top on both parties. Because there was a leadership campaign and I guess if you want to use that word both sides were out to "get" Mr. Trudeau and they both used that pamphlet. And hundreds of thousands of copies were printed of that pamphlet. Mr. Gouzenko only published I don't know what it was, five thousand or something. But tremendous quantities were printed by the two political parties.

Val Sears

The editorial was published and I do not recall any response of consequence until we were served notice that Gouzenko was going to sue. I wasn't terribly surprised. I didn't think it would be pursued. I thought it was a ploy on Gouzenko's part to get money out of the *Star*, as he had done before to others.

Alan Harris

Well, when you address a jury about a libel case and when you frame your pleadings and your statement of claim in a libel case, you always claim that the perpetrator was attempting to bring the person of whom they were talking into contempt and ridicule and into such a state that everyone else in the world should shun that poor person that they're talking about. And in effect the editorial, as I recall it, and it's been a long time, ten-twelve years, but as I recall it they virtually said it in words that all Canadians should shun Mr. Gouzenko. And therefore what they said was what most lawyers try to get a passage to be held to have said. Whereas they just spelled it straight out. And not only that but, as I recall, the editorial was one of two very large ones, and the other one in the same page was about hate literature and somebody who was publishing some pamphlets and tracts. And even to have put the editorial about Mr. Gouzenko onto the same page with that kind of literature was to, in my opinion, have tried to make the hate literature rub off on Mr. Gouzenko.

I thought it was a particularly strong article about Mr. Gouzenko and I thought it was, from a lawyer's point of view, a darn good case to take. The pamphlet that Mr. Gouzenko had written about Trudeau, Mr. Gouzenko had put his name to the bottom. Whereas no one had put their name at the bottom of the editorial about Mr. Gouzenko. I thought, certainly as I looked at it, that that would be one of the first things I would be taking a crack at. No one that read that pamphlet had to wonder who wrote it. It was Mr. Gouzenko. He put his name and signed it. Nobody did it there. And, as I say, I thought it was a particularly strong editorial or article about Mr. Gouzenko and went far beyond the bounds of proper comment.

Val Sears

When Marty Goodman [the editor] and I discussed it, I said I think we ought to stand on this one because (a) the editorial is factually defensible and (b) it would be a good cause to go to court on because we cannot lose on the basis of attacking hate literature. Newspapers are sued all the time for the wrong reasons, and this is a good one to go on and I think we ought to go. Marty was very enthusiastic. He said: "Let's go right to the end on this one. We won't pay off. We won't even talk about it." When we appeared in court Gouzenko showed up without the bag over his head and a navy blue suit and running shoes. I figured here was a guy not familiar with Canadian dress customs. He was sitting by himself but was not publicly identified.

Lloyd Tataryn

Of all Gouzenko's libel suits this was the only one fought out in a courtroom to the finish with both parties battling tooth and nail to the final decision. And Gouzenko just plain lost.

Val Sears

Then Gouzenko's lawyer, to my surprise, asked them to retire again and consider what would have been their damages had they found the *Star* guilty. So the jury retired again and came back and said one dollar. I gather Gouzenko's lawyer asked for this in the event of an appeal.

Lloyd Tataryn

I talked to the laywer of the *Toronto Star* who brought this case forward and he sent me a copy of the editorial. Although he was scathing about Gouzenko and his use of libel suits, he nevertheless requested that I not quote from the editorial. For some reason Gouzenko might decide to re-launch the suit. Even though Gouzenko had lost, he wasn't confident that if the editorial was quoted again that Gouzenko wouldn't sue again.

20 The MI5 Interview

John Picton

    Gouzenko told me shortly after his defection the British sent a man to interrogate him. He had been interrogated by the Mounties, of course, and now the Brits wanted a go at him as well. He said a British fellow arrived and he said in retrospect he recalls this British fellow approaching him with caution. He said he approached him as if he was afraid he might have seen his photograph in the files in Moscow as being a Soviet agent. He said the meeting was extremely brief, about three minutes, and the British fellow asked him very few questions and went away and Gouzenko didn't see him again.

William McMurtry

    Gouzenko felt this man was almost trying to shield his face a lot of the time and spent a very short time with him. He couldn't understand this at the time.

Robert Reguly

    He said in his original debriefing he identified a top-level Russian mole in British Counter-intelligence [MI5]. He didn't know his name but he said from clues he had he knew which office section he was in. He said it could have been narrowed down to only two or three people. That's how close he got.

John Picton

    Years later, in the early seventies, Gouzenko got a request through the Mounties that the British wanted to talk to him again. A man arrived — a different man — and had a thick

217

report with him and said: "Could you have a look at this and tell us if this is what your earlier interview with our fellow is all about?" Gouzenko said he started reading it and threw it across the room. He said: "It's all lies. It's all lies. I didn't say any of those things." And apparently some of the things in there quoted him as saying that the British had a high-ranking mole in the Kremlin. "It's not true. They couldn't possibly have a high-ranking mole in the Kremlin, not when Philby was sitting as head of MI6." And besides which, he said, the interview lasted only three minutes. He said: "I wouldn't have had time to say those things." He subsequently found out that the Mounties had exactly the same report in their files and never satisfactorily explained that.

Peter Worthington

I had never seen him so suspicious as when British Security wanted to come over and interview him. . . . He came to the *Sun* at the Eclipse Building by the Royal Alex. And just said they were coming to see him and should he see them. He was half of a mind not to because they had ignored his memo and never showed him the original stuff and was treated fairly casually. I said I felt he had got to see them. Then he was wondering why would they want to see him, could they do him damage or something. I said the RCMP had okayed it. Even I don't go that far. So he agreed to see them and then when he was on his way there he came in and asked if I would go with him and attend the meeting in the Royal York. I had mixed feelings with the thing. There was no way they would interview him with me there to begin with. It would have been kind of fun to go along to see the horror on their face to have a newspaperman there. So I told him that if he was really that concerned I would, but that I really didn't think anything would happen. So we finally left it at that, that he would go and that he wanted me to know that he had no intentions of jumping out the window like Masaryk or anything like this — to commit suicide — and if he did, he more or less gave me the story. . . . I decided not to go. The temptation to make waves and see what would happen was counterbalanced by the fact I didn't think he was in danger.

Robert Reguly

He always thought people were trying to set him up. In the 1973 meeting with the Brit he felt they were trying to get him into the hotel just to knock him off. He was very suspicious of anything presented to him, whether it was a coffee or tea or juice. The Russians have stuff you can put into a liquid which could give you a heart attack. He was aware of that.

William McMurtry

And they did show to him the statement of his first interview and it was totally fabricated. It was basically constructed to make him look as if he had nothing of significance to tell anybody. His speculation is probably true. It seemed that the only concern of this person who came over to interview him was to find out how much Gouzenko knew about this mole and could he identify him, which at first seemed to be quite legitimate. And it's upon reflection that Gouzenko realized that this fellow probably was the mole or one of the moles and came over to see whether he really posed a danger and whether they should get out.

Peter Worthington

They showed him the interview and went over it with him. He said: "I'd never say this. Any intelligence person reading this would know it's all nonsense and everything then would be then discredited." He said, for example, he was quoted as saying: "We in the Kremlin know — have a list of all the British agents who are inside the Kremlin." Words to that effect. He said: "There are no British agents in the Kremlin. It's impossible for them to be there. The British read this about me talking about British agents in the Kremlin and they will just throw out the whole thing. They know they don't have any. I know they don't have any." He said: "The only person who would put that in is somebody who wants to discredit everything I'm saying." Which I subscribe to.

Robert Reguly

He said it was a total lie. He said the transcript had been doctored. He said somebody had doctored the transcript to conceal references to a high-level spy in the British MI5 organization. Hollis was sent over and he presumes it was Hollis's hand that doctored the whole summation of it. But Gouzenko's claim was that the report of his debriefing was sent over to England and plumped on the desk of Kim Philby.

Svetlana Gouzenko

They also presented something [a document]: "But here it is, Mr. Black, in his handwriting, confirming that you did make this kind of statement." And Igor looked and saw then it is one word a little bit higher [than] the other. It was pasted on. And Igor can see then it is pasted on. It is a collection probably out of Black's letters or translations that he made out of all kinds of documents. Then it was put together. But it was just a little bit inaccurate because it was practically impossible. You write one letter with this slant, the next letter would have a little less slant. And it is one word too much slant, next little bit too straight and the next one letter a little bit too small. One letter is big, the other one small. It is not the same letter. So Igor said: "Could I have a copy of that because I have got lots of Black's letters while he was translating and all were in his handwriting."

John Picton

And he said there was some handwriting on the report and he said: "I recognized the handwriting. I have a sample of that same handwriting at home. I asked them if I could have a copy of that handwriting to compare it but they said no. They wouldn't let me have it." But he said he could tell by the furtive glances of this RCMP guy that there was something amiss. He didn't know what those glances meant, whether: "God, how the hell did we get this report if they're both wrong?" He didn't know quite how to interpret the glances.

Svetlana Gouzenko

And the Mountie — the one who gave him [the document] — said: "No, we can't give the report." But Igor was holding this letter. And I said, why didn't you grab it and put it in your pocket. He said, they could have shot me. So when I told Igor why he didn't put it right in your pocket and Igor said: "Well, all three Mounties that were there, they all have guns. We don't." Well, so the Mountie took it out of his hand. Pulled it. And Igor was holding it and he was pulling it. [He] pulled this report, folded it and put it in his pocket, and sighed. People, even men, cannot completely hide their emotions.

John Picton

Then the British fellow came back a second time and showed him photographs of six men and said: "Do you recognize any of these men as having been the man who interviewed you?" Gouzenko said it had been too long and he couldn't remember. He picked out and said: "It might have been him or him, but I can't swear to that." He had no idea whose pictures he might have identified. He was never given any names.

Svetlana Gouzenko

The thing is that there were so many people that he met and all British [people] look the same and he could not really pinpoint and say this is the man. Too many years passed by. But he said, let's do it by elimination. One man [in the photographs] had a moustache. "No, that man didn't have a moustache. Out." Black moustache. The other had something else. So by elimination he came finally to the one picture and said: "I don't say this is the man but I say it could be this [picture], but those three it could not be." So this Mr. Stewart [of MI5] went away and it was forgotten.

James Barros, *political scientist*

I think where we went wrong is that we kept Gouzenko under wraps too long. Once Stalin died we should have allowed Gouzenko to emerge and live under his own name. I think the new style in western intelligence agencies is to allow these people to surface if they wish after a number of years under their own name so that they can lead a normal life. At some point the flame was no longer worth the candle. I don't think the Russians would have harmed him. It would have disrupted relations with

Canada much too much and it wouldn't have been worth it for them just to get their pound of flesh.

Robert Reguly

He came in one day to CTV and said: "Next week is the thirtieth anniversary of my defection. How about doing a story about that?" So I took him in to see Jack McGaw and we discussed whether it was worthwhile, with him there. Jack McGaw had a vague idea who Gouzenko was but wasn't quite sure. He remembered the story but it didn't ring much of a bell with him. Jack said: "The question is, what are you going to wear on TV? People have already seen you with a paper bag over your head." Gouzenko said: "Well, what about a balaclava?" Well, it came down that he agreed to go on just with ski goggles, one of these goggles you wear for downhill skiing. We discussed it. I wanted him to do it but Jack said: "I can't see any reason to do it." He couldn't see any value in the story.

Jack McGaw, *producer*

We were talking of penetration of Soviet Intelligence into Canadian affairs and he was in a position to throw some light on that and I was anxious to establish his credibility on camera by revealing who he was. He wasn't prepared to make that sacrifice and I could understand that. The guy still believed he would be wiped out. Reguly wasn't so sure of that.

Jeff Fry, *associate producer*

There was money involved. We weren't prepared to pay money for him just to repeat his brown-bag stuff, which everybody knew about. But if he was to come on and reveal himself it would have a certain dramatic effect, even though [he] didn't have much in the way of information.

The impression in my mind is what an inoffensive little sandy-haired fellow he was. He was mild-mannered, self-effacing, a wispy little guy. This was the guy who had opened North America's eyes to what the Russians were doing here. The contrast between the events and the man was the most significant impression I had of him. I couldn't get over it.

Peter Worthington

I kept trying to get him to do his memoirs of thirty years in Canada because nobody has experienced what he's experienced. Several times he was going to leave copies of the manuscript with me for safekeeping. He didn't trust publishers and was afraid of what might happen to it. So I was only too willing to be the custodian of it, but [he] never did. I always assumed that when he died you might be able to do something with it.

. . . His second book, *Ocean of Time*, was another one of these epic novels which he kept working at and written in Russian.

Svetlana Gouzenko

There are many, many reasons [why it wasn't finished]. He first of all wanted it to be perfect — better than *The Fall of a Titan*. *The Fall of a Titan* was such a success he didn't want to spoil [it]. So he worked and worked and he had a tendency to write too much, expand it into so many characters, and finally I had to look back and [say]: "Who is this character? Where did you get it from?" . . . [I said]: "You have to eliminate because [the character is] of not great importance. If it wouldn't be really a pressing financial situation, then *The Fall of a Titan* wouldn't be finished because he would be rewriting it in longhand over and over and over and over. And you can say the same thing in ten different sentences. It would be still the same meaning. You don't have to say it in ten different sentences. Well, that was the way he wrote.

21 McGraw-Hill

James Eayrs

Out of the blue one day someone knocked on the door and it was Gouzenko. The purpose of his visit was to try and enlist my co-operation in a project to write a film script. It was very surrealistic. He looked like . . . what a Hollywood director would look like. He was dressed in a cream-coloured suit. It was in the summertime. We had a three- or four-hour talk. I remember my marvelling at the fact that he remarked as we left that his wife was waiting for him in a car that was parked across the way in a park — this was High Park. We lived next to Grenadier Pond in Toronto. I remember marvelling at what a life that woman must have led if this was the customary way in which she was treated, because there was no indication he would be at my place for five minutes or four hours. It was quite clear that for long as he was there she would be waiting in this car. He left me with an autographed copy of his *Fall of a Titan* that was effusively inscribed. So this was a very surrealistic experience.

The purpose of his visit was to sell yet again another version of his story. I suppose he was just trying to do his story one more time with one more set of royalties. But the real irony of the whole thing was how completely he had sold out to the worst aspects of the society he had defected to.

I wasn't very enthusiastic as to whether this would play, in the sense I didn't really think he had a market for this, and I was trying to break this to him gently. And he misinterpreted my negative reaction and thought he hadn't offered me enough of the proceeds for my collaboration. I remember him saying, very eagerly, that he miscalculated in saying only twenty per cent of the take would be mine. He upped it to twenty-five per cent.

Ron Besse, *publisher*

I was president of McGraw-Hill and around 1974 the idea came up at one of our editorial meetings that somebody should approach Gouzenko to publish his autobiography. We thought he would be difficult to reach. We wrote a letter to the Royal Canadian Mounted Police saying we would appreciate having the opportunity to meet with him and all of a sudden one day he arrived at the door and introduced himself. It was a great surprise. He arrived within a week of the letter.

We had quite a long driveway into the McGraw-Hill premises in Scarborough and he was never dropped off at our door and he never arrived by car. He always arrived by bus and walked in. He was paranoid about the KGB and felt he always had to be very, very careful. His wife dropped him off at a plaza and then he would take public transportation from there to our place.

The most vivid memory I have of Gouzenko are the disguises he would wear and they generally were a hat — a fedora. The first time he came he was wearing a Truman kind of Stetson and it was always variations of that hat. I remember when he was telling us about the necessity for being disguised. I said: "You're not really very disguised." He would certainly attract attention by the wide-brimmed fedoras he would wear. He said: "Yes, but how would you describe me?" I said: "Well, a short man with a big fedora." He said: "That's the disguise." So he was really caught up with these different fedoras he wore. He was quite comical about it. He wore these crazy clothes: very long overcoats. One day he came in a very short overcoat, looked like something he got out of the Junior League Shop — black-and-white checks. He was quite clever this way. "What do you remember about me?" "Your hat and now your coat." I don't think I could describe his face. He was very much into this. People would notice him but could never describe anything but his apparel.

Robert Reguly

He was square. Square in the sense he had an angular, square build. He looked like something out of Central Casting when they'd say: "Send me over a Russian." You'd pick Gouzenko. Particularly the way he wore his hat straight across his head. He had a stolid walk. He was chunky square. He looked like old photographs of heavies out of the 1930s movies.

Ron Besse

He was anxious to publish his autobiography but he was in dire financial straits. . . . He needed money, so we advanced him $5000 the first time and we signed a contract with him. The arrangement was that he would dictate his manuscript in Russian and then we would have it translated. That's how it started. We gave him the first $5000 and then I believe it was two additional $5000 amounts. He kept coming back to us for more money and we wouldn't give him any more. He was using us to bankroll him and it would have gone on as long as we would have paid him. We stopped giving him money and he stopped coming to see us. After two years and $15,000 of our money and coming back for more, he never produced a page of manuscript. He always said he needed more money so he could work on it. By that time we realized that he would never produce a manuscript.

Doug Gibson, *publisher*

Shortly after we had signed up John Diefenbaker to write his memoirs for Macmillan — this was around 1974 — we made the great mistake of actually boasting about how much money we paid to sign him up, something that we do not do any longer. That obviously is what brought Mr. Gouzenko to our door.

I was working on the fourth floor in the editorial office at 70 Bond Street. My name had been associated with the announcement that we had signed up Mr. Diefenbaker. The receptionist called up to say there was a Mr. Brown to see me. I said: "Mr. Brown. Do I know which Mr. Brown?" She said: "No, just Mr. Brown. He's waiting in the library." Like everyone, I know several Browns. I thought, is this Danny Brown, the painter, my friend, or perhaps Craig Brown, the historian? Just on the off chance it was one of the Browns I knew, I grudgingly went down the four flights of stairs to see this person waiting in the library. As it turned out there were three people waiting in the library, just standing around and reading books, and I didn't recognize any of them. So I cleared my throat and said: "Ah, Mr. Brown." And this short, sturdy, middle-aged man wearing glasses turned and indicated he was Mr. Brown.

Then he started to wink and nod and beckon. So I went towards him in a very gingerly fashion and shook his hand and he kept holding my hand like LBJ and pulled me back into the corner. By now I was becoming greatly alarmed because this strange man had been shaking my hand for ten seconds and was winking and nodding and jerking his head toward the corner. I must say I did think I was dealing with someone who was mentally disturbed because his face was twitching as he winked and his head was jerking back as he gestured and implied he had something secret going on. In the corner he leaned forward and whispered dramatically and animatedly: "Is not Brown. Is Gouzenko!" So I said: "Oh right, yes, of course. Good to see you again, Mr. Brown. Would you like to come upstairs?" We went upstairs and with Hugh Kane, our president, and our sales manager I took him into our boardroom and closed the door and [we sat] around our big walnut table to see what Mr. Brown had to tell us.

He had to tell us he was offering us the rights to his life story and said it would be a wonderful life story. He told us some good stories about life undercover and indeed they did sound very interesting. He talked a great game in a very, very thick Russian accent which was not always easy to understand. He was a very enthusiastic salesman for all the good stories he had up his sleeve. He made it very clear the reason he was here was that he learned we were publishing Mr. Diefenbaker's memoirs and we were paying lots of money. And he wondered aloud several times if lots of money would be available to him. So we hummed and hawed and said we were certainly interested and would like to meet with him later. He indicated it would be hard for us to get in touch with him but he would be in touch with us in due course. So he went away.

Hugh Kane made one quick phone call to confirm his suspicions and discovered, as he had suspected, that Gouzenko was under contract with McGraw-Hill to write his memoirs and that this contract, for which a fair amount of money had changed hands, was still in operation and that he had no right to offer this book to us. He contacted us again by phone and I simply said I was sorry but that I didn't see any basis for us to do business. That was the end of that. It was an interesting way to spend an hour.

Peter Worthington

I remember that thing. He was so angry that Diefenbaker should get such a large advance and he should get such a puny one. He was very angry at McGraw-Hill. I think McGraw-Hill had given him $15,000 eventually, and he felt that if anybody else was getting $100,000, or whatever they were getting, that it was almost an insult that he got so little, that he was far more important and significant than Diefenbaker. It was a comparative thing. He began to be almost resentful of McGraw-Hill for not giving him more.

The ethics of the thing, I don't think they did bother him. I'm not sure he even saw them. I must say I didn't get into an ethical dispute with him. It sure as hell would have bothered me. It's ethically unacceptable.

Robert Keyserlingk

He didn't understand the ethics of it. All business was evil anyways. So anybody who engaged in commerce was an evil person. If you go into a den of thieves and don't steal, you're just a fool. There was no sense of obligation. You were dealing with a completely amoral person. Under the Soviet system the only beneficiary of your actions should be the state, and since the state isn't there, then it's a free-for-all.

Ron Besse

I don't think he had the literary ability to produce a manuscript. Because it wasn't a difficult task that we were asking him to do: just to dictate into a machine and then we would work with a translator from that. I couldn't help but think he was incapable of doing anything. I don't think he was a very literate person. I think he was incapable of writing, that he was just a story-teller. I just felt he was incapable of ever producing. We would spend a lot of lunches and a lot of money for nothing. So he wasn't a totally honest person either.

John Holmes, *chairman of the Canadian Institute of International Affairs*

He walked into my office. I said I really couldn't have lunch with him that day but I would be happy to take him to lunch some day. He said he couldn't make an appointment. I said: "Well, if you want to take a chance on coming in again, I would be very happy to see you." I guess he was so anxious to talk to somebody as Igor Gouzenko that he made an appointment with me shortly after that. He wanted to take me to lunch and wanted to make sure it was in the best restaurant. He took me up to the top of the TD Tower.

Peter Worthington

The KGB could have killed Gouzenko so quickly. They could have just got hold of him by phoning me or the CBC or his trust company and say you wanted an interview with him, that you had $500, and that you were Joe Smith from the so-and-so newspaper. The amount of checking would be to call and find out if there was a Joe Smith at the *New York Times*. They do have a Joe Smith, he's not a bad guy you hear. You don't know. So he would see Joe Smith in his hotel room or some place. Joe Smith could be Boris somebody or other and pushes him out of the window.

John Holmes

I could have tracked him down so easily. When he made an appointment with me I could have easily phoned a friend of mine in one of the newspapers and had him come and take a picture of Igor. I guess he must have thought he could trust me. He also told me things about his family that I'm sure I would have been able to track if I had wanted to.

Robert Reguly

The simplest thing to do would be to trace the car licence number. I know the car he drove. I could have taken down the licence number any time I wanted. Then I would trace the ownership. It would be as simple as one phone call. Every journalist should know how to do it.

John Picton

Latterly, certainly during the days of *détente*, I'm sure the last thing the Soviets would want was for anything to happen to Gouzenko. I'm sure they dreaded the possibility of him being hit by a truck because immediately people would say the Russians did it. And during *détente* that was the last confrontation they wanted. That's my opinion. But you have to remember initially the Soviets would have loved to get their hands on him. He used to say to me: "I'm a living example their system can be beaten. I did escape and I'm still alive. I'm a bad example as far as the Soviets are concerned."

Peter Worthington

He made such a fetish of security that it almost became a parody in a way and that it was almost more useful to the Soviets that nothing happened to him. I always felt that his greatest danger was as an example to other Soviets. If they had a rash of KGB defections, this would be a way of putting a lid on it. He was such a symbol that everybody knew of him.

John Picton

One day he came into the office with a painting. It was a fall scene and a lovely painting. He wanted to sell it to me for $100. I didn't have $100 then. It was a lot of money then. I said I was sorry. I was polite and declined. It wasn't signed. He said: "I'll sign it with my real name but only after someone buys it. If something happens to me on the street and I'm carrying this painting, I don't want anything on me that suggests I'm Igor Gouzenko." I declined and I regret it now.

John Holmes

The last time I saw him was really very sad. I felt quite sick about it. This man, who had played quite a part, behaving like a poor cadger. He came in just before lunch and I was tied up. It was a Friday and he said: "Oh, by the way, my wife forgot to go to the bank. I wonder if you could let me have some money." I quite honestly said: "I'd be very happy to but I've only got $10 in my pocket because I was going to the bank myself." I said: "I'm sorry. I'd be happy to give you a cheque but I guess that isn't possible." He said: "Yes, it is." So I made out the cheque to Peter Brown and it was cashed. That was the last I saw of him and I felt rather sad. Why he didn't come back I don't know. He never paid back the $50. I never really expected him to. It may have been embarrassment about that.

22 Blindness

Alan Harris

He always had things going. It was a busy family. There were people coming and going in that house. When I got to know him in '75-'76, my goodness it was like Grand Central Station. Children, grandchildren, and people. It was amazing. A lot of people who didn't know him except under his assumed name coming and going. It was just quite a family.

Karen Milne

He had a tremendous relationship with his wife. I think they were especially close over the years because all they really had was each other and the children and were very ingrown as a family. The family was very proud of what the father had done. He was concerned about his children's safety. He was afraid that perhaps, maybe not even so much the Soviets, but maybe somebody who was very pro-communist might want to harm his children for what he had done. He was worried just as much about some of the crackpots out there as he was worried about Soviet revenge.

Alan Harris

I think they were very happy people. They loved Canada. They loved life in general and life in Canada. It's just amazing to me. We used to comment all the time. They loved life. They really did. I think that's what enthused me about them in general. I still like them to this day. Just an indomitable spirit: enjoyed life. Enjoyed so many things. Like art, ceramics, painting, sculpture, music. An awful lot of things. Very wide and varied interests. All sorts of interests. He loved to talk about all sorts of things. Just an interesting character. And loved to tell stories and anecdotes. They loved children, anybody's children.

John Picton

He was delighted in his children and his grandchildren. He was very proud of his children, most of whom, if not all, had whizzed through university with scholarships. Brilliant kids. He seemed very, very proud of that. I think it's fortunate for him that he had such a large family. He had eight children, which is another thing he never wanted me to put in my stories. It took him a long time before he told me how many kids he had.

Svetlana Gouzenko

He was always with them and was always recording, either a snapshot or a movie picture. Snow fort in the back? Daddy there with camera ready to have a snowball fight. And then when we dug the pool there was a huge pile of sand and they all built their own sand castles. Daddy's right there taking those sand castles on film for posterity.

Alan Harris

Later on he got diabetes and he couldn't drink of course. He loved to have people drink. He set a great table. They were wonderful cooks and hosts. He also set out quite a bar. There'd always be Harvey's Shooting Sherry. Always had champagne and some liqueurs, maybe Scotch and something else. He would always say: "How does it taste?" Would virtually smack his lips. He just wanted to hear how it was. It was all symptomatic of loving life. If he couldn't have it, well, at least he would enjoy it vicariously by listening to what other people thought about the food.

Peter Worthington

He always liked his food. He tucked into things. I don't know whether he liked food or looked at the prices. But he liked the most expensive. We'd go out to lunch and he'd always say: "Are you paying for this or is the *Sun* paying for this?" Then you knew what was coming. He'd go for everything expensive.

John Picton

I hadn't seen him in years. The main reception desk on the newsroom floor phoned me and said: "There's a Mr. Brown here to see you." So I went out and there was Svetlana, whom I had not met before. She said: "Are you John Picton?" I said yes. She said: "We're going to lunch." So I said: "Where's Mr. Brown?" She said: "He's outside waiting." We went down the elevator and out the main door and Gouzenko was standing outside the front door, the most conspicuous place to be standing. And he was standing there alone. And I suddenly spotted the white cane. I was shocked. I must have taken a step back. She said: "Diabetes." He was blind.

Arthur Cole

He had changed the last time I saw him in that he was certainly almost blind. I think he told me he had ten per cent vision or something like that.

Robert Reguly

I knew he was going blind. He was wearing glasses. He'd be walking up and down the street. He'd look like a stage Russian — stolid walk, the way he wore his coat and especially his hat. He couldn't see very far. You could tell his eyesight was going. . . . He just said it was diabetes.

George Burnett

I was sitting with him when he went blind. He just looked at me and said: "I can't see you." We were in the Fifty-Fourth at the top of the Toronto Dominion Centre. He had just had strawberries and cream. He looked at me and said: "I can't see you." I took him downstairs and he reached into his pocket and pulled out a wad of bills. He said he wanted to take a cab home and asked me to get a twenty out of it. So I got a twenty and gave it and he put the balance of the money into his pocket and took a cab home. I had to guide him to the door.

Peter Worthington

He insisted for years that it was strawberries, that curious Russian superstition. He had strawberries when the blindness came and, I suppose, blamed the strawberries. He fought diabetes. He wouldn't take any injections for it. He fought diabetes by exercise and would spend hours — he would say this — would exercise for five, six, seven hours on end and do nothing but exercises.

George Burnett

I had a striped tie and he used to maintain he could see the stripes. He thought the eyes were getting better. I know he used to love strawberries. He'd be looking for them in midwinter. He did have a weakness for strawberries.

John Picton

He was afraid to take medication in case somebody slipped him something. And he was afraid of doctors. He just didn't trust them. He was afraid of them slipping him something too. He didn't trust anybody. He always claimed that's why he stayed alive for so long.

Alan Harris

He made a couple of comments to me that he really didn't believe in insulin, felt that if you were in good shape you didn't need it, also that because he took it in pill form I think he felt that possibly maybe somebody could give him the wrong pills or some darn thing. And consequently he didn't take it.

Svetlana Gouzenko

Igor didn't need it. Again the idea that he was afraid to go to the doctors is such nonsense. Just unbelievable. But if he would report it to the Mounted Police, they say: "Which doctor? You're taking pills? What kind of pills?" They were just pestering us all the time because they have to have all the information. However, we consider that there are Soviet agents inside the Security Service. This information would go to the Soviets and then they will arrange for some pills to be mixed up and he will be dead. What we did was to go to a doctor under a different name and he got full treatment.

Alan Harris

As I understand diabetes and diabetes blindness, it is a needless situation that you go blind these days, I think. But it never stopped him. He learned braille. He got himself a braille typewriter. "Brailley" he used to call it. They had a funny way of pronouncing some of these words. If there was an "e" at the end, they pronounced it as a hard "e". So he called it "Brailley". Just as he called Yale University "Yaley". Or actually he called it "Yawley". I had a hard time sometimes catching some of the words at first.

Svetlana Gouzenko

Listen, Andropov had diabetes. He went blind in the last — in his picture you can see that Andropov is blind. He is held by two men on each side and making steps down. The man was blind. . . . So he had the best medical treatment and he could get anything that is invented in the West. He had it. He still had diabetes and he still went blind.

George Burnett

He used to say he exercised a lot. He ate apples. Apples are a natural source of sugar and with diabetes your sugar level has to be maintained. I know he ate a lot of apples.

Peter Worthington

He would weight-lift and all that stuff. He would always claim what great physical shape he was in. I gather this offsets diabetes somewhat, because to go as long as he did with diabetes and live as long as he did and finally be killed by a heart attack defies medical science in a way. But he wouldn't take medical treatment.

Alan Harris

I've never seen anybody as fit as he was. I remember him suddenly flopping down on my living-room floor as stiff as a board and catch himself on his fingertips and then do ten quick push-ups and clap his hands together at the top of the push-up and catch himself before he hit the ground again. He was in tremendous shape. But that was part of his problem. He thought he was in good shape and didn't need to take insulin too.

Svetlana Gouzenko

When he first went and detected diabetes, the doctor told him in 1951-52, then: "Diabetes is such a thing then your veins will get weak and will start bursting. If your vein will burst somewhere in the heart area you will have a heart attack. If a vein bursts in your brain you will have a stroke. And if a vein will burst in your eye you will go blind." So he was prepared for it. All these years he would gradually prepare to thinking that he could go blind. It's we that didn't prepare ourselves really.

Robert Reguly

His wife was his seeing-eye dog. He had problems eating at first. In restaurants his wife would turn his plate. The meat would be at twelve o'clock, the vegetables at three o'clock. That's the way they do it for blind people, so she would rearrange it in this blind pattern at restaurants.

John Picton

She would cut his food up for him and he would grab it with his fingers and stick it in his mouth. We were at the Imperial Room, the Poseidon Room, and at the swank restaurant in the King Edward Hotel, and he would sit there and eat his meals with his fingers. And he would feel around the edge of the plate to see if it was a potato or whatever. His tie would be off, which you would expect of a blind man. And he had lost many of his teeth, which was a symptom of his diabetes, too. He wore pretty shabby clothes. He wasn't stylish by any means.

Svetlana Gouzenko

He was shaving himself. . . . [He tried] to put the hot tea from the kettle into his own cup and it upset on his hand and the whole hand came into blisters. It was so horrible I rushed him to the hospital and all. But his independence. That independence.

Peter Worthington

Whatever qualities the guy had, there wasn't an ounce of crybaby about his blindness. He just rolled with it and adopted it and kept living his life. At that age he learned braille and it didn't slow him down a bit. There was no remorse saying "if only, if only". He just adapted to the circumstances. If I were in his position and couldn't see — you'd be terrified all the time. He really wasn't. He'd stumble and go into restaurants blind and flounder around. He'd miss the food, then jab himself with the fork. He was unselfconscious about it and laughing about it. You had to admire the panache that the guy had in the thing.

Alan Harris

That was a great tragedy, I felt, and of course it really slowed him up on his second book. He was writing *Ocean of Time*. It must have thrown him for a three-year delay. So it really threw him off course on that book. It takes, as you know, a long time to write a book. He'd been writing it for ten years, that *Ocean of Time*. So it really threw him for a loop.

John Picton

Of course, after the story broke alleging Sir Roger Hollis was the mole, Gouzenko was blind. So when the photographs of Hollis were in the paper as a possible mole, Gouzenko wasn't able to see them and say whether they were one of the two photographs he partly identified.

. . . What I could not say in that story — this is when the Hollis thing had broken — was that Gouzenko was blind and can't identify Hollis. I couldn't say that in the story because he pleaded with me — always — "Never say I'm blind. Because the moment you say I'm blind, it narrows down the number of people it might be. I've got a foreign accent, and there aren't that many blind people as an overall percentage of the population." So it wasn't until his obituary that I was able to say he was blind. Although I had seen a reference in the London *Sunday Times* several years ago where they said Gouzenko was blind.

Svetlana Gouzenko

He was the boss. You don't think that I was the boss. Oh no. Whatever he say, it's the law. Even the kids, even [when] they're older now, say he was the Rock of Gibraltar. And he was always right. In so many details now I find it, that I come across and say: "My gosh, he was right and I thought he was wrong."

John Picton

He would rehash the old things, the old names, the old civil servants, the old events — preaching that communist moles were hidden all over the place. He kept up very much with day-to-day events. In latter days his wife would read items in the newspaper, so he was very much aware of what was going on. He was a very bright man. He had a very quick mind. Certainly on anything to do with the Soviets and espionage and developments in the Kremlin. He would say: "Ah, you know what they mean." He would espouse his theories on various scenarios and so on. So he was very much up on current events.

Peter Worthington

Gouzenko would always call on me after a Picton article. I must say I was generally in tune with what Picton was writing and was always amused by the intimacy that was built up between the two. Gouzenko would always call and say it was invention, that this and that wasn't so. He used Picton, no doubt. They used each other, as we all do. I suspect Gouzenko had a lot of good friends.

John Picton

He always phoned me after one of my articles appeared. "Brilliant journalist," he said. "Brilliant journalist."

Jim Littleton, *radio and television producer*

When I was researching and producing the film series "On

Guard for Thee" I got a call from an Australian film-maker named Bill Bemister who was producing a film on international espionage. He had come to Toronto to interview Igor Gouzenko. I was struck by the fact he had come all the way from Australia to interview this figure who had taken on mythic proportions. But he figured it was an important thing to do. I told him: "It's not hard at all. Just call his lawyer and tell him you have a little money to spend. You'll have no problem at all." We went up to his hotel room in the Harbour Castle and he made the call. Bill thought he'd have to wait around several days for a reply while Gouzenko checked him out. We went to the bar, and literally ten minutes later the person at the hotel desk came over and said there was an urgent call for him. It was Gouzenko, and he would be glad to meet him any time. He had no way of knowing who Bill was, whether he was an agent of the KGB, the CIA, or anything else. All he had was Bill's word that he was a film-maker and had money to spend. So he invited Bill to come to his house that night and told him how to get there. When I saw him the next day he said he had had a wonderful evening and had consumed a lot of alcohol in a long, long session.

Ian Adams

Up to the year of his death the media still phoned him up to ask him about his view when a high-level KGB defector had moved over to the CIA. Gouzenko would be pontificating. It was quite ludicrous that journalists would still take him seriously. I think the media is responsible for mythologizing the man beyond all reason. I guess it is a desperate search for myth in our own society.

Jim Littleton

Bemister got in touch with me the next morning and told me he had this wonderful time with Gouzenko and everything was fine and he'd be able to do as much interviewing of Gouzenko as he wanted to. We had him over for dinner and in the course of the evening he said: "I have a souvenir from Gouzenko," and produced the pillowcase that Gouzenko wore over his head. It was a cloth bag with the eyeholes and I think the nose hole cut out. It was autographed. It said something like: "To my good friend Bill Bemister from Igor Gouzenko" in ballpoint pen. We had some good laughs over it. Right at that time Ian Adams was running his "Igor Gouzenko Look-Alike Contest" in *This Magazine* and it occurred to me this was the perfect chance to enter the contest. So I put the bag on and had my picture taken wearing an FBI T-shirt and holding a copy of Karl Marx's *Das Kapital* in one hand and a glass of brandy in the other. Sure enough, it won the contest.

Ian Adams

We would run a photograph saying it had been sent to us by a retired officer of the [RCMP] Security Service and it was a true picture of Gouzenko. The picture was always somebody with a bag over his head. Someone sent in a wonderful family photograph, circa 1920 — a very formal portrait of seven or eight people and there was a bag over everyone's head. The caption read that Igor Gouzenko was the young lad who was second from the left. We continued in that vein. Strangely enough, Gouzenko never sued. He sued everyone else at the drop of a hat. But I heard from some sources that he was quite hurt by the "Igor Gouzenko Look-Alike Contest".

Jim Littleton

The day after Bemister spent the evening at Gouzenko's house, Gouzenko and one of his daughters showed up at the Harbour Castle Hotel and knocked on his door. He didn't know they were coming and they just strolled in. They went down to the bar and shot the breeze with him. When I say he didn't take security seriously I'm not kidding. Bemister could have been a KGB agent and it wasn't very hard for him to get him.

23 More Libel Suits

John Picton

According to Gouzenko, a Mountie came to him one day and said a professor at the University of Toronto wanted to contact him and the Mountie said: "I'll go ahead and hire a room at the Royal York Hotel for you to have the interview." Gouzenko said he became suspicious and phoned this professor himself and asked why he wanted to see him. He claims the professor said: "I didn't want to see you. I just wanted to contact you on the phone and ask you a couple of questions. In fact I don't have time to see you. I'm just packing my bags to go to New York." Gouzenko read into that that the Mountie was trying to set him up. "Push me through a window."

James Barros

My wife and I were packing to go on a research trip to New York and Washington when the telephone rang. The chap on the other end said: "I'm the chap you want to talk to." I just for the life of me couldn't figure out who the fellow was who I wanted to talk to. He repeated it several times. It finally dawned on me that it was Gouzenko. I put my hand over the mouthpiece and said [to my wife]: "You know, it's Gouzenko. I think he's crazy calling me." I never thought that Gouzenko would take the initiative and call me up on the phone. I explained to him we were leaving and couldn't see him now but would see him when we returned.

John Picton

The inference [from Gouzenko] was that the Mountie was in

242

the pay of someone who wanted to see Gouzenko rubbed out. This is his scenario, that he would have gone to the hotel and into a room and waited for the Mountie and suddenly somebody else would have turned up, the window would have been opened, and Gouzenko would have gone out head first. Then it would have come down to who booked the hotel room. Presumably nobody ever would have known who booked the hotel room. That was the scenario.

James Barros

He alleged this four years after the event. Certainly there was no attempt by the RCMP to suck him into some hotel room for the purpose of killing him. The RCMP certainly wasn't using me as a patsy in this alleged assassination plot. This is all a figment of his imagination. . . . How in heaven's name in December 1980, four years later, did he get the thing all messed up? It's like a plumbing job done by some yahoo. All the pipes are going in the wrong direction, the up pipe is down and the down pipe is up.

Arthur Cole

He certainly didn't have very much money. I can tell you one Christmas not long after I had him on the program he didn't have enough to buy a Christmas turkey. I got him $150 from CFRB just because he was down and out. That wasn't too long ago. That was '77 or '78, around in there.

James Barros

He asked me for money. He talked about how he was going to publish his memoirs and how some of the information I was asking for may detract from the value of his memoirs. His letter said: "I therefore would appreciate if you would pay me $10,000 for any comments on Mackenzie King's diary. You have or could have, I would think, the backing of some wealthy organizations such as the Ford Foundation with their multi-million dollar funds out of which is especially reserved for historic study research and publishing." He went on in this vein for a page and a half. He concluded the letter by saying: "The New York Times has said that I have changed the course of history. My comments therefore have great historical value and should be paid for generously. This is logical, fair and decent." I think I told the RCMP corporal that, if anything, the Ford Foundation was liable to pay $10,000 to blow his brains out.

Lloyd Tataryn

In 1981 Gouzenko sued author June Callwood for her book *Portrait of Canada*. Callwood's book has a passing reference to Gouzenko and I was astounded that he would sue Callwood over such a passing reference.

June Callwood, *author*

Portrait of Canada is a linear and social history of Canada and moves very fast to cover the landing of the Vikings up to the election of Lévesque and the Parti Québécois in 1976. Maybe three paragraphs in all deal with the period of Gouzenko's defection. I knew that Gouzenko was litigious. I've been a journalist forty-four years and you couldn't possibly not have heard people saying: "Be very careful, Gouzenko likes to sue." So I wasn't naive. So I referred to his behaviour as, he "seemed erratic and unstable" at a certain period.

Svetlana Gouzenko

What did she say? "Despite the startling nature of documents he carried from the Soviet embassy, there was little evidence to convict Canadians of any crime." She should be charged with contempt of court. Eleven men were sent to jail. Eleven people. Some were men. Eighteen were arrested but there was not enough documents. Not enough documents to prove their guilt. That doesn't make them really not guilty once they were mentioned in the documents. But it's not enough to convince the people and they went free. When eleven people are put in jail and June is stating then it is not enough evidence to convict of any kind, she should be charged with contempt of court.

June Callwood

About six-eight weeks after the book was published, Gouzenko's lawyers sent a letter to Doubleday in New York saying he took exception to that. . . . The letter said he wanted *Portrait of Canada* withdrawn from distribution immediately. I thought it was not at all actionable. I was told that in the United States the case would never have been started. The American lawyers told me they were amazed Canadian libel laws were so tight that that could be taken seriously.

Peter Worthington

Gouzenko got quite cross with me when he was suing June Callwood. I don't know if you read June Callwood's book, but there's an area there where I think she was terribly wrong. He sued and she was distraught over it. She was defending herself and falling right into his hands, I thought. And I tried to persuade him not to do it. June Callwood's son had just been killed and her daughter had been run over by a cement truck and there was a lot of sadness. And Gouzenko expressed great sympathy and concern, but he said: "It has absolutely nothing to do with my case. What has her personal life got to do with maligning me? It's two different things." And he wouldn't equate the natural sympathy with the other. And he's right, I guess. I suppose it's a sign of a flaw that you do overlap certain areas. I just dropped it very quickly. There was no way of getting him off it.

June Callwood

When our son was killed I had a very thoughtful letter from Gouzenko's lawyer saying everything would be suspended for a time in view of the tragedy and that I was to freeze the process at that point. Nothing changed, except nothing went forward.

John Picton

I know he was concerned about the book *Wilderness of Mirrors*. It was I who sent him that book. I knew it had just come out and our then Washington correspondent sent it to me and said perhaps your pal Gouzenko would be interested in this because there's a reference to him in it. The book arrived and I didn't even read the book. I just phoned him and said if you're interested you can have it. They came and picked it up one day. He phoned me some time after that, ranting and raving about this book. Apparently it made some disparaging remarks about him. So he sued them.

William McMurtry, *lawyer who represented Gouzenko in the* Wilderness of Mirrors *libel action*

I guess I had a prejudice against him when I first met him. There was no doubt I was one of those people who had been reached by the hearsay stories that I thought he was extremely litigious. When I told people — my colleagues, my partners, my friends — that I was acting for Igor Gouzenko, because it's common knowledge once you appear in court, it was amazing how many people cautioned me: "Oh, he'll wind up suing you." I was a little bit leery at first. It seemed to me he was suing people right and left. But when I actually looked into the individual cases, he seemed to have a very legitimate reason in every case. I've had a lot of clients who have had very good reason to sue newspapers but for whatever reason decided not to, which I could also understand. But in every case where he brought an action, if you looked into the facts we felt he was justified. Now, whether he felt justified in thinking it was as important as he did, that's open to argument. That's not for me to say. But he had certainly been wronged in these cases, if you accept his version, and I certainly did.

. . . I remember when I wrote the first letter and I outlined why we were aggrieved. I got a letter back from Mr. Gouzenko: "Thank you very much for the copy of draft letter which was sent for my comments. I appreciate your kind remarks and deep understanding of the motivations of my action." That letter really stressed that we were more concerned about his place in history. He was very concerned that the first editions of these books would go into libraries and wouldn't be changed, and anybody doing research on Gouzenko would keep coming up with these things.

Karen Milne

The defendants all agreed they were to make an apology. What took so long was hammering out the details of how it was to be worded. Gouzenko being the way he was was very particular every single punctuation mark and word had to be perfect from his point of view. Actually for a while he drove me a bit crazy because he was always sending back drafts and he wouldn't sign until it was perfect. So we went through all these drafts. The publisher and David Martin were also particular, I guess, at least their lawyer was, because they didn't want to give in to his every whim either. So figuring out the wording took a long time. And then, after we did that, it took a couple of months working out what page in the newspaper it had to be on. He was very concerned that it end up on page two of the *New York Times*. He didn't want it to be shuffled to the back of the classified ads. So we had to be very careful as to the settlement agreement we reached on that. The size of print was of concern to him because he was afraid the publisher was going to use the size of print they use for birth notices and he didn't want that. He didn't want the type of apology that would just be buried in the middle of a lot of advertisements. He wanted it right in the middle of the news section so that it would have attention. All those sorts of details he was concerned about.

William McMurtry

At one time they proposed more money. I think it was thousands of dollars more if we'd forget — and they said they would do a bigger ad in the *Globe and Mail* but they didn't want to do it in the *New York Times*. If we would just change a few lines, they were prepared to pay. He was not interested. That was not a consideration as far as he was concerned. This is why today I am morally certain that what he told me from the very first was true. He felt a great hurt that people would not accept his motives for defecting.

Karen Milne

One of the things he most wanted to have in there were some comments about his five-point program. The publisher was really balking at that because to apologize was one thing but to propagate his philosophy is another thing. In the end they certainly cut down what he originally wanted. He was very proud of his achievements. I wouldn't say he was overly egotistical. I would just say he was proud of what he had done. I guess like any person who has been a celebrity for a long time they get used to it and expect it to continue. He liked it when his interviews were in the paper and would phone up excited when there was an article, for example, about the case we were involved in.

William McMurtry

The longer settlement negotiations dragged on, the more I realized that money was a very small consideration compared to the form of retraction. They could have doubled the sum and he wouldn't have accepted changing one line of that retraction.

Karen Milne

One of the problems the defendants faced was that he wanted it published within a certain time period, but they couldn't guarantee that. The *Globe and Mail* wasn't too hard, but a large paper like the *New York Times* had a hard time guaranteeing that it would be within a certain number of pages. I forget the exact details but I think it had to appear between page two and page fifteen, and the *New York Times* just couldn't guarantee on any given day if he wanted it published on Day X that they could do it; for all they knew the president could be assassinated that day, so they couldn't make any promise. Gouzenko worried that somehow this apology would be buried in the paper.

Lloyd Tataryn

The publishers of *Wilderness of Mirrors* eventually published an apology to Gouzenko. Harper and Row bought space in the *Globe and Mail* on April 26, 1982, and apologized for printing "one short passage which Mr. Gouzenko has found objectionable". Gouzenko pocketed $10,000 for his efforts against [author David] Martin.

John Picton

He said he was going to take us out for a slap-up champagne dinner when he got the money. We went to the King Eddie. He had his sole. It wasn't on the menu but he got it. And he insisted I have sole, but I wanted something on the menu that I really felt like having. He said: "No, you must have sole." I said I'd prefer to have something else. "No. No. We have sole." And he ordered sole and that was the end of it.

Jean Picton, *John Picton's wife*

Everybody didn't have sole. He just insisted that John have it.

Lloyd Tataryn

I was interested in the Igor Gouzenko phenomenon and talked to *Canadian Forum* to see if they would be interested in an article on the fact that Gouzenko wasn't being properly scrutinized by journalists because he sued a lot. *Canadian Forum* was really interested. They said: "Yeah, go ahead. It sounds like a great piece. It will tell us something about libel suits and the tactical use of libel suits to prevent anybody from examining a given situation."

Sam Solecki, *then editor of* Canadian Forum

I assumed when I commissioned the article that we would be sued. But given that the Callwood suit was still pending, ours would be left alone until he died or the Callwood suit was resolved. I also assumed our lawyers would look at it first. So I had no compunctions about letting the thing go.

Lloyd Tataryn

Once I began looking into Gouzenko it was a bigger story than I imagined. I did not know, for example, that the *Toronto Star* had to apologize and publish a complete retraction of an article first put together by Jocko Thomas on October 30, 1953. I called

Jocko and he told me he was very confident when he went in there that they would win the suit.

. . . I couldn't say in my article what his article was about. That would have raised the points which led to the original suit that was settled out of court. So I couldn't say that Jocko Thomas wrote that Gouzenko was on the verge of bankruptcy because of overspending. I also couldn't write that in January 1965 the Toronto *Telegram* had to settle out of court and apologize for suggesting that *The Fall of a Titan* was ghost-written. All I said in my article was that he sued the *Toronto Star* in 1953 and the Toronto *Telegram* in 1965 and there were out-of-court settlements and so on. If some interested reader wanted to go to the library and look up these articles it was up to him.

James Dubro

I asked him a number of times why he sued. He said it was not for the money — he would have to say that — but if he let any story that was untrue go, history would accept it. If he fought a libel action, then it would be known that he challenged that version. He also felt there was some conspiracy by certain Mounties who were putting out these stories. He would never admit to the reality of the stories, such as being a spendthrift. And yet at one of the dinners he certainly spent a lot of money, which was rather nice. He gave me a bottle of Dom Pérignon for Christmas.

Lloyd Tataryn

Frank Rasky wrote a book called *Gay Canadian Rogues* containing two chatty chapters describing Gouzenko's flight into the Ottawa night. The book was sympathetic with Gouzenko's decision to adopt a country where he could, in Rasky's words, live in air that is perfumed with freedom. What I couldn't understand is why anybody would want to sue for those two chatty chapters, because, if anything, it depicted him in the usual way: as a hero. I called Rasky and talked to him. His wife was very reluctant for him to talk to me. She said: "Look, we don't want to be sued. He sues and we're very angry over what happened. So if you quote us, don't quote us saying anything negative about Gouzenko because we don't want to be sued. We'll comment on how disappointed we were and that sort of stuff." But Rasky was extremely angry. His book, he said, which was selling quite well, was pulled from the shelves and Gouzenko apparently settled with the publisher for $12,000.

I found it very interesting that when publishers decided to go to court that Gouzenko actually fared badly. What he did was take them to the brink and then settle out of court. It seemed pretty hard for me to imagine that Rasky would have lost that case.

Ken Lefolii

Nobody wants to spend money, time, emotional and creative energy necessary to pursue these suits to the bitter end. This becomes a problem with people who sue at the drop of their name. Suing becomes a winning tactic. Eventually no one wants to write about them in any depth. Just like you can train rats to react reflexively to a stimulus, you can train publishers to react automatically to the possibility of a suit. Publishers aren't interested in publishing material which leads to suits and neither are editors. Editors won't tell you that because they're supposed to be fearless but they know what publishers want. Both editors and publishers reflexively have been trained to shy away from stories on people like Gouzenko.

June Callwood

Self-censorship is so sinister because you never say to yourself: "I'm not going to write about this because Gouzenko sues." You never think that way or else you would go ahead and do it. What you think is: "That's an interesting time in our history and I really must get to it."

Lloyd Tataryn

I then found out that Gouzenko had served writs on three books in the last two years. And he had also threatened the *Toronto Star* with legal action over references to him in an article by Daniel Stoffman that appeared under the headline: "Libel: The Dark Cloud That Hangs Over Every Writer". When

I called Dan Stoffman he asked me how I knew that a suit was launched by Gouzenko. He didn't want to talk about it at all and referred me to his lawyer, and his lawyers didn't want to talk about this particular case and so forth.

Daniel Stoffman, *former* Toronto Star *reporter*

It was a short feature article and it was listing a number of cases where suits had been brought against publishers. I interviewed publishers, for example, Linda McKnight, the editor of McClelland and Stewart, saying they were not interested in fighting suits, it just costs too much money and they would rather avoid it at all costs. So what it meant was that they would be censoring books or taking it out of books or not publishing books rather than get into trouble. And the conclusion was this was obviously a form of self-censorship that would limit the freedom of self-expression of authors. In many cases these lawsuits weren't very serious. . . . In the one suit that he brought against that particular article, they [the *Star* editors] had no intention of writing an apology or anything. They were just prepared to fight it if they had to because there was nothing wrong with the article.

Lloyd Tataryn

As I was compiling the research — and it was a massive amount of material when it comes to looking at his litigious history — I phoned *Canadian Forum* at least twice and told them what I was finding. They were intrigued by it. At one point I said: "Look, the lawyers I'm talking to are all saying you're taking a chance if you publish this article because Gouzenko will sue." I wrote the article deliberately in a low-key manner and told them I wasn't going to be inflammatory and would take every precaution to make sure they wouldn't get sued. But I said that if they publish the article they would have to assume the legal costs. That was one of the agreements I required to go forward with the article. They said: "Okay. It sounds great. Keep on writing. It sounds like a good controversial piece."

Sam Solecki

Each time he called me he had new stuff which all had to be

checked out. So the thing dragged on past my tenure as editor.

Lloyd Tataryn

I wrote it and sent it in and got a letter back in effect saying: "Sorry, we're in a financial bind right now and we'd go broke if we published this article, because we'd certainly be sued, even though you're probably very, very correct, and the magazine would go under." So I called them and asked them: "What's the score here? You said before you were going to do it." And they said: "Well look, we liked it. It was well written and well researched. We liked the organization and the materials but — " They gave me the money for the long-distance phone calls and said: "I'm sorry. We just can't do it." Which I thought proved the point I had made all along, that Gouzenko prevented people from examining his past and he did it by very deliberately and meticulously intimidating people through libel suits.

John Hutcheson, *editor,* Canadian Forum

I thought Gouzenko was going to sue. Lloyd partly got caught with us because I had just taken over as editor and the article had originated with the previous editor. Lloyd felt he was more likely to do it. I said: "Even if we win, we can't afford to do this."

. . . I had a feeling that while the article was probably accurate, the story wasn't big enough to justify the whole hassle that it would likely produce — given that our resources are very limited. Even if it's a case that you're going to win, it's so destructive to be involved.

24 Death

Robert Reguly

The last time I saw him was over the show *KGB Connections* when he was scheduled to be interviewed. I was a consultant to that program. He was suspicious of the cameraman. Could his grandson operate the camera? The cameraman might pull a trick and have a gun come out of the lens, that sort of thing. We bogged down over that. Money was involved too. I forget how much. He wanted $2000. They offered him $500. He was holding out for more than the money agreed upon.

Peter Worthington

I guess ever since his blindness he had been deteriorating. And he had bad feet. His feet were always swollen. He would wear sandals. And he would only buy good clothes. He would buy very expensive suits and things and wear these terrible old sandals with green socks or something. It was a most astonishing sight — with his commissar fedora. He was very dapper in a sense. It wasn't the great Brezhnev fedora. It was a little snappy one. Even wearing a fedora these days is unusual.

Svetlana Gouzenko

He had the flu and I was concerned then. Oh my gosh, that was a terrible flu. He finally had blisters on his legs even come out. And I was pouring this boric acid so it would not get infected. In order to have blood circulation he was in a bathtub sitting in a hot tub of water, cold tub of water, hot tub of water, cold tub of water, because of poor circulation — and those blisters. And then after manipulation like this, pouring over boric acid so it wouldn't infect, because with his diabetes the infections are healing very, very slowly. Then I'd massage his feet around all those blisters — massage four or five times a day. And once I was clipping his toenails and he said: "Annie, if anybody would tell you in university you were going to clip the nails of this fellow, what would you do?" I said more likely I would be laughing unless I would die laughing right there. How things change. How they change.

John Picton

He had been trying to get me to get copies of each edition of the *New York Times* on the day in which his apology was due to appear. I phoned the *New York Times* on his behalf several times and no one down there seemed to know which editions they had and where they came from. I was referred to several desks and the advertising department and no one seemed to know anything about their edition times. It was incredible. I never got a satisfactory answer for him. He said he thought they had slipped the apology in an obscure mid-west edition but that they had either dropped it or changed it in some way for the New York and Washington editions, the important editions. I have no idea what made him think this. But he certainly thought they would try to get around their legal obligation.

Karen Milne

The only time I went to a restaurant with him was at the King Eddie when we went to celebrate the final settlement in the Harper and Row case. We went out to supper, and true to his usual style it was cloak-and-dagger just getting to the restaurant. He came in one car. We came in another car, and at a street corner we all transferred into a cab and took a circuitous route to get there. At this point I had known him a year and wasn't even told the name of the restaurant until we arrived there. There would have been a more elaborate scheme involving one of his sons, but at the last moment his son's girlfriend came to town and that scheme fell through and he was frustrated because he had to have an alternative plan worked out on how we were going to get to this restaurant, which was only two blocks from where we started out. But it took all these manoeuvres to get there. What I found kind of amusing was that while we were in this restaurant — it was in the King Edward Hotel — and it was quite a quiet night. There weren't many people there. Because Igor was blind he wasn't aware of his surroundings and sometimes he forgot where he was. My parents were there, too, and at one point in the conversation he was talking about why he defected and getting into areas that could very clearly identify who he was. He kept referring to himself as Igor and would say things like: "Such-and-such talked to me and said, 'Igor, why don't you do this or that?'" He was talking in quite a loud voice. Any of the waiters or people sitting fairly close by, if they were listening, could immediately identify him. On the one hand he took all these security precautions to get to the restaurant and as soon as we got there he was eating and talking and basically blowing his own cover.

John Picton

Sometimes I would have to caution him in a restaurant. He would be mentioning his own name. In a loud voice he would say: "Oh, people say this about Gouzenko and that about Gouzenko." He would get carried away and sometimes people would be looking, not because he was Gouzenko but because he was talking rather loudly. I'd have to caution him and say: "Peter, people are sitting around us." "Oh-oh," he would say.

James Dubro

I was dining with him in the Royal York just a few days before he died. We were in the Acadian Room. There were people all around us. Mind you, he couldn't see them because he was blind but he was aware of it. His daughter, a second-year student in college, was there. He was telling me some story and he screamed at the top of his voice: "And I told him, I, Igor Gouzenko, tell you this." His wife was kicking him. He just forgot. He had total lapses of security. People would just look over.

Svetlana Gouzenko

On a Thursday night we went out for a dinner with James

Dubro and he wanted some movie [made] and he tried to persuade — attacking — my husband [that] he would appear without a hood. And my husband said: "What do you want to see in me? I lost my hair, I lost my teeth, I'm an old man. What do you want to see in me? I look handsomer with the hood over my head." He was in a good spirit.

James Dubro

It was the last supper, so to speak. It was a celebration. Now, his reason for having a meeting was quite different than mine. I wanted to convince him to have an interview full face for *The Fifth Estate* and he was beginning to come around to the idea of doing it. I was using the argument that he owed it to history. He was trying to sell me on the idea of a film being done on his novel *The Fall of a Titan*.

Karen Milne

I told his wife I'd help him set up an account in her own name because the cheque [from the Harper and Row settlement] had been made payable to Igor Gouzenko and he endorsed it as Igor Gouzenko. She didn't have an account in her own name as Svetlana Gouzenko and there were some problems in opening up an account because she didn't want any bank records showing her name and address. She also didn't have many documents proving who she was under that name. So she came to my office that Monday and I thought she was upset about something. She was very tense. But she was talking in a businesslike way and went over to the bank and made the arrangements and then came back to the office. And it was at that point that she said she had something to tell me and told me about her husband's death. It obviously affected her very much. I think even she was in a state of shock and that's why she was able to handle things the way she did. She was very, very broken about it. They were so close. She just couldn't believe it. She was totally broken up by the fact she had lost him. They were such close companions, not just husband and wife. They were always together.

Svetlana Gouzenko

We had a big dinner with Dubro. The whole [next] day he
didn't even have an appetite and all he was drinking is consommé and eating salad. . . . I had just read him the horoscope
and he said: "Where is the cash in this horoscope? What's the
horoscope if there's no money in it?" And I just said, there's no
cash for tomorrow. And he said: "Cash, how about you make for
me right now kasha?" Kasha is buckwheat porridge and that's
his favourite. But that's not something he should eat. And I
said: "No, I can't give you now because 'eat now, then go to bed'
that will be bad. But I will make for you tomorrow morning.
Then you will exercise all day. Then it will be all right. So you
can have it. What do you want now?" And he said: "Okay. Give
me a glass of consommé to drink but after I listen [to] this
[radio] program."

John Picton

He was conducting the orchestra when he had his heart attack.
He was listening to CFRB. He clutched his chest, she told me,
and let out a gasp and fell. Svetlana and her daughter were
there. They rushed over and one of them was trying to give him
mouth-to-mouth resuscitation and the other ran for the phone.
As he was being taken out the door on a stretcher he let out a
gasp and she said: "I knew that was his last gasp. I knew he was
dead."

Svetlana Gouzenko

[He was] just listening. Conducting. And then he bent over.
"Ohhh." Bent over on the table. [Mrs. Gouzenko re-enacts the
scene, leaning on the dining-room table where Gouzenko had
stood supporting himself with one hand on the table and covering the eyes and forehead with the other.] "Ohhh." [He] put his
hand like that. Then he stood up and he said: "Ohhh." I was
there — after reading the horoscope — and I jumped to him.

Peter Worthington

He was a very musical person. He used to listen to this thing
and was conducting it and in the middle of conducting he had a

heart attack. I always felt it was fortunate he died at home. If he had died in the streets of Toronto, who's to tell it isn't a cyanide gun or something like that? I probably would have been the first one writing about it. But there was nothing really suspicious in his death.

Svetlana Gouzenko

Wendy was at the telephone and she dropped the telephone. [I was] yelling: "Hang up. Call the ambulance." I have to call the ambulance. And she rushed here and [there was] this "Ohhh". Was a real strong "Ohhh". And that's [what it] was like: "Ohhh". Wendy was here: "What is it?" And he just took a deep breath and collapsed in our arms. We put him down on the floor. We're blowing and pushing, blowing and pushing. Wendy had to call the ambulance. I was blowing, pushing — out of breath myself. Then Wendy, after calling the ambulance, was blowing and I was pushing. We kept him like that until the ambulance came. And they came very fast. Seemed to be very fast. And right away they put oxygen on. I had my dressing gown on, so I had to rush upstairs, put some clothes on. [They] took him on a stretcher and took him [away]. The ambulance was rushing. And I looked at him in this oxygen mask and I just knew that he is not alive any more, because that was his last breath. And Wendy thought too that that was [his] last breath.

We rushed to the hospital very fast. Everything was very fast. And I touched him and he was still warm on the stretcher when they wheeled him away. And I kept asking all the attendants how long it takes a body to cool off. And they all said that it is quite a long time. So he was dead anyway but he was still warm.

Karen Milne

Apparently he died in a moment of intense joy. Mrs. Gouzenko was very pleased about that because she said there were so many other circumstances that he could have died under — I guess she was thinking of his earlier years when he could have been shot by the KGB, and over the years there could have been so many other ways he could have died. I think she was concerned that earlier that day she was out running errands for him. She was just very happy that she was there and some other family members were there and that he would die in a moment of peace and happiness — he was very happy about the settlement in the lawsuit. There was something else in the works that he was very pleased about. Considering the hard and difficult times he went through, it was one of the better periods.

Svetlana Gouzenko

He was so full of life. So many plans what we were going to do tomorrow and "Annie, you have to find this." And I had a big list of what I have to find, what to put down, and what to write and what to take. And three seconds and he was gone. Actually the pain [he felt] probably could be maximum only two seconds. The doctor's explanation was that he had a vein burst in his head which was in control of the heart. So all our blowing was for nothing because the nervous system already stopped working.

Karen Milne

She seemed very surprised by his death. She said she couldn't believe he died then and wanted him to live ten years longer. She thought they would have more time together. Apparently he had stated his preference for a small funeral. He didn't want the media there for the safety of his family. He specifically mentioned he wanted me there. In the last months we had been close, but specifically I think one of the reasons is that he felt I was a lot younger than most of the people who knew Igor Gouzenko. I guess I'd just live longer and talk about it longer for history. There was something about my youth that appealed to him — as well as the fact that we were close.

Svetlana Gouzenko

[His death was on] Friday night, the 25th of June, 1982. And he arrived in Canada on the 25th of June, 1943. Thirty-nine years later to the day.

Peter Worthington

The news got out because when I was taking the phone call

[about Gouzenko's death] I was on the phone to Barbara Amiel, who was associate editor then [of the *Toronto Sun*]. And she was on her way to CJCL radio station. She had a radio program that she did once a week. She was calling me about something and my secretary came into the office and said I was wanted on the phone, that another call had come in. I gestured that I would get around to that later and she wrote a note that Igor Gouzenko had died and that this was the phone call. So I said: "Oh Christ, Barbara, I've got to go. Igor Gouzenko has just died." She was interested. I went onto the other phone.

Andy Barrie, *broadcaster*
Barbara was in on my show and called her office just to see what was cooking and got word about Gouzenko's death. I forget what we were supposed to be discussing that day. She came in and said she could think of absolutely nothing that would be more important than to pay adequate tribute to Gouzenko. I wasn't sure we ought to do this, but she insisted it was so important and if I didn't agree that would be an excellent thing for us to talk about. So she went on the air and said she had just learned that Gouzenko had died and it really became in the course of her conversation a eulogy.

Peter Worthington
Meanwhile, unbeknownst to me, Amiel is so distraught over the loss of this legendary counter-espionage coup that she scrapped the text she was going to give and launched into a eulogy into the death of Igor Gouzenko and what he meant to free men everywhere. It's interesting the radio station didn't want her to do it. They said: "Who's Igor Gouzenko? What does that mean? Why do you want to waste all this time on that?" Anyway, she insisted and gave her eulogy to Igor.

Andy Barrie
We talked for about fifteen or twenty minutes and by the end of her item the newsmen from our own newsroom were coming in to say they were getting calls from the wire services and could they confirm it. There was no other way to confirm the story.

Nobody knew where Gouzenko's family was.

Peter Worthington

The next thing that happens, apparently, is that she isn't off the air when other people start calling back asking: "When did he die?", "How did he die?" Now other news stations are starting to call. So Amiel says: "Peter Worthington told me." By this time I'm getting calls saying: "Amiel says you know." I'm saying: "If Amiel says the thing, you ask Amiel. Don't ask me." I wouldn't talk to them about it. Gouzenko's executor from National Trust calls me: "What's this I hear?" I told him. Then the Mounties call. They don't know. So then the agencies are calling.

Andy Barrie

She was really scooping herself. It was going to be page one news in the *Sun* the next day and it's likely if she hadn't discussed it on my show it would have stayed out of the news for another full twenty-four hours. . . . It was one of the major stories the *Sun* was going to break. It was made out to be funny later and people felt it was cute she scooped herself. But to be fair, I don't think she realized that Worthington at that time was the only one in possession of that information. For all she knew, it had come over the wire services.

Peter Worthington

This was happening at noon and then I'm dashing off [to the funeral] wondering if I'm going to be trailed. But nobody was thinking of that. Basically I could see no particular need for the secrecy except that the family has lived so long in secrecy that they can't live any other way. They feel comfortable with it. And if they want a quiet funeral it's their privilege.

Karen Milne

[It was] a very quiet family funeral. It was at one of those chapel funeral homes in the west end. His immediate family were all there, the children and the husbands and wives and some of the grandchildren were there. . . .

I came early and spent a little time in the anteroom off to the side where the family was. I spent quite a bit of time talking to Mrs. Gouzenko and the children whom I had met. From time to time some of his older children came into the office with them. So I was expressing my grief.

Peter Worthington arrived. He came just before it started. He was the other person Mrs. Gouzenko was quite concerned that should be there.

Peter Worthington

It was a small funeral home out in Mississauga at a certain hour. So I went out there and there was myself, this woman lawyer, and the family. Big family, they had about ten kids. They were all up there. The body was up at the front of the chapel, an open coffin. The minister was wearing World War Two medals and maintained the legend about Mr. Brown from Prague. So it was Mr. Brown. I'm sure the minister didn't know, but he maintained this legend to the family, myself, and this woman lawyer, and we kind of looked at each other. Then the minister went into a eulogy about the fact that I was there, which puzzled the bejesus out of me, why he would centre on the outsider. I suppose he knew who he was, I don't know. He must have known. But he gave no indication he knew whom he was dealing with.

Karen Milne

It was a very simple service. There was a pastor from some church, I don't remember which one — someone who had known the family. The family was seated up front. Peter and I were seated a few rows behind.

Peter Worthington

The family then went up and in Russian tradition lined up in order of rank and kissed the corpse. It was a very touching kind of moment. I remember wondering whether his life had been worth it — would he do again what he did then with his life? Because there were no friends there; there were no contacts there; he was being buried anonymously and he had not had a comfortable life; he was not a tranquil man, he was always a fighter. Would he have done it if he had to do it again? Really it answered itself. Because here was a guy with this family around him and they were clearly just devoted to him. They thought he was wonderful. The outside world may think one thing but his kids and the grandkids and in-laws thought he was really something special. That is the mark of a fairly successful parent. And the other thing is that all his kids were doing well. When you produce ten or eleven kids in this world and they're all living free, contented, and successful lives, if that means anything that's a successful life. Then the third thing, which is his own personal triumph, I always figured, was that he died peacefully. He beat the system. For big-name defectors to die quietly — a lot of them die violently, car accidents or jump from windows or other strange things. But Gouzenko defied the odds that way.

Karen Milne

The service in the chapel couldn't have been more than half an hour. They had a few songs and then we all went out to the cemetery.

Peter Worthington

After the ceremony, which was relatively brief, we all jumped into the funeral cortege with the black cars and everything. I took my car because I was going to work after. All these cars had these little cloth funeral flags up and we were going to inconspicuously drive to the cemetery, which was along the 401. Well, this funeral was straight out of *Monty Python*, I got to say. We went sedately with our lights on up to Highway 401 and then went at about sixty miles per hour for about ten minutes, racing along at break-neck speed and all the flags flew off. Anything it was not was inconspicuous. Then we raced through whatever town it was into the cemetery, and to the scream of brakes we all pulled up outside and hustled out quickly and buried him in a small ceremony. The minister leapt into his car and vanished very quickly and the family had a few brief words with me and then everybody scattered. Twenty minutes later it was as if it never existed.

Jack Batten, *author*

I had finished writing *In Court,* which had a chapter on the great litigation lawyer Joseph Sedgwick, who successfully defended Eric Adams in the spy trials and cross-examined Gouzenko and didn't think much of him. The chapter was written through Sedgwick's eyes. It was to come out in the fall of 1982 but in late June that year, on a Saturday night, I was at a party and met June Callwood. Gouzenko had recently started suing her over her history book and we started talking about Gouzenko. I said: "I've just written this chapter," and I told her what was in this chapter and she said: "He'll sue. He'll sue." So the following Monday I phoned Macmillan and said: "Listen, I've got to change part of that chapter. I've got to soften it up." They said: "Well, it's going to cost money." I said: "Look, June Callwood says he'll sue. We better avoid this." Right away I'm thinking there will be some kind of injunction. The book won't come out. It won't earn any money. It's censorship but I've got to get the book out.

Anne Holloway, *editor*

He came to me and said: "I'm really worried. I had this conversation with June Callwood and Gouzenko is really ruining her life and she was warning me how litigious he is." He already knew that and thought he had put in only the very necessary references to Gouzenko. Even so he was nervous. Jack is a lawyer and knows how long and complicated a suit can be.

Jack Batten

I went down to Macmillan's offices and went through the galleys. The book was in the late production stages. I couldn't cut lines, so I had to fit everything out to the same length. I couldn't take Gouzenko out but changed all this stuff that I thought Gouzenko might go after. I softened up everything.

Anne Holloway

As we were sitting there doing this he was saying: "If somebody would bump off this son-of-a-bitch. He's the biggest problem for Canadian writers." We joked back and forth in this vein for a while.

Jack Batten

I finished it and went down to the parking lot and got into the car and started the motor and drove out and switched on the radio right at the five o'clock news. The first item was "Igor Gouzenko is dead." I thought: "That son-of-a-bitch. He's done it to me from the grave." I got home and phoned down to Macmillan. Nobody was there, so I phoned the next day and said: "Let's put all that stuff back in." They said: "It's too late. It's gone to the plant." So that's how Gouzenko had reached out.

Franc Joubin

He was quite revealing when pressed with questions. He told me from his early teens he dreamt of becoming a great writer in the field of historical novels. I've often wondered if he found himself in a situation where he thought: "By God, I can exploit this into my novel and be the hero of the novel." When it was all over, that was the impression I was left with. I often wonder if in his strange mind of fantasy he wasn't living the role of the hero he might have imagined.

What the Neighbours Say

Karin Middleton

I think there were some neighbours, especially the new neighbours, that didn't know. But I suspect quite a few knew. But I never talked to them until after he died.

Margaret Hale

I think we felt that this was just something between ourselves and we wouldn't breathe a word to anyone else who they were just because we didn't want any harm to come to them. No, it was just kind of a neighbourhood secret, if there is such a thing.

Ruth Gilmore

No one really talked about it that much because everyone was trying to let them lead as normal a life as possible. . . . We just always assumed that he must know [that we knew]. But I don't know. He never talked about it.

Karin Middleton

I heard it through the grapevine. Some of their friends said something and I think they knew they could trust me. They told me: "I think I can trust you, Karin, but did you know that such and such — " I said: "Oh." I said: "Well, this is as far as it will go because I think it's safest for me that way in case there is any problem that I am aware of." And I heard through another branch of the grapevine, shall I say, something and as I say we strictly kept it to ourselves. I didn't even tell our immediate family.

Marilyn Maxey

Even before I knew who he was my kids were playing back and forth and just as a matter of conversation I said to the kids: "Where does your dad work?" They said in a hardware [store]. That didn't stagger me. The voters' list would come out and they'd have him down as a mining engineer. And I thought, "That's strange." Things just never added up. My suspicions led me to believe that's who they were. But my husband did tell me that's who they were. I don't know how he found out.

Karin Middleton

He was very interested in us, where we came from, what nationality and so on. . . . He was very interested, and yet we were not able to get that much information from them. Well, you asked him what he did or what his occupation was, he was an author or a writer, he wrote things, but you couldn't get much farther ever. So, in other words, what we knew about him was vague, whereas we were able to tell him my husband did this and did that and so on.

Marilyn Maxey

I had only moved into the neighbourhood a couple of weeks or maybe a month or so and a lady came down and said to me: "Don't let your kids go over there to play," she said, "because they're going to throw a bomb at the house." I thought the woman was off her stick. I said: "Why?" and then she said something about he's a Russian spy or something. And, oh God, I phoned my husband at the office and I said: "My God in heaven. I thought you said this was a good neighbourhood." And, of course, I was terrified. My one son chummed with one of their sons and my daughter chummed with their daughter.

And I was just sick. I was just a little too young to remember the story. But I was very, very worried. And they were such nice people. And I thought, well, I've always been a fatalist and if that's the way it's to be I guess it's going to have to be. Because how could you hurt little children?

Margaret Hale

I was standing at the bus stop and I tried to make conversation on one occasion and I didn't get any response from him at all. So, of course, I just ignored it. And I realized that perhaps that he had every good reason for not wanting to speak to a complete stranger. He didn't know who I was. And under the circumstances knowing who he was I wasn't offended by him not speaking.

Marilyn Maxey

They had to tell an awful lot of lies to cover an awful lot of things. It was a terrible way to have to live. Believe me, he paid an awful price for defecting as far as I'm concerned. I can remember one time the kids were out where the school is now — it was just a field — and there were some men in there and they left their cars on the street. He [Gouzenko] came to the door and he was very, very nervous. My mother was here at the time. And he said: "Oh, where's Mrs. Maxey? Where's Mrs. Maxey?" She said upstairs. And, my God, he flew upstairs. I was making the bed. And he said: "Please go out and see what those men are doing out there. Cindy's missing." That was his daughter. I just knew they had a fear that his kids would be taken or something would happen. You could tell. You could feel it. I went out there like a nut and asked them what they were doing. They were picking grape leaves. They were making something like a cabbage roll. We even checked it out. Another person and myself had a cookbook and sure enough it was true. They were really doing that. But it did look very suspicious. Men in suits picking grape leaves.

Margaret Hale

I read many accounts where they were complaining about not

getting enough money from the government, but the children never seemed to do without things, so I didn't give too much thought to that.

Marilyn Maxey

I had been to the house many times. I could see that they were in need. I think it was through Stan. He came to the door one night or something. I'd even lent them money. They were in need. She asked me and I gave it to her. And she always paid back.

Ruth Gilmore

He made no secret of it [his financial difficulty] when you talked to him. They were always having a hard time with one thing or another. Now and again he'd be exasperated. I mean, this wasn't very often because we didn't see him that often. But I think our government had more or less promised him some things that weren't forthcoming, because for a long time I don't think people realized how valuable the information was that he'd given them. And I think they're only beginning to realize now what he'd tried to tell them that many years ago.

Margaret Hale

I had a great deal of admiration for him. I felt he did Canada a great service, one I don't think people know enough about. Not everybody has read the book [*This Was My Choice* by Igor Gouzenko] and realized what he went through in order to provide Canada with the knowledge that he imparted. He put himself in a great deal of self-imposed danger.

Marilyn Maxey

He was an excellent father. If there was a movie and the children, when they were small, wanted to see it, he would always go to that movie before the kids did. He went and saw the movie before the kids were allowed to see it. There's not very many fathers who would do that, let me tell you. He didn't like obscenity. He was fanatical against communism. He was a real straight guy.

Karin Middleton

[He was] mild-mannered, good sense of humour, easy to talk to, but certainly [had] very definite political views about the different parties in Canada and who he thought was good or bad. He always tried to make his guests feel very much at home, made sure they were happy, had enough to eat. I always remember sitting there munching our cheese and caviar — little crackers sprinkled with caviar. Caviar you don't have often, but it was just a sprinkling, of course. But he said: "Oh, take more. Take more." He was always anxious that we were well satisfied.

Marilyn Maxey

She would come over to the house. We were really good friends, really good friends. Personally I think it was an honour to know them and to know her and to know the family, because I think they're terrific. Just terrific. They were wonderful neighbours to me. And wonderful to my children. She is one of the kindest people you'll ever meet. She is a lover of children. She's a super, super lady. Of course, a lot of people might have seen them as telling lies, but they had to tell a certain amount to protect their own self.

Ruth Gilmore

He had built this giant fountain in the backyard and used to spend a lot of time fiddling with that. I guess he spent a lot of money on that that seemed kind of foolish. It was about twenty feet in diameter and I don't know if it worked. But it was meant to shoot a great fountain of water in the air.

Marilyn Maxey

I had raised a baby bluejay my daughter found in the field. And he came to take a picture of the bluejay when I fed it and when it grew up. It was nothing for him to sit down at the picnic table and have a chat with you. I always thought he was a very nice person. He took out a pad and pencil one day and sketched my granddaughter. He was a very talented artist.

Ruth Gilmore

The children all played together and they had an enormous backyard. It used to be all grown up in tall grass. Those kids got out there and you couldn't see them. So you had to go out looking for them.

Marilyn Maxey

He'd walk through the fields. But I never, ever, saw him walking on the street alone. Not to my knowledge he never walked alone. This is my opinion, it's terrible to walk around a corner and think a gun's going to be pointed at your head and blow your brains out.

Did Mackenzie King Fumble When Gouzenko Defected?

J. L. Granatstein

Mackenzie King at first felt the appearance of Gouzenko was very curious. If this man was a defector with documents, there was a potential for trouble. If he wasn't a genuine defector, there was again a potential for trouble. Mackenzie King, as we all know, was not someone who liked trouble. He avoided it, unless it had to be faced and dealt with. I think Mackenzie King, like [Norman] Robertson, was sceptical. Robertson, however, was much more willing to grab Gouzenko to see whatever he had. You could always give him back if you had to. The important thing in Robertson's view was to find out where he was and what he had. For the moment, nothing happened. The government did not act and Gouzenko was left to wander the streets.

Gary Marcuse

When Gouzenko defected, the matter of spies in the civil service was not a large issue in the mind of the Canadian government. There were bigger issues: the explosion of the atomic bomb; the enormous tension at the United Nations; the difficult questions surrounding the withdrawal of Soviet troops from the Middle

East; and the formation of governments in Eastern Europe. All these took precedence in King's mind when he considered what embarrassment Gouzenko could cause his government. He didn't want the Canadian government to cause the disruption of these much larger world events.

J. L. Granatstein

It has always struck me that Mackenzie King's response was (1) typical of Mackenzie King — cautious, and (2) fairly sensible in the circumstances. At this point no one knew who Gouzenko was and what he was carrying, whether he was a crackpot, a crank, a lunatic, or an *émigré* out to cause trouble. Nobody knew anything about him. So it seems on September 6 that for the Canadian government to be sceptical was entirely right and proper, and not least because the Soviet Union was a friendly country at that point. It was an ally and we had good relations with it, and for the government to have acted in any other way on September 6 would seem to me to be highly unusual.

Jack Brayley

You had to put yourself into the situation of the time. We were admiring the Russians for their stand at Stalingrad and for what they were doing. There were regular meetings of the Friends of Russia and right-wing people, Roman Catholic priests and the Bronfmans were in on it. I can remember covering a Friends of Russia rally in the Forum in Montreal where Eleanor Roosevelt spoke. That was the feeling at the time and that's why I think Mackenzie King didn't want anything to do with Gouzenko. He didn't want to spoil this great wave of love for Russia which was sweeping the country. I'm no champion of Mackenzie King, but he's not being treated fairly by some of the biographers who have suggested Gouzenko was forgotten, which he was, but there was a reason for it. The attitude at the time was that we love the Russians and it mustn't be forgotten. And no Korean plane had been shot down to disturb people.

Arnold Smith

When I first came back from Russia in December [1945] — this was before I knew about Gouzenko — I had been warning about a lot of the post-war plans based upon the false assumption there was going to be close co-operation between the so-called Great Powers. I said there was not going to be a lot of co-operation, that there was going to be a lot of trouble with vetoes at the UN and you better do a lot of rethinking. I was advocating collective security, if possible, to get the Americans committed in advance to an alliance with Western Europe. And I wasn't getting replies. I would also put this into personal letters. I got one saying they knew the strain of no holidays during the three years there were very grave and after the war I would get a very long holiday. So when I came back — I was third secretary; acting second secretary — Mackenzie King asked me to come and see him in Laurier House. And I saw him alone one evening. And he talked. He said he was very impressed by the things I had written. And he said: "I'm inclined to agree with you. But I wouldn't have dared say these things to Parliament or to my cabinet. You must understand that a democracy must not make the all-out effort that is necessary to fight a war if it didn't believe that victory is going to be heaven, that we will live happily ever after. You must understand this. This is a cardinal rule of psychology."

Don Page

Mackenzie King . . . [believed] if we don't antagonize them [the Soviets], then they will be able to talk and we can have an accommodation. It goes back to his view of labour-management in terms of conciliation through arbitration and conference diplomacy. He was applying this in this particular case. He didn't want to antagonize them in any way that they would then break off diplomatic relations. If they don't talk to the allied side, then there would be an irreparable breaking of relations which would lead to nothing but conflict. He wanted to try and prevent that.

Consequences: The Impact of Gouzenko's Defection

Robert Fulford

I think the Gouzenkos' defection and the fallout, taken together, were a major historic moment in modern civilization. Until the moment of the Gouzenko defection the West was more or less settling into the public view of the Soviet Union being maybe not perfect but benign and very friendly. We had had to think that way during the war. From 1942 until the end of the war the Soviets were our dear friends and brothers, and even the most vehement anti-communist western statesmen, for example, Winston Churchill, were promoting the idea of brotherhood with the Russians. That continued after the war. I don't think we understood the nature of the beast, and Gouzenko changed that.

J. L. Granatstein

The simple answer is to say that the Gouzenko case started the Cold War. On one level that's true. But there's no doubt that relations with the Soviet Union were already entering a difficult period even before the war against Hitler was over. There were differences on how the Eastern European countries were going to be treated. There were differences on policy to Germany. There were conflicts on virtually everything. What Gouzenko did was to make the public aware of the fact for the first time that the Russians are not entirely our friends. What Gouzenko did was to make a propaganda, public-relations-type effect. Gouzenko was the beginning of the Cold War for public opinion. The Cold War was already under way for governments before Gouzenko, but for the public Gouzenko was very important.

Robert Fulford

If you were to say aloud during the war among any group of moderately liberal or forward-thinking people the Soviet Union is a giant concentration camp and they won't let people out and they are ruled by the secret police, you would be considered at best eccentric and probably a warmonger and maybe a maniac. Gouzenko changed all that. He changed the atmosphere of the West and its attitude towards the Soviets.

Merrily Weisbord

It had an effect on the world. Political dissent became subversion at that point. If you said anything that could at all be smeared with being red, it was subversive. The left-wing unions were purged. There was a very strong lobby for civilian and international control of atomic weapons. It was made up by all the top atomic scientists. The senate committee on atomic legislation was meeting and forming atomic policy and the spy trials came out in the middle of that and the civilian and international control lobby was wrecked. It was discounted. The concept of national security as opposed to global security became paramount. There were witch hunts in all the scientific centres in the United States.*

Ian Adams

I have come to the conclusion that if Gouzenko hadn't existed

---

*Read Merrily Weisbord's *The Strangest Dream* for an authoritative and detailed account of how the Gouzenko defection affected communists in Canada.

they would have had to invent him. His defection came at a wonderful time when there was tremendous resistance from the scientists involved in developing the atomic bomb. They wanted to see an open book on the development of nuclear power with everybody collaborating so that it wouldn't become the ungodly arms race that it did become and is today. So if Gouzenko hadn't fallen into the western intelligence services' lap, they would have had to invent somebody like him.

James Barros

That the Cold War started with Gouzenko is utter nonsense. The Cold War started in 1917 when the Bolsheviks took over Czarist Russia. But I think we really owed him a great debt. He alerted us more than ever before to the fact that the Russians are a threat to the national security of western democracy and that they would use every device and tool at every opportunity to do us in. I think the wartime alliance had dulled people to similar Gouzenko-type incidents which had occurred in the 1930s. We forgot all this with the war, and Gouzenko, with all this documentation and with his memory, shook us when we needed to be shaken. In that sense we owe him a debt.

Jim Littleton

You have to look at the defection in historical terms. It happened at an opportune time for Gouzenko and for the people in the West who wanted to make much of the Soviet threat. I see it more as a fairly minor event than as a cause of anything. It helped certain political processes occur that probably would have occurred anyway but I don't think it caused them to occur. He happened to be the right guy at the right time with the right kind of shocking revelations.

Peter Russell, *historian*

I think it's saying too much to say without him the alarm wouldn't have been raised. I think the alarm was going to be raised. It's just that his was the incident that did it. There were other espionage agents apprehended in Great Britain and the United States soon after Gouzenko and there have been plenty since, and any one of those would have raised it. But I think I'm right in saying that Gouzenko was the first major one in the West.

Robert Fulford

It [the Cold War] probably would have happened with Czecho-slovakia if Gouzenko hadn't come along. Many, many things happened after that but this was in fact the time it happened. Many other things could have caused it to happen. So you can't say it changed what would have otherwise been a period of happy relations between the West and East into a time of bad relations. But you can say the moment this change came about was the Gouzenko defection. I'm absolutely certain the Cold War began in Ottawa. I've argued that in terms of geopolitics it was the most important thing that ever happened in Canada — in terms of geopolitics.

Don Page

The operation of the [Canadian] legation in Moscow was virtually finished because no Soviet officials wanted to communicate with us. . . . [Canadian Ambassador] Wilgress was out of the country at the time and when the story broke he never went back to the Soviet Union. It was because of the strained relations and because the Russian ambassador had been withdrawn in protest about our revelations that we never sent our ambassador back to Moscow. In fact we didn't re-establish those kind of relations until 1955 when Pearson went to see Molotov in Moscow. We had a chargé d'affaires in those early days.

Arnold Smith

I think this was — apart from pre-war show trials — the West's first real awakening from the dream we would live happily ever after at the end of the war. I think it played an important part. It was not a sufficient part. It took Stalin's seizure of Czecho-slovakia and those things before we got a North Atlantic Treaty. It took several things, but they were all the sort of things a few of us had been forecasting.

Jim Littleton

The revelations were shocking. Nobody apparently thought the
Soviets were running a spy ring. Although there was a certain
amount of interest in the possibility of that, contrary to what a
lot of people have said about it. I have seen documents that
make it very clear that, for example, the U.S. State Department
and the Office of Naval Intelligence were keeping a fairly close
eye on what the Soviet Embassy in Ottawa was doing as early as
1943 and were pretty sure that [Second Secretary] Vitaly Pavlov
was an NKVD agent. Nevertheless, King was shocked, as one can
see by reading his diaries, and Robertson was dismayed. But at
the same time we know from the diaries and other documents
that they didn't immediately draw the conclusion there was a
vast conspiracy or effort to undo the country. The shock was
more that Canadians would do this, that there were civil servants
who would betray their country. That was the shock.

Merrily Weisbord

They were the first of the ideological show trials in the West.
They polarized the scene. It was "us" and "them". Traitors and
patriots. There was no grey area in between. It was treasonous
to talk about co-existence and co-operation and international
control of weapons. It took until very recently for a broad-based
anti-nuclear lobby to come back. The trials were the first western
volley of the Cold War.

Robert Fulford

I can remember night after night the headlines in the *Toronto
Star* and the building up of what seemed to be an appalling
mountain of evidence that the Soviets were involved in something extremely devious and dishonest. I was in my early adoles-
cence and the feeling was in the air. One reason it was so appalling is because we had at that time a more naive view of
espionage. We didn't understand that people do spy even on
their allies. Today if you were to discover that Washington was
spying on Paris, for example, I don't think you would be very
shocked. At that time nobody believed in such things. So an ally
spying on another ally was in itself shocking. Beyond that, they

were subverting government officials and acting generally in an extremely duplicitous way in Ottawa of all places. It seemed to reveal the nature of the Soviet Union in a way nothing could have at that time.

Stuart Keate

The whole case polarized a lot of the press. There were some lefties around who I think were quite innocent of any treason to Canada but they went around espousing left-wing views. And some on the right thought this was too serious to be kicking around, so they took their stand. You would go to a Montreal cocktail party or a reception at the Press Club and you would find half the guys there weren't speaking to the other half just because of this story. Gouzenko was the issue they polarized on. Some took the view he was a great servant of democracy and others saw him as a Russian spy and a traitor to his country.

Don Page

Canada had not been involved in intelligence operations prior to the Second World War. It was only because of our unique position as a member of the British Commonwealth and our closeness to the United States that we at this time got into cryptanalysis — the deciphering of enemy messages being transmitted by wireless telegraphy. Throughout the war this became a very valuable means of knowing what was going on internationally as well as getting a source of information apart from diplomatic reporting. At the end of the war a decision had been taken virtually to wind up the examination unit, our crypt-analysis effort, and our whole effort to be involved in international intelligence activities. Because of the Gouzenko revelations, that decision, made by the Privy Council Office, was overturned. So the operations that were scheduled to be wound up continued. That meant that when we got into the era of the Cold War we now had liaison with allied intelligence sources which we would not otherwise have had. That was important to us because it allowed us to know what the other major powers were thinking and on what basis they were making their decisions, and much of it was coming from intelligence sources which we would have been totally unaware of. I think a great deal of the credit as to why Pearson was able to astutely present proposals he knew would be accepted by the major powers was that, because of intelligence sources, he understood the basis on which they were making decisions and therefore could offer realistic proposals.

J. L. Granatstein

For the first time in our history there were genuine secrets in Canada that were worth passing to a foreign power. We are now used to being part of NATO and NORAD and having relatively good information about what our allies are doing. In 1945 we had been part of the grand alliance against Hitler and we had played a major role in war production and in the development of the atomic bomb, and there were things in Canada that were worth finding out. That too was unusual. If Canadians expected that the post-war world was going to be different, those sorts of secrets would again be in our possesion. What Gouzenko meant to the Prime Minister was that the post-war world was going to be, if anything, more difficult than the pre-war or the wartime world had been.

Don Page

We knew at that point [as a result of the Gouzenko disclosures] that the Russians had sufficient information about the atomic bomb that it was only a matter of time before they could develop an atomic bomb. Recognizing that, the whole tenor of inter-national negotiations took on a different atmosphere. . . . Had it not been for that, the Allies would have negotiated in all of the important international forums in the belief that the Soviets did not have the potential for this capability, and therefore they could have directed the Soviets into areas they might not have otherwise done.

Peter Russell

In 1946 in direct response to the Gouzenko spy revelations the Canadian government introduced a program of security screening in the federal public service to ensure as far as possible that people with access to secret information were trustworthy. Once that program of security screening is introduced it creates an intelligence requirement — they have to have information about the candidates for positions in government with access to secret information and also they have to have information about the activities they are worried these people might be engaged in. So Canada greatly expanded at that point the security and intelligence operation of the RCMP. I think you will find the same thing happened simultaneously in the United States and Britain, that the security screening programs were introduced in a much more formal way after Gouzenko and again with the need to expand the intelligence-collecting capability of their security agencies.

Don Page

Up to this time there had been no security clearances for public servants. People were known by their friends or by an old-boy network when they came into the department. Most of the officers came in because they were known by an officer in the department or they were known by a professor who was well known to the department and who wrote a letter of recommendation. But as far as the clerical and secretarial staff was concerned there was never any attempt made to do a security check on them at any level. Immediately after the Gouzenko affair they started to take the current secretarial and clerical staff and conduct security checks on them. And later that was done on officers, too.

J. L. Granatstein

In Ottawa nobody paid much attention to security. You had a simple padlock on filing cabinets. After Gouzenko there were safes, security officers, and classification levels on the documents which *are* taken seriously. There was a whole panoply that we now come to understand — if not entirely to accept — of the right of government to declare some information sensitive and the right of government to declare that some people are not trustworthy and with the right of government to try and pry into the attitude of those people who work for it. So the impact of Gouzenko was a major one in this area.

Don Page

The security of files and documents was notoriously weak in the department. There was an RCMP guard placed at the main door of the East Block, but that was the only hindrance to anyone walking into the East Block and taking virtually anything they wanted. Indeed, when they went around to inspect the filing cabinets, George Glazebrook's favourite trick was to kick the cabinet in a certain place which sprung the lock and all the doors flew open. Furthermore, it was traditional practice not to take the key for these cabinets with them or to guard them but that they would hide the key behind curtains or in some other place in the office so anyone with a little bit of knowledge of the operation or with a strong boot could have opened any of these cabinets. Well, of course, these cabinets were all replaced with secure ones.

Gary Marcuse

The Communist Party of Canada was totally devastated. The obvious involvement of senior members of the Communist Party laid the responsibility of the Gouzenko affair on the Communist Party as a whole. They tried to reverse that damage by disowning Sam Carr and Fred Rose, but clearly the damage was done. It outraged some members of the Communist Party who were much more interested in traditional political activities. A lot of members said: "This is stupid and ridiculous," and they blamed the Soviet Union. They said: "Why should the Soviet Union use members of a domestic political party to gather information? If they want it they should get it through traditional means which all countries engage in. Why use public political people?" They felt it was a waste and irresponsible. There was a lot of anger within existing party members. And if there was anger among the people who remained in the party, think of the people who left. Members were demoralized and it set back the party a lot.

William A. Reuben

In the fall of '54 I did three articles in the *National Guardian* [in New York] on the Canadian case in telescoped form of what I said later on in my book *The Atom Spy Hoax*. The interesting thing, I thought, was that the paper had a visit from Canada of two officials of the Communist Party of Canada, then called the Labor-Progressive Party. This was nine years after the story had broken. The editors kept me away from them and they talked to them and relayed the information to me. . . . All that I know is that the *Guardian* editors apparently believed enough in me and my documentation so that whatever the complaint that the Canadian left-wingers had, I never had to publish a retraction or a withdrawal or an apology or change a semicolon or anything. But these guys came down from Canada to talk to the editors and said: "You're running this stuff. You're ruining the whole Communist Party of Canada by challenging Gouzenko's story." They had bought the accepted version.

The Accused

Convicted

Fred Rose, Member of Parliament (Labor-Progressive Party)
Convicted by a jury in Montreal and sentenced to six years. Released in 1952.

David Gordon Lunan, Wartime Information Board
Convicted in Ottawa and sentenced to five years.

Edward Wilfred Mazerall, National Research Council
Convicted by a jury in Ottawa. Given four years.

Harold Samuel Gerson, Department of Munitions and Supply
Convicted in Ottawa and given five years. Conviction was quashed on appeal. Convicted in new trial and sentenced to four years.

Philip Durnford Pemberton Smith, National Research Council
Convicted in Ottawa and sentenced to five years.

Emma Woikin, Department of External Affairs
Pleaded guilty and given two and a half years. Also given six months for contempt of court in the Fred Rose trial.

Kathleen Mary Willsher, British High Commission
Pleaded guilty and given three years.

Dr. Raymond Boyer, McGill University
Convicted in Montreal and given two years.

Sam Carr, Organizing Secretary, Communist Party of Canada
Arrested in New York. Tried and convicted in 1949 in Ottawa and given six years.

Allan Nunn May, British scientist working in Canada on the Atomic Energy Project
Convicted in England.

John Soboloff, Toronto medical doctor
Charged with making an untrue or misleading statement to procure a passport and convicted. Fined $500.

Charges Withdrawn
Freda Linton, National Film Board
William Pappin, Passport Office

Acquitted
James Scotland Benning, Department of Munitions and Supply
Convicted; sentenced to five years; overturned by appeal court.
Henry Harris, Toronto optometrist
Convicted; sentenced to five years; overturned by appeal court.
Eric George Adams, Bank of Canada
Matt Simon Nightingale, Royal Canadian Air Force
David Shugar, Royal Canadian Navy
Agatha Chapman, Bank of Canada
Frederick Poland, Wartime Information Board
Israel Halperin, Canadian Army, Directorate of Artillery

W. Kenneth Campbell
I had to swear these people in to testify [at the Royal Commission]. I would look at them and think: "My God, why did you ever get mixed up in this thing?" Their testimony would unfold and you would find the reason. Some of them I felt were relatively stupid people. There was Willsher — Eric Adams persuaded her to do what she did — and there were several others who were stupid people. There was Mazerall. They were misguided and thinking that this was the right thing to do. Boyer was a professor at McGill and he said we were allies with the Russians and Canada should give the Soviets the RDX.

J. L. Granatstein

Some of them were ideologically convinced that the Soviet Union was the future of the world and anything they could do to help the Soviet Union was a good thing. Some others were Jews who were convinced that only the Soviet Union had fought the Nazis vigorously, that there was too much anti-Semitism in North America, and that Russia was different. Others were scientists who thought that it was a scandal that here the West was developing nuclear weapons and not sharing them as a matter of course with the Soviet Union when the Soviet Union was suffering so many casualties in the war. Others were people who were simply lonely. Kathleen Willsher, for example, strikes me simply as a lonely woman who was looking for something to do in Ottawa and found her way by chance into study groups that talked about Marxist literature and current events and from there slipped into passing information to Fred Rose. At least one of the people was sleeping with Fred Rose. I suppose he simply seduced her into passing information. The reasons vary, but it wasn't money. They did it either out of a straight ideological conviction or a misreading of current events and history that for them amounted to a kind of ideology.

Peter Benning, *son of Scott Benning*

My father wasn't a Marxist in the sense that the people in the movement in the seventies were. When he joined the party it just wasn't giving that kind of education to sympathizers and later to members. My father was an anti-fascist. His feeling, beginning with the war in Spain, was that the only people who adopted a consistent and effective anti-fascist position was the Communist Party of Canada. That's how he went into it. He went through the same agonies everybody else did during the Hitler-Stalin Pact and was happy and relieved when that ended and [he] could get back to the serious business of fighting fascism.

In the course of the work that he did, which was as secretary of the Department of Munitions and Supply, he was appalled to sit in on meetings of the department which were attended by fairly high-ranking members of the American, British, and

Canadian armies — colonels and above — who very openly said that the war against fascism was a temporary thing and once the war ended we would get back to the serious business of dealing with the communists. He had some horror stories to tell about attempts almost to subvert the Soviet efforts during the battle around Stalingrad. Treaties which called for the shipment of arms and ammunition to the Soviets were subverted in the sense that there were plans to send field pieces and ammunition of a different calibre, or weapons and no instruction manuals — that kind of thing — on the theory that they would let the Nazis and the Commies beat the shit out of each other on the eastern front and then come afterwards and mop up. That was what appalled him. There wasn't any serious dedication to the fight against fascism.

Merrily Weisbord

I think the wartime was an absolutely special time for people who were communists because there was an alliance with the Soviet Union. The Russians were the heroes of the Second World War and they were acceptable. Representatives of the Red Army were in Canada speaking on platforms with respected political leaders and cardinals. Eaton's flew the hammer and sickle. Stalin was on the cover of *Time* magazine as Man of the Year. In Ottawa the Soviet Embassy was one of the liveliest places to go. A Canadian colonel who testified at the Royal Commission hearings said Lt.-Col. Motinov was "a very cheery chap" and he liked him "immensely". It was a completely different world, and the communists had a vision of a post-war world where all the allies would work together and co-operate. They saw a different post-war world, one with significant social change even in Canada.

Ben Dworkin

Kathleen Willsher was a very mousy type of person. I lived next door to her for three years and never said hello. Her sin at the time was not giving away military secrets but giving economic information which was freely available from the Department of Trade or from the financial papers or anywhere else. In my opinion she would never be convicted today. It was almost a McCarthy type of atmosphere.

Merrily Weisbord

The newspaper headline at the time was: "Party Will Expel Rose If Appeal Fails — Buck". It's like the spy novels. When somebody is caught, they're out in the cold. That was what happened to Fred Rose. The Communist Party leaders cleaned their skirts of him. Their feeling was that it was a choice between the party and him. They tried to dissociate themselves from Rose and Carr. And Rose and Carr protected Tim Buck, the leader of the Communist Party. Fred Rose never named Tim Buck. Fred Rose never named anybody. Fred Rose never said anything because he didn't want to name anybody. He never took the stand at the trial.

Had it been up to Fred Rose and Raymond Boyer, among others, the trial would have been a political trial. They would have said what they did and why. But the decision was made by the central committee of the Communist Party not to have any joint defence or any political defence. It was to be fought individually with the use, for the most part, of establishment lawyers strictly according to law. There was a local Quebec Fred Rose defence committee but it was squashed by the central committee.

Peter Benning

My father was one of the accused who thought these trials ought to have been conducted politically before a jury. In 1947-48 you just couldn't put together a jury in which a father or a brother hadn't been killed or wounded in the war. And just set out very clearly what it was that these people had done. What kind of information had been communicated. Under what circumstances. And for what reasons. But the party made it very clear from the outset: "You're on your own. You are to make individual defences and you are not to claim any party affiliation." It didn't want to claim any affiliation with any of these people. The dilemma my father found himself in was that he found himself still loyal to the party as he was coming to the conclusion it was making the wrong decision about this as it had about a lot of other things. In the end he backed off.

Robert Keyserlingk

Boyer was another one of these guys. He just couldn't lie. He was an amazing idealist. He certainly didn't need money because I think his mother was a Fourget and he had the millions of the Fourgets behind him. But he was a complete and utter idealist who was doing it because he believed in it.

Merrily Weisbord

Raymond Boyer was working in a lab at McGill University. It was the lab developing the new process for making RDX which was later touted as this top-secret weapon. But the doors were open and students wandered in and out. The concept of security was completely different as far as Raymond Boyer was concerned. Security at the National Research Council was a personal oath and an ID card.

Despite the fact there was an agreement with the Russians to supply weapons, the new process for the mass production of RDX wasn't given when it was asked for in 1943. The Canadian government made it accessible to the Russians in 1944 but wasn't given at the time Raymond Boyer took it upon himself to give it to the Russians.

Doug How

You had this fellow Boyer . . . I don't think I covered his trial. This was in Montreal. He was one of the ones who knew that the Allies had developed the super-explosive called RDX and that they weren't going to give it to the Russians. He decided that the Russians should have it and that if the government wasn't going to do it he'd do it. Again, as I remember — maybe I did cover the trial — the judge said: "This is not your place to do that, rightly or wrongly."

Merrily Weisbord

Some of them felt Canada wasn't helping Russia with the war as much as it should, especially those involved with the military. And from the moment they had become communists, the Soviet

Union had always been the geopolitical centre of communism. There was also the myth that everything in the Soviet Union was perfect. Everybody worked and everybody had the right to an education. There was no racial prejudice. Everybody achieved according to his potential and got according to his needs. That's what they believed was really happening in the Soviet Union. When they saw that the Soviet Union was threatened, as several of them said to me, "Any one of us would have helped the Soviet Union."

Doug How

Benning, as I remember it, had a notebook with Fred Rose's phone number and the Mounties had seized it. The question that arose was, why did he have Fred Rose's phone number? He said that when he had come to Ottawa he asked Fred who might help him find an apartment. As I recollect the trial, it came down to: did the jury believe that it was the reason he had Fred Rose's phone number or did he have it for less honourable reasons? The jury looked at him and found him guilty, but a higher court eventually threw it out.

Peter Benning

If you read his case in appeal, it's a judgment in law. It's not that the jury came to a wrong verdict. The presumption created by either article three or article four of the Official Secrets Act sets out that anybody who is shown to have a document which establishes he is in communication with an agent of a foreign power is presumed to be acting for that foreign power. If that's reduced to the bare bones of its logic, you can have a telephone directory with Fred Rose's name in it — you can go that far. That's basically what the Ontario Court of Appeal found — to the extent that the judge at the trial charged the jury on the basis of that presumption, he did it wrongly.

Jack Brayley

Fred Rose was one of those arrested.* I used to ride home in the

---

*This happened a month after the other arrests, when the Gouzenko story had already been made public.

streetcar with him regularly. He was the Labor-Progressive Party Member of Parliament. I had a tip he was to be arrested, and at that time I went up to his office and said: "Fred, I understand they're going to pick you up." He said: "Oh no. Parliamentary privilege," or something like that. I said: "I hear you're going to be arrested." He said no. I said: "Well, I'm going to keep a check on you." So every once in a while I phoned from our parliamentary office to his and he said he was still okay. I think we went home on the Lindenlea streetcar together and when he got home I kept calling him from my home. I phoned regularly, and one time I phoned and said: "Are you still a free man, Fred?" He said: "Yeah. You've got it all wrong. You're wasting your time. Oh, just a minute, the Mounties are coming through the door." The phone hung up. I'll never forget that part of it. So I ran over there and saw the police whisk him away in a car.

Merrily Weisbord

Fred Rose and Sam Carr were a whole different kettle of fish. I just found out that Fred Rose during the war gave a letter to a man in uniform to deliver to somebody he said was a friend in Europe. The man he asked to deliver this letter saw Fred Rose's "friend" in the newspaper after the war arrested as a Soviet agent. That was a completely different level of involvement. . . . Fred Rose knew what he was doing.

J. L. Granatstein

It was quite extraordinary that the Royal Commission's report with its clear presumption of guilt was released before they were tried in court. I think one could argue that it was almost impossible for these suspected spies to have a fair trial after the Royal Commission report. What is so striking is that, despite that, so many of those people were found not guilty in court. That has always tended to confuse the issue. If they were found not guilty in court, then clearly they were not spying. That seemed to be the usual public response. But first, some of the evidence given at the Royal Commission could not be used in the courts. The government decided it was too sensitive and didn't introduce it. Secondly, there were legal questions involved in using stolen embassy documents as the basis of a prosecution. There were some real legal problems in using the material Gouzenko had brought out. What it came down to was that unless the people came clean and confessed their guilt, they almost all got off. If you read the transcripts of the Royal Commission, you will see that as time goes on — the hearings stretched from February to May — people began to say: "I won't say anything unless I can have a lawyer. I won't say anything to incriminate myself. I deny flatly everything I'm accused of." And when people said that, there was very little evidence that could be taken to court against them, whether they were guilty or not.

Vera Rosenbluth, *writer and broadcaster*
The commission report talks about some people not committing any crime but having the character so that they would have if asked to. They asked one man how many feet of Marxist literature he had in his library. He tried to explain he had a very vast library. They still insisted on literally measuring the number of Marxist books he had. They obviously intimidated the women. One of them particularly was asked: "Do you know what can happen to you?" She said: "Yes, I know I can be shot." In terms of what was written there, no one disabused her of that.

Wes Harvison
I think it was Durnford Smith who broke down in court and denied the things the defence were trying to say about third degree and so on. I don't know if this ever has been printed but the defence was trying to make out that they had been held in deplorable conditions which amounted to third degree and all the rest of it. In fact, where they were being held was exactly the place where my father himself either a year later or a year earlier did the Canadian Police College course. It was officers' quarters. It was barracks. It was where their own people were housed. And they were not threatened and they were not abused, although obviously the defence is going to try to make that claim. Durnford Smith broke down in court and said: "No, it's not true; Harvison is a hell of a swell guy."

Merrily Weisbord
Most of them belonged to Section 13, which was the secret

professional section of the Communist Party of Canada. It was made up of professionals — scientists, teachers, architects, artists — the darlings of the movement, people the Communist Party felt could lead the popular-front groups that were growing up in the late thirties. For example, Raymond Boyer was the president of the scientific association. Dr. Norman Bethune worked in a broad-based health group. Others led the Civil Liberties Union, the Committee to Aid Spanish Democracy. And, as communists, they had a history of working in illegality. Until 1935 you could be jailed in Canada under Section 98 of the Criminal Code for being a communist. Then came the Padlock Law in Quebec. So a lot of them in Quebec were mimeographing leaflets in their basement and handing them out at the factory gates while one of them kept a lookout for the cops. They were publishing *Clarté* and *The Clarion* in the Laurentian mountains and smuggling it into town and dropping it into different houses. There was a whole clandestine life going on. Then came 1939 and they were illegal because they were supporting the Nazi-Soviet Pact. So they were banned under the War Measures Act and internment camps were set up and the whole party went underground from 1939 to 1941. They had safe houses and all this shtick.

Then came the war. And Soviet Intelligence chose Section 13 to draw upon because they weren't known. First it was always the soft approach. To the guy who ran the National Research Council information network, the approach would be: "Write something about Canadian politics so we can clue them into the post-war world." This guy was a writer, so he started writing about politics so the Soviets would have a better idea of Canada. The next thing was: "Why don't you speak to a few other guys and find out what's happening in radar?" That's one case.

Two things were operating. One was a tradition of working in illegality. "You have to take chances. You have to fight for what's right." Then the second thing was this beginning soft touch. But that's not true for all cases. Some knew exactly what they were doing and they thought it was right. But none of them knew that there was a network. That's a fact. Each one of them thought they had made an existential, unique decision. The only ones who knew there was a network that I know of were Fred Rose, Sam Carr, and Tim Buck.

W. Kenneth Campbell

The other one I thought was quite wrong was Pappin — the passport office. If you read the evidence of Madame Soulière — she was in charge of the dead-file section — she was the corroboration of the evidence against Pappin. She appeared before the Commission and there appeared to be no question about her evidence. She gave it forthright. And on that basis the Commission named Pappin. But at the trial she changed her story. She couldn't remember anything or she was sick or didn't appear. Anyway, that vital evidence was missing.

Gary Marcuse

Information about submarine warfare was turned over, but it is less dramatic when you realize what was being discussed was information concerning the type of paper being used in a certain type of subsurface detector. The information was not particularly secret or exotic. A lot of the information passed on was definitely a violation of the Official Secrets Act. But John Cartwright, the prosecutor in most of the Gouzenko spy trials, whom I interviewed in 1978 two years before his death, said he found that none of the information was of any value. In addition to that, he said he thought the sentences handed out by the judge, McRuer, were certainly severe enough. He shook his head a little and said: "Though obviously Justice McRuer wouldn't have thought so, because he was the one who gave them." Cartwright gave an example of this fellow who was over in a café in Hull and had given to a Russian chap some information that a week later was released at an air show in Britain. That was typical of the kind of information. If you scrape away the rhetoric and look at what actually happened in court, the information wasn't really of any value.

Merrily Weisbord

Most of them didn't realize at the time of the trials how crucially the world was going to change. During the war there was an informal Liberal-Labor coalition. Communists helped the Liberals organize their election. They spoke on platforms with Liberals. Some communists were elected to municipal and provincial bodies. Almost every major city had a communist alderman. People like Raymond Boyer didn't realize how much the mood would turn. I think that's one of the reasons why when he was arrested he talked.

Doug How

One thing struck me as I was covering the trials, that was the number of accused who had gone to McGill in the thirties. I would think half a dozen. Fred Poland, I think, had. Matt Nightingale had, as I remember it. David Shugar had. I think Durnford Smith had. It made you wonder that perhaps there was a little Cambridge that went on there, probably on the same basis that there were a number of people who were honestly conviced that the capitalist system had had it. I don't find it terribly strange that they would have been, but I guess the strange thing was that they had pursued this and the Russians had come in and exploited it for their own purposes.

Merrily Weisbord

For example, one of those later arrested was editing the Canadian army newspaper during the war and he was deeply involved in post-war social issues — housing, education, medicare for returning veterans. Everything was forward-looking. At the time he was arrested he was helping Paul Martin write his speech at the first plenary session of the United Nations.

Hon. Paul Martin, *retired cabinet minister*

I was in London in January 1946 for the first General Assembly meeting of the United Nations as head of our delegation. Mr. St. Laurent had been our head but had to leave because he had to return to Ottawa in connection with the Gouzenko matter. It was so secret even I didn't know why Mr. St. Laurent went back. And Gordon Lunan, who was one of the suspects, was the communications man for our delegation. He left the delegation a month later to return to Ottawa so he could be arrested. Of course, he didn't know what would happen to him. We told him he was getting a new assignment.

Merrily Weisbord

Raymond Boyer said to me: "Today we know we won the war. But the end of '42 was a low point. We were losing everywhere. German subs were sinking almost all the ships on the way to the front. The Nazi army was on the Volga. The United States hadn't even started to get going. Victory was a long way from assured." There was a certain exigency that they felt about helping the Soviet Union. They were naive about the context in which they were making their decision, but there was an exigency, a real exigency.

Greg Guthrie

I remember a terrible confusion arose with the interpreter. The word at issue was "network". I remember a tremendous dispute between the lawyer and interpreter. Apparently there are about twelve words in Russian for network depending on what sort of a network it is. They have one that applies to railway lines, another one for fishing nets. There was quite a hot dispute about that.

Doug How

No two trials were exactly alike. I remember these two brothers-in-law . . . Gerson and Benning. The Crown lawyer was John Cartwright, who eventually became the Chief Justice. He was very gentlemanly. He always reminded me of Mr. St. Laurent. They were unusually gentlemanly versions of their callings. I think he finally one day stooped to calling the Russian Embassy "this house of infamy". You could almost see him reeling back thinking: "Oh my God, what have I done?" The evidence was that these two brothers-in-law had been providing the Russian Embassy almost daily with copies of typewritten accounts of every bloody munitions sent out by the munitions department, which was C. D. Howe's department.

Wes Harvison

My main recollection of my father's attitude towards the defendants was that they were decent people. Now, this doesn't go for all of them. He had nothing but contempt for Fred Rose, but for the engineer types, Durnford Smith and Ed Mazerall and so on, he almost felt sorry for them because they were really victims. They were culpable, of course, but he said these people were politically naive, as the Russians themselves said in their files on them. They were taken in and in a couple of cases made to feel they were really big-time stuff. Between genuine concern for the issues the Russians put in front of them and a certain romantic feeling, they were thoroughly sucked in. Now, there were others he didn't have that feeling for.

Don Page

The impression Emma Woikin had given people in the Department [of External Affairs] who knew her was that she had had a most unfortunate life. She married when she was sixteen into a very desperate situation with just no money in the household. Her husband had gone mad and hanged himself. She discovered him hanged in the house and had to cut him down. Her child had died young and she had come into the Department quite recently, probably around 1944-45. She had been known as a quiet employee and just a couple of weeks before the Gouzenko revelations had been given a promotion for her work. But she had been really struggling in life and people felt sorry for her. When her defence came up, her argument was: "Well, I understood that the Russians could do something about poverty and I wanted to help them do this." And that fitted in with her character. It wasn't as if she was a committed communist or anything of that nature.

Merrily Weisbord

She knew she was doing something secret. She knew she was going into those telegrams and taking them out. Just as Scott Benning knew he was taking stuff from the Department of Munitions and Supply through the security — because there was some security there. Sure, they knew they were doing illegal stuff. But they had done illegal stuff before. And the confusion in their minds was that helping the Soviet people was helping the Canadian people, since it was helping the brotherhood of man and the evolution of the working class. In their minds they weren't helping the Soviets as opposed to the Canadians. They were helping the world.

Wes Harvison

One thing my dad couldn't get over during the pre-trial detention was that there never was a night that Durnford Smith didn't sit down and write a delightful children's story for his kids. My dad said how a guy with what was on his mind could write really delightful material like that for his kids really got to him. And he said it told him something about the sort of man he was.

Doug How

One day I was walking down a corridor and M. J. Coldwell, the leader of the CCF, stopped me and asked: "Aren't you covering the spy trials?" I said: "Yes." "Have you covered the Mazerall one?" I said: "Yes, I have." I knew him fairly well and had a great respect for him. Everybody in Parliament did. He said: "I'm very troubled about that case. You know, he never really gave the Russians anything." I guess this was true. He was a classic case where the Russians come to him and he decides to have it both ways. He'll give them something but it is something that is going to be made public almost immediately. And this is what he did. So I think he thought: "Well, okay, I haven't let down the side. At the same time I really haven't let down the NRC [National Research Council]." And Coldwell said: "I find that sending a man to prison for four years and ruining his career on that basis, I find that pretty hard to take." I said: "Well, I don't think I can do any better, Mr. Coldwell, than to quote you what the judge said. He said 'That wasn't the point at all. He had sworn an oath of loyalty to the government of Canada, and if he had carried out his oath of loyalty, his real task was to report immediately the fact that surreptitious efforts were being made to get information.'" In other words, he had been disloyal to his own country. Coldwell said: "That satisfies me." He walked away quite jauntily. He said: "That's right. That's true."

Merrily Weisbord

When the Royal Commission examined the trial suspects they tried to prove that the suspect was a communist, and a lot of the interrogation was about study groups, *Tribune* subscriptions, support for the Ford strike or for the Soviet Union, friends who were communists. The Royal Commission wasn't supposed to prosecute. It was supposed to be a fact-finding body, but in fact it attempted all the time to create statutory presumptions — the burden of proof — in favour of the Crown. They tried to set it up for the trials. They tried to do so with Agatha Chapman proving she was a communist even though she was later acquitted. And in doing so they quoted 3-2 of the Official Secrets Act and this is it: "On a prosecution under this section it shall not be necessary to show that the accused person was guilty of any particular act tending to show a purpose prejudicial to the safety or the interest of the state and notwithstanding that no such act is proved against him he may be convicted if from the circumstances of the case *or his conduct or his known character is proved* [their italics] it appears his purpose was prejudicial to the safety or the interest of the state." And that's where Gouzenko came in. He set up the reality as strongly as he could all communist purpose was prejudicial to the interest of the state. Simply to be a communist was prejudicial to the state. That was the new Cold War reality. And that's why Gouzenko was so important.

APPENDIX E

The Accused Revisited

Jim Littleton

They're up in their sixties and seventies now. Most of them are still in Canada. Allan Nunn May wasn't Canadian and he left the country and didn't come back. Fred Rose left and died.

Merrily Weisbord

It was very difficult to speak to anybody about the trials. People had gotten burned so badly that they didn't want to talk. Among the first, I guess, was Raymond Boyer and we talked about many things before we talked about his trial. He had two trials, each one for about a month. Same judge. He didn't like to talk about the trials and would have rather have forgotten the whole thing, which is how I think most of them feel.

Vera Rosenbluth

They weren't making philosophical arguments. These are people in their seventies now who still shake with fear and anger too when they think about it. It's not a rational debate: "Should we talk about it or not?" It's terrifying for them. The nightmare didn't end at that point. It just began for them.

Jim Littleton

In the course of doing the research for the film series *On Guard for Thee* I tried to find as many of the people arrested as I could and try to persuade them to appear in the film. I talked to seven or eight of them either in person or on the phone. What struck me most strongly was the way in which all these people had been traumatized by the experience of having been named by the Royal Commission. Some were charged and some weren't. But in every case it was an experience that even thirty-seven years later was clearly the most important experience in their lives. This was true of every one of them separately. Usually they were unwilling to talk about it. With a lot of discussion and persuasion they would talk about it to a certain extent, providing I was very careful with them. They had an extremely deep resentment of that entire episode. I would say everyone who would talk about it felt they had been treated tremendously unfairly and were tremendously resentful of the way they were arrested and held incommunicado and confronted with the facts from sources they didn't know and that they didn't have legal counsel and all that sort of thing. Those who were charged and tried then faced Gouzenko in the courtroom and they had no respect for him whatsoever and did not think he was speaking truthfully. They did not think he was speaking of anything he knew directly.

Vera Rosenbluth

Gary Marcuse and I together set out to investigate the events surrounding Gouzenko's defection and the spy trials. We wanted to do a radio documentry and very soon into the research wanted to avoid naming names and that a documentary was going to be difficult, so we ended up doing it as a documentary-drama on CBC-Radio called *Official Secrets*. . . . I talked to people who are now in the late sixties and seventies and they were so upset they couldn't continue. I was very surprised by that. There was some ambivalence: Should we talk about it or shouldn't we? It was a tortured decision. They are bright people and they know it needs to be talked about and their fear is it won't bring out the entire truth as they suspect it. So they feel that if the whole truth can't be known, to let it be and not dig up old ghosts.

Merrily Weisbord

I bothered and harangued and harassed one guy who knew me

who refused to speak to me for three years. In the process of the final rewrite of my book I said: "I have to talk to you. I don't understand. I just don't understand. I have to come and talk to you." So he said: "Okay, you can come tonight." I had found a deposition he had made at the time of his arrest which was most dramatically written. It reads like a play. You get the whole set-up of what an arrest was like. But it still didn't tell me why he had talked. His talking was crucial in Commissioner Harvison's breakthrough. Although I had a clue from Benning's wife. When Scott Benning was arrested they could get no information at all about him. They didn't know where he was. They didn't know how he was. He had a landlady who was going out with an RCMP agent. She said: "Find out how he is, please, please." So the landlady came back the next day and said: "My boyfriend said everything is all right. The worst thing that can happen is he'll get shot." That was the reality this guy spoke about. I drove out to his house and spoke to him and his wife. I slept there. We spoke late into the night. His reality was that he was in the army, was commanded home, followed by a guy from MI5, was arrested at the airport, was taken to a barracks. The lights were on. The windows were barred. He was kept cut off from friends and the outside for days. He was told there was a large fifth column giving atomic secrets to the Russians. He was told that many other people were similarly detained. He was shown handwritten stuff from the Soviet files. He was threatened and intimidated. He was told he would never see his wife again if he didn't talk. He couldn't have counsel if he didn't talk. And he really thought that because he was in the army, because everything told to him was so dire and so treasonous, that he might be shot. He was terrified and the evidence presented to him was overwhelming. So he talked.

Wes Harvison

Ed Mazerall, whom I myself knew later on, when he got out of jail came to my dad, who was in Winnipeg. He had applied for some kind of government job that involved a security recommendation and would my dad give him one. Dad said: "Look, I'll do what I can to help you, but there's no way in the world as a Mounted Policeman I can recommend you for a job with any kind of security clearance when you're just out of jail on an espionage rap. If it's any other kind of job or recommendation or whatever, I'll be glad to help you." My dad made a habit of doing that kind of thing. He often did give people a leg up when he could.

Merrily Weisbord

I wanted to see Fred Rose, who was the provincial leader of the Communist Party in Quebec. He agreed to see me but told me he probably couldn't be very much help in what I wanted to know. He had never spoken to any journalist about the trials — ever. He agreed to see me basically because he had known my parents. I went to Poland and we met in his house in Warsaw over a period of a week. We worked every morning together and we went through the history of the party and his involvement in it until he was jailed. And if I asked him anything after that, he'd say: "Listen, sweetheart, I was in the coop at that point." He didn't tell me much about the trials except what he felt the political forces were during and after the war. He certainly didn't tell me anything of any import as far as his own involvement in the network was concerned. In fact, a year before he died he told his grandson who was visiting him for the first time that he hadn't done anything, that there was nothing to it.

. . . He wouldn't deny it with me. But he was pinned by political forces. He was living in Eastern Europe and getting a pension for work he had done on a Polish newspaper and living in a home which had something to do with the state. His contacts in Canada were people who were still communists. He wasn't at liberty to speak either against the Soviet system or the Communist Party of Canada. He never said he had made a mistake to anybody publicly. He was always a very proud and a very political person with a strong sense of what he saw as his place in history. In fact, just before he died, when his daughter was trying unsuccessfully to bring him home to die, he said: "They're determined to do a job on me, but I'd match my political reputation against any one of them."

. . . What I wanted to know is why he had done it. And his

answer was never directly why he had done it but only to discuss
the military and political situation at the time. It was understood
that we wouldn't discuss the details of his role in the network. I
would sometimes get around it or near it by throwing in questions. But his answer would always come back in general terms.
Which doesn't answer the big questions one has: how does
somebody take upon themselves involving other people and
risking their lives? Or how important was it to be respected in
the international communist community? What part did that
play? You would need somebody's full co-operation and desire
to delve deeply into their own psyche to get that. For Fred Rose
I'm sure until the day he died his own emotions and psyche
were secondary to larger political concerns. They were something you tried to put aside for bigger issues.

Jim Littleton

It was very moving to hear what happened to some of these
people. One told me quite a bit about his life since then. He had
been a capable young engineer in 1945. He went to prison and
when he got out he moved to a different part of the country and
re-established himself and made a new career in a different field
and had been quite successful. This person at first agreed to be
in our film — the first one to agree. He told me when he went to
this new city he got in touch with the RCMP Security Service and
let them know he was there and where he would be working and
agreed to keep in touch. Then he got a job shortly after and
discovered the reason he lost it was because the employer was
told who he was. He kept having experiences like that. Nobody
wanted to employ him. For instance, he had to go to the United
States in connection with this job. Before going he went to the
Security Service officer in charge of that region and told him
when and where he was going and was told, according to him,
that everything would be fine. He got on the train. When he got
to the border, U.S. Immigration officials came onto the train
and went straight to him and confronted him with his identity
and said: "You're not allowed in this country," and took him off
the train and took him back. So he was quite bitter about a

whole series of experiences of that kind. After talking about this for a long time, he agreed to be interviewed on film. I think he wanted to set the record straight about a number of matters. Just before the interview he asked me for a copy of the Royal Commission report. I sent him photocopies of the appropriate parts. When he got them he called me up and said: "Look, I'm going to have to cancel the interview. I was so upset reading that and the allegations that were made against me by Gouzenko that I just can't go through with it." He was tremendously upset. This was from a man who had lived a very respectable life for the last thirty years and is a respected member of his community. His case was a little more compelling but not really very different from the others. Each of them had a similar kind of very strong emotional reaction and feeling they had been harmed in human terms. They still felt it very hard to come to grips with that and were unwilling to talk about it on the record.

Merrily Weisbord

In most cases their lives were totally uprooted. Nothing was the same after. Marriages were destroyed. Families were broken up. People became sick. Jobs were lost across the board. Careers were wrecked. They were ostracized. Even rank-and-file communists were often scared to speak to them. I don't think any of them could say their lives weren't stamped forever by the event.

I'll give you some specifics. One family couldn't work anywhere and was harassed and left for Eastern Europe and the wife, a Canadian from Ontario, went nuts because of the tension and the isolation. A scientist, a top-ranking physicist, couldn't work anywhere in Canada. Friends got him a job in France and then eventually he ended up working in Eastern Europe. He had to leave family and friends. Scott Benning was always hassled and harassed by the RCMP. He was chased from job to job. The RCMP would show up and say that he was a spy. Even now, for example, one of those who did time has a company and every time an article comes out in the newspaper — and they come out on a fairly regular basis if you follow it — he'll lose four or five clients.

Peter Benning

My father from the period of about 1948, which is when the appeal decision came down acquitting him, for years after that was followed from job to job by the RCMP, who would inform the people he was working for that despite his acquittal this guy was a commie spy. He lost a number of jobs. It got to the point where, when I was five, in 1954, we moved to Toronto. It was the only possibility he had of getting a job. . . . For a time he wound up working for my uncle because my uncle was the only person who would give him a job.

Lola Benning

My husband was not a college graduate and [during the war] he worked with college graduates and they were all amazed that he got one promotion after another. In fact he was told he would get a big job in Ottawa in the civil service. He also had offers from two firms and we were discussing whether we should stay in Ottawa or take one of these offers and go to Montreal. Then it all fell through. Scott was a very bright guy and he was respected for what he did and how he did it — until this happened.

Peter Benning

The last job my father had was working in Montreal for the same guy he had moved to Toronto to work for and then his employer expanded the plant in a suburb of Montreal. My father was a fairly competent manager and that's why he got the job in Montreal. The company went bankrupt in about 1976, I think, and my father was laid off. I remember my father never made more than about $22-23,000 a year and his designation was manager of research and development in a fairly small electronics outfit. It was the kind of job that even then would have been worth a great deal more than that, and the reason he was working for the salary he had was that the person who hired him knew he couldn't get a job anywhere else. My father had no choice. He needed a job and was able to do good work and this was the best offer he could get.

Jim Littleton

All the people I talked to have rebuilt their lives in a fairly successful way. Some of them were university professors. One was a journalist. They were intelligent, well-educated people. The only one who impressed me as a serious and highly committed revolutionary was Sam Carr, and he did impress me as being that even though he was pretty old when I met him. He, it seemed to me, had thought through his political position with great care and was able to articulate it in an extremely clear way. In a sense I would have to say he was very different from the others in that he was a very serious revolutionary. He was far more sophisticated in his thinking than I would have ever imagined. I had imagined him as a dull apparatchik of the Soviet machine and in fact he was extremely bright and amazingly well-read. But also very tough in his thinking.

Merrily Weisbord

Everybody considers him one of the most brilliant people in the Communist Party. Very articulate. Very tough. Certainly knew what he was doing all the way through and was doing it consciously and probably more expertly than anybody else. There is a feeling he warned his guys not to talk. The people who didn't talk were not convicted. The people who talked were. It's as simple as that. And most of the guys who didn't talk were the guys in his charge.

Peter Benning

The one thing that's most important to me is that despite everything that happened to my father they weren't able to break his spirit. Up to the time he died, even though his political beliefs became more and more funnelled until they expressed themselves as a rabid anti-Americanism and not a whole lot more, he was convinced until the end that he had done what any right-thinking person would have done. He never repudiated it. He was bitter towards some of the other people who had been accused along with him who either talked or renounced what they had done. My father in the end decided to testify before the Royal Commission but didn't give anybody else away. The

Royal Commission was a frightening thing. I guess I'm more forgiving than my father was. I know my mother and my aunt were always appalled at how bitter he was towards people who just didn't have the same kind of control that he did. But despite it all, the fact is my father never regretted it. People like me — I'm in my mid-thirties — and friends of mine who were politicos in the late sixties and early seventies, the best we can do is say: "Well, I don't regret it. I learned a lot." But it's not as if I'll be able to look back and say: "Those are the best years in my life." And that's what my father said.

Merrily Weisbord

There is no common thread about their feelings afterward. Some feel really as if they had been lied to and used. And others feel that they did the right thing, that it is a choice they would make again today. I don't know if getting caught would be a choice they would make again today, but that they did the right thing at the time.

Peter Benning

When I talked to Merrily [Weisbord] she was very deferential. "Can we talk about what your father did?" I know my mother was very hesitant about it. Because she thought it would hurt me in my new career. I had to convince several members of the family. If there was one thing my father was proud of, it was this. I'll be damned if I'll be a party to a conspiracy to keep it quiet. I feel very strongly about that.

Vera Rosenbluth

Some of them thought we were investigating in dangerous waters. I never could figure out explicitly what they thought the danger was. But there was an overriding fear that it could happen again. There was also some ambivalence.

Merrily Weisbord

It's odd that none of them really talked very much about Gouzenko. I think they just saw him as a stooge, actually. He testified at the Raymond Boyer and Fred Rose trials at great length. He said the same stuff over again and over again. In fact, Raymond Boyer mentioned seeing him in the corridor during a cigarette break. Gordon Lunan was in the corridor waiting to go on and Jim Lemieux, the Quebec RCMP officer, jokingly told Lunan not to chat it up with Gouzenko or he'd get a bad reputation. Boyer remembered this as a light moment. I don't know what they thought of him except nobody seemed to care very much about him.

Vera Rosenbluth

I don't think they were at all bitter toward Gouzenko. They didn't view him as a particularly important player. They were angry at the process but I don't think it was focussed on Gouzenko as an individual. The lawyers had some pretty uncomplimentary things to say about him.

The People Quoted

Adams, Ian — writer
Agostini, Lucio — orchestra leader, *Front Page Challenge*
Anderson, A. Clare — Ottawa neighbour
Argyle, Ray — former staffer with the Toronto *Telegram*
Baker, Philip — friend of Gouzenko
Barrie, Andy — broadcaster
Barris, Alex — broadcaster
Barros, James — political scientist
Batten, Jack — author
Batza, John (Jack) — retired RCMP non-commissioned officer
Bayfield, Cecil — retired RCMP officer
Beavis, Don — former Privy Council Office security official
Benning, Lola — widow of J. S. "Scott" Benning
Benning, Peter — son of Scott Benning
Besse, Ron — publisher
Black, Lydia — widow of Mervyn Black
Blackstock, Peggy — former editor
Brayley, Jack — retired Canadian Press reporter
Burnett, George — former trust officer with National Trust
Callwood, June — author
Campbell, W. Kenneth — secretary to the Kellock-Taschereau Royal
    Commission
Chalmers, Floyd — retired publisher
Chaplin, Charles — former Canadian general manager of United
    Artists

Cole, Arthur — retired broadcaster
Conlan, David M. — Ottawa neighbour
Coulson, Fernande — retired secretary to the Crown Attorney in
    Ottawa
Cowan, Bernard — announcer, *Front Page Challenge*
Cronin, Fergus — retired journalist
Crysdale, G. B. — neighbour
Crysdale, Minnie — neighbour
Dalrymple, Alla — former wife of John Dalrymple
Dalrymple, John — journalist
Davis, Fred — host, *Front Page Challenge*
Dean, John — retired RCMP officer
Driedger, Elmer — former Deputy Minister of Justice
Dubro, James — film and television producer
Dworkin, Ben — former reporter, Ottawa *Citizen*
Eagleson, Alan — lawyer
Eayrs, James — historian
Eustace, Irene — wife of Cecil Eustace
Eustace, Phil — son of Cecil Eustace
Fast, Don — retired RCMP officer
Fisher, Barbara — wife of Doug Fisher
Fisher, Doug — columnist
Fisher, Mark — son of Doug Fisher
Fraser, Elizabeth — former reporter, *Ottawa Journal*
Fraser, Graham — son of Blair Fraser
Frolick, Stanley — lawyer
Frowde, Chester — former night city editor, *Ottawa Journal*
Fry, Jeff — producer
Fulford, Robert — writer and editor
Fulton, Hon. E. Davie — former Minister of Justice
Ghent, Dave — former reporter, *Ottawa Journal*
Gibson, Doug — publisher
Gilmore, Ruth — neighbour
Glasgow, Robert — former *Time* correspondent in Canada
Glazebrook, George — retired External Affairs officer
Goodman, Eddie — lawyer
Goodman, Walter — author
Gouzenko, Svetlana — widow of Igor Gouzenko

Granatstein, J. L. — historian

Griffin, Eugene — former correspondent in Ottawa for the Chicago *Tribune*

Guthrie, Greg — former *Ottawa Journal* reporter and assistant to Opposition leader John Diefenbaker

Guthro, Jim — former producer, *Front Page Challenge*

Gzowski, Peter — writer and broadcaster

Hale, Margaret — neighbour

Harris, Alan — lawyer

Harris, John "Hap" — retired RCMP officer

Harvison, Wes — son of late Cliff Harvison, RCMP Commissioner

Higgitt, W. L. — retired RCMP Commissioner

Holloway, Anne — editor

Holmes, John — former director-general of Canadian Institute of International Affairs

How, Doug — former Canadian Press reporter

Howland, Dr. Robert — Ottawa neighbour

Hutcheson, John — editor, *Canadian Forum*

Jackson, Richard — former *Ottawa Journal* reporter

Joubin, Franc — acquaintance

Joy, Roma — former house caretaker to the Gouzenkos

Keate, Stuart — former *Time* correspondent

Kelly, William — retired RCMP Deputy Commissioner

Keyserlingk, Robert — publisher

Lefolii, Ken — former *Maclean's* editor; producer of *This Hour Has Seven Days*

Littleton, Jim — radio and television producer

McClung, Mark — former RCMP chief of research

McConnell, Ray — producer, *Front Page Challenge*

McCulloch, John B. — retired Ottawa policeman

MacDonald, John — Ottawa neighbour

MacDonald, Margaret — Ottawa neighbour

MacFarlane, Andy — former managing editor, Toronto *Telegram*

MacFarlane, J. D. — former managing editor, Toronto *Telegram*

McGaw, Jack — producer, CTV

McGillivray, Don — financial columnist

McIlraith, Hon. George — former cabinet minister

Mackay, George — retired RCMP officer

McKechnie, Bill — son of Laurie McKechnie
McKechnie, Leslie — widow of Laurie McKechnie
MacLeod, A. J. — retired Department of Justice lawyer
McMurtry, William — Toronto lawyer
Macpherson, Duncan — cartoonist
Main, Harold — Ottawa neighbour
Main, Mildred — Ottawa neighbour
Marcuse, Gary — broadcaster
Martin, Hon. Paul — former cabinet minister
Maulsby, Del — retired Mountie
Maxey, Marilyn — neighbour
Middleton, Karin — neighbour
Milne, C. C. "Chuck" — former assistant city editor, *Ottawa Journal*
Milne, Karen — lawyer
Mockett, John — former *Ottawa Journal* reporter
Morris, Robert — former counsel to U.S. Senate committee
Nichols, Marjorie — columnist
O'Brien, Andy — retired reporter
Olsen, Bob — photographer
Orford, Ann — former publisher's representative
Osler, B. B. — lawyer
Page, Don — historian, Department of External Affairs
Parks, Ken — former reporter, *Ottawa Journal*
Paterson, George — former night editor, *Ottawa Journal*
Pickersgill, Hon. Jack — head of Prime Minister Mackenzie King's
    office
Picton, Jean — wife of John Picton
Picton, John — reporter
Rasky, Frank — author
Reguly, Robert — freelance journalist
Reuben, William A. — author
Robertson, Peter — picture editor, *Toronto Star*
Robinette, John J. — lawyer
Rosenbluth, Vera — writer and broadcaster
Russell, Peter — former chief of research, McDonald Royal
    Commission into RCMP wrongdoing
Schnobb, Marcel — retired sports deskman, *Ottawa Journal*
Sears, Val — reporter

Sinclair, Gordon — longtime panelist, *Front Page Challenge*
Smith, Arnold — retired External Affairs officer
Smith, I. Norman — former editor, *Ottawa Journal*
Solecki, Sam — former editor, *Canadian Forum*
Sourwine, J. G. — former counsel to U.S. Senate committee
Spanton, Herb — retired RCMP officer
Starr, Hon. Michael — former Minister of Labour
Starr, Nelles — lawyer
Stephenson, Sir William — wartime head of British Security
   Co-ordination
Stoffman, Daniel — former *Toronto Star* staffer
Tataryn, Lloyd — journalist
Temple, J. W. — lawyer
Thomas, Jocko — reporter and broadcaster
Thomson, Lorraine — co-ordinator, *Front Page Challenge*
Weisbord, Merrily — author
Westwick, Bill — former sports editor, *Ottawa Journal*
Wilson, Phyllis — former reporter, *Ottawa Journal*
Woodside, Willson — former writer with *Saturday Night* magazine
Worthington, Peter — journalist